THE GOSPEL IS ENOUGH

Rediscovering the Good News of Jesus Christ: His Kingdom, His Power, His Sufficiency and His Grace

Scott Wallis

Lighthouse Publications, Inc.

The Gospel is Enough
Rediscovering the Good News of Jesus Christ: His Kingdom,
His Power, His Sufficiency and His Grace

by Scott Wallis
Printed in the United States of America
ISBN 9781933656120

www.TheGospelisEnough.com

www.Gospel-Revolution.com

Publisher
Lighthouse Publications, Inc.
PO Box 6462
Elgin, IL 60121
www.Lighthouse-Publications.com

Cover Design
Arbëresh Dalipi
www.99designs.com/profiles/arbereshdalipi
web.facebook.com/ArbereshDalipi

Inside Layout
Scott Wallis & Associates
PO Box 6462
Elgin, IL 60121
www.ScottWallis.net

Bible Versions & Copyrights

Dedication

This book was inspired by a prophetic word spoken to me in March 2015. While at Andrew Wommack's annual ministry conference for the newly formed Association of Related Ministries International (ARMI), I was challenged by the Lord with these words: *"Heal the sick, Cleanse the lepers, Raise the dead, Cast out devils..."* Matt. 10:1. This took place while Barry Bennett was preaching about his experience of being challenged by the Lord, *"You feed them,"* from Mark 6:37. At that moment, I realized the words in Matthew 10:1 were actually a command. I was convicted, challenged and changed by Barry's message. From that experience, I wrote this book. So, Barry, thanks for faithfully sharing your experience. It has borne good fruit in my life and, I trust, in the lives of those who will read this book.

I want to acknowledge and thank those who have helped me with the editing process. Mom and Dad, your insights have made this a better book. Robert-Dale, your proofing and editing and layout of the design process enabled me to move from words on a page to an effective tool for believers and churches to walk in gospel power and share the gospel message. I also want to say a special thank you to all of those who have endorsed this work. I pray that a special award is delivered to you from heaven. And, I cannot forget my congregation members: you have been such a blessing to me throughout the years. Your faithfulness to hear the calling of God on my life has enabled me to reach the wider body of Christ with this work.

I want to thank my wife, Cecile. You are a gift from God. Your support has been invaluable. You make me a better man. You love me. And, you care about me – the me that no one else sees. I am grateful that you came into my life when you did and chose to partner with me in life. I am excited about what the future holds for us. And, I believe this book is just as much a fruit of this marriage with which we have been blessed. Our marriage was prophetic, took place suddenly and miraculously and inspired many as they saw two older saints join together in holy matrimony. You preserved yourself for me, and I for you. Truly, love can happen at any time and in any place. God is awesome.

I want to thank you, the reader, for choosing to read this book. Your choice to learn the gospel is celebrated and appreciated. I trust and hope that my thoughts will inspire you to greater pursuits of him, his will and his works. We're all part of the great gospel army that God is raising up in this day. I pray that the anointing of the Holy Spirit will rest on you, just as it did Jesus, when he was anointed by the Spirit of the Lord *"to preach the gospel to the poor... to heal the brokenhearted, to preach deliverance to the captives, and recovering of sight to the blind, to set at liberty them that are bruised. To preach the acceptable year of the Lord."* Lk. 4:18,19. Together, we can change generations and nations for the glory of God and His Son, Jesus Christ.

Finally, I want to thank Jesus, my Savior and Messiah, my best friend. You saved me from the hellish pits in which I was destined to walk and the snares set for me by Satan himself. I am eternally grateful for Your love that You have shown me continually throughout the course of my life. I can never say thank You enough for what You have done for me and how You have blessed me, even when I sinned and did evil against You. I bless Your Name and call You, my Lord. I trust that this work meets Your approval above all else. I ask that you confirm its message with signs, wonders and miracles, supernatural demonstrations of power. We're hungry, Lord. And, together, as the Church, we say, "More!" Let your gospel revolution begin in this generation! May this book be a part of that revolution, for Your glory, Lord. Amen. To join the revolution, visit: *www.gospel-revolution.com.*

Endorsements

Scott Wallis is so timely in this release. It is a great teaching tool and needed in this hour as many water down and stray from the truth of the gospel. I was excited to go from chapter to chapter. The Word warns of false teachings and I want to encourage you to weigh this word... absorb it... and obey, so as not to be guilty of "ticklish ears." I Loved Every Word!

Gail McCrory, Pastor
Solomon's Porch Ministries

I am extremely honored to endorse such a work that I believe will influence the next generation of believers for the better. This book takes the reader on a very transparent trek through the unfiltered lenses of the author, Scott Wallis, in relation to the gospel of Jesus Christ. He skillfully navigates through the carnal complexity of a man- or me-centered "gospel" to one that embodies the essential character of Jesus Christ. Scott's writing is mindfully and spiritually proficient in articulating exactly what the true gospel is and what it is not. He achieves this by interjecting personal testimonies of how he was seduced by somewhat flawed teachings, only to have his eyes opened through divine prophetic revelation!

Upon reading the first couple of pages, I immediately realized just how similar Scott's journey was to my own. I was essentially impregnated by the Word of Faith movement during the late 1990's! I bought it hook, line and sinker! I comfortably used phrases such as: "Name it and claim it!" and "Blab it and grab it!" as if they were actual scripture. I basically lived by these words until, like Scott, my eyes were opened. I had mistakenly equated the gospel of Jesus Christ to the Word of Faith movement, not realizing that they were really two separate entities. To me at the time, following Christ equated to getting what I wanted through the sheer power of my words being uttered in faith! I found that to be untrue more often than not. This "gospel" had more to do with pleasing me than it did with pleasing "He"! In time, this manner of Christian living became unacceptable for me. *The Gospel is Enough* exposes the simplicity of Christ's message to the world and the fallacy of many to translate it to the local church. Historically, there have been far too many leaders who have traded in this simplicity for complexity rooted in carnal values. Instead of God's will being done, man's will is being established with the house of the Lord. This book shines the light of His divinity upon this much over-looked topic. Scott boldly addresses issues that few are willing to even acknowledge exist. The result of such investigation is a manuscript that is interesting, thought-provoking and challenging.

Scott has released a clarion call to all believers! He's urged us to trim the "fat," so that we can have access to the true intent and meaning of the gospel of Jesus Christ. He refreshingly illustrates that through all the religious fads that come and go, the message remains the same. This fact becomes more evident with each chapter. This one is definitely a page-turner! It possesses the ability to shift previously existing paradigms. Romans 1:16 lets us know that the gospel is the power of God for salvation. It is, in essence, the sinless life, the sacrificial death and the resurrection of our Lord and Savior. This concept is affirmed and reaffirmed in this labor of love. Throughout this book, Scott gives credence and evidence that the gospel is truly enough!

John Veal
Enduring Faith Christian Center, Pastor
John Veal Ministries, Prophet

Scott Wallis very clearly writes about the importance of the gospel, as it is the Power of God unto Salvation. Everything we need is contained in the gospel. I encourage everyone to read and understand this awesome book on the gospel. Your life will never be the same again. You will be blessed.

Sudhakar Rao, Pastor
Christ Ministries

Scott Wallis is a prolific writer with a message for the Body of Christ today. I have read several of his prior works and have always been stirred and encouraged in the Lord by them. His current work, *The Gospel is Enough*, is a battering ram to the religious system that seeks to water down the all-sufficient gospel of Jesus Christ. Scott explains how the gospel is proof of the living hope that Christ offers and that true change comes only through a converted heart. Miracles and healings are not the gospel. Prosperity and wealth aren't either. Yet, everywhere these signs appear, the gospel is evident. Scott makes these points and others in a way that is simple, yet profound.

This book is a must read for all students of the gospel to see what God is up to in our present generation. With prophetic insight, Scott elaborates on what the Gospel is and the grace it offers, all within the context of the Kingdom of God. Scott speaks within the timeline of history, preparing us for the last days of Jesus' return. I would highly recommend this book to all who want to be challenged and inspired to go deeper in their understanding of the full satisfaction of the Good News of Jesus Christ.

Rusty Wimberly, Pastor
Elgin City Church

Preface

When Scott asked me to endorse his wonderful new book, I had to just take a few moments and reflect on the amazing friendship we have, and how that began back in 1988. Scott showed up at the church I was attending in Iowa City, and almost immediately he joined our small circle of friends, most of whom were students at the University of Iowa. One of the things that truly stood out to me about Scott, even from our earliest years of walking with God, was his genuine love and heart-hunger for God. It was great to hang around someone hungrier than I was! Another outstanding trait was his bold character, unafraid of what anyone thought of him, coupled with compassion and the seeds of a powerful prophetic gift. This prophetic gift has touched my life at various times in our friendship.

For example, I remember in those days I had moved into a new apartment in Iowa City and just sensed a strange presence there. It was like an uncleanness in the spirit, but you wouldn't know it by looking at it. It was a quaint, little one-bedroom place in an older home. One evening Scott came over and was sitting in the living room. He looked at me and said, "Bill, there are two evil spirits in this apartment." It totally shocked me that he would have that insight, and it affirmed and clarified what I had already been sensing. Wow. We prayed and he cast them out. There was a notable difference after this! Another time, the Lord used Scott in my life while eating lunch under the huge oak trees in front of Schaeffer Hall at the university. I had been working on a Master's Degree in Classics, and contemplating getting a Ph.D., but felt the call to the ministry stirring in my heart. In an almost matter of fact tone, he said to me, "You know you're called, Bill. I mean, look at you! You even look like a pastor!" And he laughed in his very distinctive laugh that belonged to Scott alone! Well, whatever a pastor "looks like," I didn't know, but those words touched that call in my heart, and at that moment I knew I would never be a university professor. I would follow God and obey that call!

Finally, after graduating and going our separate ways, he back to his hometown of Elgin, Illinois and I to RHEMA Bible Training Center, we eventually lost track of each other. Then, 17 years later, we were able to reconnect. I was a missionary in Peru, and he was a pastor, prophet and writer, living in Elgin. I had been sensing the Lord leading us to move back to the States and start a church – a very radical move for me with a wife and three children at that time. I was really struggling over this transition, and seeking God for confirmation. Scott graciously invited me to come minister to his church and reunite after all those years. And, just before leaving his office after the weekend, as we prayed, he gave me a word (I hadn't said anything to him at all about what was in my heart about a change). He said, "In your heart you have said... such and such." What he spoke were the exact same words that I had said to the Lord in the middle of the night in prayer. Again, I was shocked at the precision of the Spirit of God. He used my friend Scott once again to deliver a supernatural confirmation that would strengthen and hold us steady to make that transition. It's now been nine years since we started our church in Sioux City, Iowa, which is making a great impact in our community for the Gospel.

In light of this, I want to endorse Scott's new book, *The Gospel is Enough.* In the introduction of his book, he recounts different moves of God in our nation and around the world – the positives and negatives. As I read his analysis and experiences, especially with the Word of Faith movement, I could see that our journeys differed. I was influenced in a very positive and powerful way by that movement, not incurring the abuses and extremes that Scott experienced. Over the years, I have come to realize that every move of God, including the Word of Faith, has excesses and extreme doctrine that can be hurtful and misleading. Satan would like to take anything that God is doing and pervert it as much as he can. Therefore, I believe that Scott's message of rediscovering the "simplicity of the Gospel" is perfect for the Church at this time. He reestablishes honor for the pure Gospel of Jesus in an inspirational, at times, corrective and thorough way. It is a scripturally-based book, full of great stories and solid truth that will bring wisdom and revelation to every believer!

Bill Yanney, Pastor
Family Worship Center

• The Gospel is Enough •

Foreword

I was born and raised in the hills of West Virginia. Life was hard. I was surrounded by poverty. My father worked in the coal mines for approximately 35 years. He was a hard man. In those early years, my relationship with my father was one of fear. I was never able to have a close relationship with him. In his later years, he had a joyful salvation experience and was a different man than I had previously known. By God's grace, the power of the gospel and the prayers of a praying mother, we both entered into a place of salvation, peace and rest. I will explain.

My family owed a farm of approximately 65 acres in West Virginia. I was raised in a family of 13 children. My father earned less than minimum wage. And, most of our food came from the farm we worked. Life was hard. The work was hard. Everyone was required to work; it was essential. But, we survived. Even thrived. There is so much that could be said about those early years and God's grace on my family, but time and space doesn't permit this.

In 1963, I finished high school. Shortly thereafter, I joined the military, and served as a personnel management specialist until I was discharged. When my tour of duty ended, I did not want to go home to West Virginia. I had a sister living in Chicago, Illinois whom I hadn't seen in several years, so I went to visit her. My years in the military brought out the worst in me: violence, alcohol abuse and womanizing. I was a train wreck. On Christmas Eve of 1969, I was involved in a barroom brawl. A gun was involved. I was shot. And, I nearly lost my life. But, God had other plans. So did my mother.

My mother was a praying woman. She believed God to work in my life. She didn't preach at me. She loved me. Often, she would say: "Son. You need Jesus." My response to her was: "I'm not ready for that." But God was tugging on my heart. That Christmas night, while I lay dying [I was shot in the stomach and left arm], an "unknown person" spoke to me and assured me that I would be alright. I am fully persuaded that person was an angel. Shortly thereafter, I was released from the hospital. My left arm was permanently damaged. As a result, I could no longer rely on my physical strength to carry me. I had to change my life, my line of work and the plans for my future.

A different track was set for me. I became involved in the steel industry. I worked in an office position for a company that produced metal parts for modern commercial airplane engines. I liked the work. And, it changed my life: I had to dress differently, think differently and even talk differently. But, it was during that period that I met a woman with whom I fell in love and married. We, Beverly and I, were married for 43½ years. We had 3 children: 2 boys and 1 girl. My family has been the source of my greatest joys and pain. Yet, through it all, I learned that the gospel is enough.

My wife was raised in a Roman Catholic church and I was raised in a tongue talking, snake handling, poison drinking, "Holy Roller" church. Neither my wife nor I were religious. And, neither one of us liked what we had experienced. We knew there was more, but we didn't know what that more was until we moved to Florida. It was those five years in Florida that became the incubator of God's work in our lives. We were born again, gave ourselves wholly to the study of God's word, faithfully attended church services and small group meetings, and even went to Bible school. There was so much grace on our lives. And we prospered, spiritually and financially. I ate the blossoming fruits of practically living out the gospel message. But, a test came....

I was involved in a business at the time. That business was very prosperous. But, two of the men involved in the business, who also happened to be married to the daughters of the owner of that business, conceived a plan to steal the business from their father-in-law. They approached me to join them in their scheme. I said, "No." I was pushed out of the business. Life became hard. Bitterness entered into my heart. I felt like Job. I was angry at life... at God. We moved back to Chicago from Florida. For two years and three months, I worked as a security guard for $8.00/hr. from midnight to 8:00 am on Chicago's south side. Dangerous. Difficult.

By God's grace, I held on to my hope in God and clung to his promises. And, I went back into the steel industry. I founded Dove Steel, Inc. It was during this difficult period that I met Scott Wallis. Scott shared with me that he had written a book, *Decade of Destiny*. I was fascinated by his prophecy of the coming season. We became friends. I would often call Scott and ask him for prayer for my life and business. He prayed and things turned favorably. I started prospering financially again. I saw God's hand move in my life and on my behalf. I began to see once again that... the gospel is enough.

In 1996, I moved to Texas and opened a steel service center. And, the business prospered and grew. After several years, I was impressed to leave Texas and move back to Illinois, which I did. I gave the warehouse business to my daughter, Lisa. She was so faithful. But, debt had accumulated. I owed over $800,000. I had no way to pay what I owed. But, during this time that I received a prophetic word from Scott that I keep in my wallet to this day: On a sticky note, I wrote $800,000, the amount I owed, and Scott wrote the words, "Paid in Full". That was good news. And, I received it.

Since then, I have had to bury a child, my daughter, and my wife. My wife died on December 16, 2013. I cannot express how hard this loss was. I cannot adequately express how I was impacted by this experience or how God mercies comforted me in my hour of great need. I began to ponder the "what if" of 49 years previously where I almost lost my life. I would have died a sinner lost for eternity. It was then that I remembered the words of my mother: "Son, you don't know how close to death you were." And, that was true, I didn't.

I thought back on a vision I had shortly after I had been born again. In that vision, I saw myself in quicksand. It was at my neck. I was sinking fast. Suddenly, Jesus walked up to the edge of the pit and said, "I am going to throw you a lifeline. I will pull you out of that pit. I will clean you up. I will tie this lifeline around my waist, and yours. Don't ever disconnect it!" I have been brought to tears numerous times through the years when I think of that vision, and again as I write this Foreword, I can humbly say, surely, the gospel is enough.

Scott, your book, *The Gospel is Enough,* is a definitive work. You walk through the gospels with a basket, harvesting fruit and then presenting that fruit to each of us individually. I think of the Scripture: "O taste and see that the Lord is good." Ps. 34:8. "...His mercies endure forever." Ps. 136:1. I was truly blessed by *The Gospel is Enough.* This book encouraged me, and stirred and stoked the fire of my desire to know Jesus more intimately, and that resurrection power that raised Him from the dead.

To the reader, I want to encourage you. Come and dine, the Master is calling you. A feast has been prepared for you, the reader, of the Lord's goodness. Just as God sent manna from heaven daily for 40 years to the Jewish people, He has sent manna from heaven to you in the Person of His Son, Jesus. Partake of Him, daily. If you want life, seek the Giver of life, Christ. As you read this book, join Scott as he teaches the gospel, where we learn how to live and move and have our being in the living Christ Jesus, to the glory of God the Father. I can guarantee that if you take the words of this book to heart that your life will never be the same again. You will experience the wonders of this simple truth: the gospel is enough. Amen.

Dan Blankenship, CEO
Business Owner

Introduction

I am concerned about what I see taking place in the Church today. I hear many men and women of God who have departed from the simplicity of the gospel message to another gospel. That drift, in some cases, may be accidental but is significant to the future of the church. The gospel being preached today is far different from the gospel I grew up with as a new believer in Christ.

Prior to becoming a Christian in 1987, I had never heard the gospel message. I didn't attend church. I didn't know Jesus. Nor did I know who He was/is. I was lost. I needed salvation, healing, deliverance and much more. I needed Jesus Christ. But, I didn't know I needed Him. No one ever communicated to me the gospel message. I attended the Catholic church three times prior to February 23, 1987 (my spiritual birthday): 1) as a baby, where I was baptized and dedicated, 2) as a child of 7 or 8 years old, sitting in the crying room with my Aunt Marsy and Uncle Chick, and 3) as a college student with a close friend, Juan Valdez.

I was interested in knowing God. Though I didn't know him, sometimes, I would pray to him at night. In college, I attended a home group of college students affiliated with the Navigators. I had fun. I liked it. Yet, I was still lost, I needed the gospel. But, I didn't know it. I had never heard the gospel message.

My Date with Destiny

On February 23, 1987, at midnight, I heard the gospel for the first time. God spoke. I heard him say, "You're a sinner!" [This conversation was internal, but audible. And, I knew God was speaking to me.] I was shocked by what He said. I thought I was a good person. I always sought to do good. In my heart, I said to that voice, "How can this be?!" Immediately, by divine download, I was given a revelation of Adam and Eve and the original sin. At that moment, I knew I was a sinner. I knew was lost. I knew I needed a Savior. I needed Jesus. In my heart, I said, "Lord Jesus, I ask you to come into my life." Immediately, I felt my sins lifted from me [it felt like a car lying on top of me was removed]. The next morning, I had joy like I had never experienced. I had been born again.

I was radically saved. I couldn't stop reading my Bible. I read the New Testament in two weeks. I began attending church services: The Assembly of God church located on Keokuk Ave in Iowa City, Iowa. In fact, I sought ways to attend the services, daily. Prior to Sunday morning services, I attended a Bible study. Prior to Bible study and Sunday services, and on Wednesday, I attended a prayer meeting. I connected with other believers who were on fire for God. We prayed, read the Bible, shared excitement concerning the things of God and those things God was doing in our lives. I even went on retreats in difficult conditions to learn more about God. I loved God. I loved His Word. And, I loved His Church. Everything was so new and exciting to me. I began to have visions, dreams, prophetic words and tongues and interpretations of tongues. The supernatural became natural to me. And, I wanted more. I was hooked.

Falling into Religion and Bound by Christianeze

I read Christian books, listened to teaching tapes, watched and listened to ministers on television like Lester Sumrall, Marilyn Hickey, Robert Tilton, Dr. Paul (David) Yonggi Cho, Kenneth Copeland, Kenneth Hagin, Sr., T.L. Osborn, Jerry Falwell and numerous others. I took Bible college courses from the Word of Faith Bible College that was located in Dallas, Texas and Columbia University in Columbia, South Carolina. I grew in knowledge and understanding of the Bible. Gradually, subtly, I drifted into Word of Faith, hyper faith, teaching.

I began reading books by E.W. Kenyon, Kenneth Hagin, Sr., Kenneth Copeland and a host of other Word of Faith Bible teachers. I wanted more of God. I thought, and was taught, faith was **the** key. I bought in – hook, line and sinker. I sought to gain more and more faith. I became preoccupied with the faith message. I read, studied, meditated on and memorized the Bible: to gain more faith. I wanted more of God, And, faith, I was taught and thought, was the key. And, faith is *a* key in our relationship with God, but it's not the **only** key to walking in relationship with God and divine power and authority from God.

Gradually, I moved from the simplicity of the gospel message to a different message. That message was the word of faith. Faith is a good topic: it's important, but it's not the gospel. From 1987 to 1991, I was stuck pursuing a pseudo message of faith, a false faith. Don't get me wrong, I learned a great deal from the ministers of whom I'm speaking, and I have great respect for them, and much of their teaching is good, but I also lost something as a result of the hyper focus on faith: the simple gospel message I had audibly heard preached by God Himself. That was the message that excited me and brought me to faith in Christ.

Regaining Destiny, Fanning Revival and Finding Freedom

Thankfully, God, by and through His grace, sent someone into my life to deliver me from this hyper faith teaching, Tom Slone. Tom, a wonderful prophet of God, was radically saved at a Vicky Jamison-Peterson meeting in Chicago, Illinois. When I met Tom, after leaving a Faith church where I experienced spiritual abuse, he spoke words that challenged me in my understanding of faith. That challenge turned me from a false faith to a true faith: one built on the solid foundation of focus on the person of Christ. I heard Tom's loving rebuke. From that point, I, like Paul, the Apostle, determined not to know anything save Christ and Him crucified. I rediscovered the simple gospel message and rediscovered the person of Christ.

In 1991, I received a series of prophetic words concerning a coming revival. I wrote those prophecies and published them in my first book, *Decade of Destiny*. I spoke of a coming revival that would engulf the world. From 1993 thru 2000, America and the nations experienced revival: Toronto, Canada; Pensacola, Florida; Smithton, Missouri; and Lakeland, Florida became synonymous with that revival. By God's grace, and a series of supernatural miracles, I published that book under my own publishing company, Lighthouse Publications, in 1994. I gave hundreds of copies to ministers and ministries. My hope in writing and publishing that book was that leaders and ministers would see the importance of the prophetic word I received, believe it and use that word as a blueprint to prepare for the coming season of revival.

At each of the aforementioned locations, the yearning in the hearts of believer and non-believer alike culminated into a thunderous roar to hear the gospel. The gospel message was preached, and it sparked a revival. A new generation became acquainted with the presence, power and person of the Holy Spirit, and the gospel message. A flame could be seen in the church, again. News media descended on those revivals: to inspect and, if possible, critically analyze those revival meetings. Revivalists such as Rodney Howard Browne, Todd Bentley and the Steve Hill caused a resurgence in churches and attendance. Believers were on fire, and for good reason, God was in our midst. We rediscovered the person of Jesus. Millions came to Christ's mercy seat because we heard the gospel message, again.

Sadly, and slowly, over the past 20 years, the Church has slipped from the simple gospel message into a host of other messages: positive attitudes, political action and passionate pursuits. I cannot remain silent: The Church today must move from the rot and rut that religion is to the true gospel message. But, we have lost that message.

In 1987, I heard that gospel message. It changed me. I became hungry for God and His Word. My desire in writing and publishing this book: to help believers and churches, especially preachers and teachers, rediscover this simple message. I want to acquaint and equip a new generation of believers with the power associated with the gospel. As such, I do not come to you with wise and persuasive words of man's wisdom, but in the demonstration of the power of the gospel of Christ. 1 Cor. 2:1.

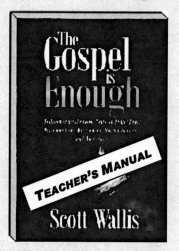
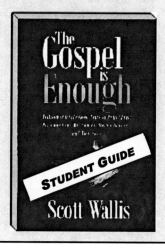

Table of References for Bible Versions

KJV	King James Version
ABPE	Aramaic Bible in Plain English
AKJV	American King James Version
BLB	Berean Literal Bible
BSB	Berean Study Bible
DBT	Darby Bible Translation
DRB	Douay-Rheims Bible
ESV	English Standard Version
GWT	God's Word Translation
HCSB	Holman Christian Standard Bible
ISV	International Standard Version
JUB	Jubilee Bible 2000
NASB	New American Standard Bible
NET	NET Bible
NIV	New International Version
NLT	New Living Translation
WBT	Webster's Bible Translation
WEB	World English Bible
WNT	Weymouth New Testament
YLT	Young's Literal Translation

Contents

Chapter One

The Gospel is Enough

I can still remember the morning I walked down to the family room in my home. It was around 9:30 am. I was still waking up. I'm more of a night owl than an early riser. So, I turned on the television and, suddenly, booming from the television, came a voice: "America needs a prophet like an Elijah – a prophet who will have the ear of America and will say to her now: If the Lord be God, then follow Him! But, if Baal, follow him... and go to hell!" Needless to say, I immediately woke up.

My reasons for waking up: I'm a prophet. I live in America. I've prophesied over our nation. I've prophesied over other nations. At the time of seeing the movie, *A Man Called Peter*, I had been embroiled in litigation before both federal and state courts in over 100 cases. I faced severe corruption before numerous federal and state judges. The evidence of that corruption was/is overwhelming. Eventually, in 2012, I published a book, *Secret Corruption*, describing a smidgeon of the corruption I discovered in our legal system. So, this movie and its message really spoke to me.

America's Elijah Moment: One Message, One Movement, One Gospel

Since then, I've learned that the voice speaking from the television was the voice of Richard Todd, the actor who played the late Peter Marshall, Sr. in *A Man Called Peter*. Peter Marshall, Sr. was well respected as a man of God. He was the pastor of New York Avenue Presbyterian Church [known as the church of Presidents] located in Washington, DC, and twice was Chaplain for the United States Senate. Abraham Lincoln regularly attended that church. So did John Quincy Adams and Andrew Jackson. Just to name a few. This movie is one of my favorite movies. I've watched it countless times. But, none were as shocking, or compelling, as that first time.

Marshall's message, although he being dead, still speaks today. It spoke to me. Millions have seen this movie and heard its message: America needs a prophet! God grant us prophets like the days of old, like Elijah, who called fire from heaven to consume holy sacrifices and offerings, and enemies, and demonstrated the purity of the God of Abraham, Isaac and Jacob. We need such prophetic voices to arise today and declare the pure gospel and its sufficiency. That is why I wrote this book: to bring back into focus the simplicity of the gospel message.

Paul said, "Not that we are sufficient of ourselves to think any thing as of ourselves; but our sufficiency is of God; Who also hath made us able ministers of the new testament; not of the letter, but of the spirit: for the letter killeth, but the spirit giveth life." 2 Cor. 3:5-6. Paul understood the source of his sufficiency – that he, in and of himself, was unable to meet the demands of preaching the gospel. Paul understood that his sufficiency came from only one place: Christ. The question is: do we?

Falsity, Fraud and Fanaticism in the Church

I've been a Christian for 30+ years. I've been a minister of the gospel for over 25 years. I've been a prophet for 25+ years. I've pastored for 17+ years. During that period of time, I've witnessed numerous changes in the church. I've seen many leaders and movements rise and fall. I witnessed the fall of Jim Bakker and his restoration. I witnessed the rise of revival, which I prophesied of in 1991 in my book, *Decade of Destiny,* and its waning. I witnessed the rise and fall of Robert Tilton, Ted Haggard, Jimmy Swaggert, Paul Cain,

Roberts Liardon, Rory Alec and numerous others. Some have been restored. Many have not. This concerns me.

I've read about and studied the failures, and successes, of other prior leaders, and movements. The shepherding movement was led by Derek Prince, Charles Simpson, Bob Mumford, Ern Baxter and Don Basham, also known as the Fabulous Five. Each one of them was a man of God. But, they were in error; they were preaching a different message. Kathryn Kuhlman saw their error, and she refused to take the stage with Bob Mumford at the Conference of the Holy Spirit that took place in Jerusalem in 1975.

In the 1950's and 1960's, the Church experienced errors in the healing movement. William Marion Branham was possibly the most well-known of the healing ministries, and he eventually came to believe that he was the prophesied Elijah for the Seventh Church age identified in Revelation. Today, an entire movement revolves around Branham called Branhamites. During that period, many others faltered and failed: Jack Coe died at 38 years old, A.A. Allen died of acute alcoholism (his blood alcohol level was .36), and W.V. Grant was imprisoned for tax evasion.

The Simple Gospel: Raw Power

I'm concerned by the message we preach, for I know the gospel is sufficient. How do I know the gospel is enough? Because I've experienced the true power of the gospel in my life. My salvation experience showed me God's reality. In an open vision, I saw his glory (brighter than 10,000 suns rolled up into one). My life was changed by his reality invading my reality. Then, I experienced intense spiritual warfare.

From 1989 to 1991, I came under great torment in my mind. I felt like a mental paraplegic. I suffered greatly. I sought help. But, no one really understood how to help me. So, I prayed and prayed and prayed. I prayed 10 to 16 hours a day. I was under intense spiritual warfare and I didn't know what to do about it. But, God did. He had a plan.

In 1991, through prophetic ministry by Tom and Tammy Slone, I was set free. That prophetic ministry lasted for 30+ minutes. Much of what was spoken has come to pass. During the time where prophecies were being given, I can be heard on the tape of those prophecies laughing and laughing. There is also a period where the holy reverence of God descends into the meeting. So, I know the power of the gospel. I have experienced it.

In 2004, I was invited to Lagos, Nigeria. While there, I saw miracles take place. God healed people, and many were delivered. I also remember preaching and prophesying at an Assemblies of God church located in the heart of Lagos, Nigeria. As I prophesied, a woman on the front row jumped up, spun around several times and fell to the ground. In the same meeting, a young man rolled back and forth under God's power. So, I've seen God's power. And, we need that power today; it's the power of the gospel.

Many outstanding miracles occurred in meetings but more prior to, during and after the meetings took place. For example, I did not know I needed a travel visa to enter Lagos, Nigeria. Less than two weeks before my trip, I discovered I needed a travel visa. I contacted the Nigerian embassy. I was told that it would take two weeks. My friend, who invited me to Nigeria, contacted the Nigerian Ambassador on my behalf. He was told the same thing: two weeks. In three days, I received my travel visa. Further, when I went to Lagos, Nigeria, I didn't know I also needed a malaria shot. I did not receive one. But, God protected me, I was not bitten by one mosquito. Now, that's a miracle.

The Stigma of the Gospel

The gospel I preach has power. I've seen many individuals touched by God's power. I've seen signs, wonders and miracles. I've experienced God's sufficiency. The gospel brings God's sufficiency into our lives. The gospel is enough. God does miracles. He doesn't fail. The failures I previously mentioned were not God's failures. No, they were Man's failure. I believe their failures, in large part, occurred due to misunderstandings and lack of knowledge regarding the gospel message and its application. Those men, and those movements, were targeted by the enemy of the gospel. By smearing them, he smeared their message. This still happens today.

I've personally witnessed deliberate attacks like this in my own life and ministry. Not everyone likes me. Some actually hate me. I've been slandered, libeled, lied about and shamefully treated. I've been accused of being a "con man" – with biting sarcasm, I've been called, "The prophet." I've been called a host of other names. I was called what I was called because I'm a minister of the gospel. Men and women will often seek to use your profession as a gospel preacher to game you. Some will seek to make you feel guilty over perceived wrongs. Others will "play victim". But, the gospel is enough; it is sufficient.

Billions have been saved, healed and delivered by the gospel message. The failures of the men and movements I previously mentioned did not occur as a result of lack of faith. No, it was something far worse, it was a lack of understanding concerning the gospel message, and, in some cases, wrong motives in the heart. Yes, some men and women have used, and continue to use, the gospel to further their own lavish lifestyles: they "pick the pockets" of those who support them for personal gain and greed. But, many gospel preachers suffer for lack of support; they have given their all to proclaim God's gospel.

The Gospel: Our Common Need

The gospel isn't about money or fame. The gospel isn't about personal gain and profit. The gospel is about much more. The gospel is more than a positive message. And, not every positive message is the gospel. False prophets and preachers can bring positive messages with disastrous results. Jeremiah, the prophet, declared, *"They dress the wound of my people as though it were not serious. 'Peace, peace,' they say, when there is no peace."* Jer. 6:14, *NIV*. The gospel is more.

The gospel is enough. It is sufficient. Once again, we, as ministers of the gospel, must learn to rely upon the gospel's sufficiency: no hype, just power. The gospel has the raw unadulterated power to save and deliver us from the power of sin, sickness and Satan. And, we need Christ's salvation. Mankind needs a redeemer. We need Jesus' delivering power. No one but He can set us free. We need healing from the brokenness so many of us have experienced, and do experience, by living in this fallen world. Yes, healing is in the gospel. So is prosperity, deliverance and much more. Ultimately, the gospel demonstrates our need for Christ. The simple gospel reduces us into the state of being one in need.

We need. Then, we discover we need Him. In 1987, I learned this amazing truth. I realized, by revelation, I was a sinner in need of a savior. No one told me I needed a savior. I realized my need when confronted by my sin. I wanted to sin. I liked my sin. But, I thought I was a good person. I didn't know that one sin could keep me from heaven. I didn't know that I couldn't save myself by my own good works. No one can. God doesn't offer work release programs. No, hell is the prison for sinners. I had no hope without Christ. I had a one-way ticket to hell. That scares me. And, I was ignorant of my condition: lost, helpless and hopeless... without Christ.

The gospel has the raw unadulterated power to save and deliver us from the power of sin, sickness and Satan.

But, my eyes were opened. I saw the light. I heard the gospel. God spoke to me. My life was changed in a moment of time. And, I've never regretted taking my present path. I'm not saying that I haven't experienced ups and downs. No, I have. But, in the middle of my pain, I remember what Christ did for me. And, it brings me hope. That's the language of the gospel. The gospel brings hope. That hope is the hope that I share in writing this book: Salvation can be found in no other Name, place or person than in the matchless Name of

Jesus. Today, salvation is coming to your house. Just believe the good news, and watch God work.

The Gospel Goes Primetime: America's "Tebow" Moment

The gospel is God's work. God made the gospel possible, not Man. The Gospel is God's idea: it originated in His mind and heart. No one else could bring us a message of hope like God could, and did. He, in the middle of our lostness and hopelessness, gave us His Son, Jesus Christ. John 3:16 says, *"For God so loved the world, that He gave His only begotten Son, that whosoever believeth in Him should not perish, but have everlasting life."*

John 3:16 is possibly the most famous Bible verse in history. That verse received heightened notoriety during America's "Tebow phenomenon," which news commentators called "eerie." What happened? In 2012, the Denver Broncos and Pittsburgh Steelers played in the playoffs. Tim Tebow was the quarterback. In that game, Tebow threw for 316 yards and averaged 31.6 yards per completion. Pretty amazing. And, the Bronco's intercepted the Steelers pass on Third and Sixteen, CBS's television ratings for that evening were 31.6 and the Steeler's finished the game with a time of possession of 31:06 minutes. Beyond amazing! And, all this took place three years to the date of the BCS Championship game where Tebow wore, under his eyelids, John 3:16. Wow!

Tebow, without uttering a single word, spoke to an unbelieving world: John 3:16. In a hardened world, certainly not one favorable to Christ or Christianity, on national television, John 3:16 was elevated to the nation's consciousness. Coincidence? Random? Such random acts had even cynical NFL executives saying, "Is that true? I'm converting," according to ESPN senior writer, Adam Schefter. The gospel is relevant and powerful. God still speaks. On January 8, 2009, God spoke through the 3:16 under Tebow's eyelids. On January 8, 2012, God spoke in more profound ways. Interestingly, Tebow, despite his obvious ability, has been unable to find a home in the NFL. Could it be the gospel message came through loud and clear? And, it was rejected. Only time will tell.

Rediscovering the Gospel's Sufficiency

That being said, the gospel message is not dead. No, God still speaks, and He will continue to speak the gospel message to a hurting world. America, and the world, desperately needs the gospel message: the gospel alone contains the sufficiency necessary to meet every human need. The Church also needs the gospel message, and we must be delivered from those false gospels that pervade the Church today. We must rediscover Biblical truth.

But, many believers have been diverted from the gospel. Much of the Church doesn't know or understand the gospel message. Most of the Church lacks the demonstrable power that results when the gospel is preached. We're more plugged into the world through our social media connections than we're plugged into the gospel message and its resultant power. Paul said, *"For I am not ashamed of the gospel of Christ: for it's the power of God unto salvation to everyone that believeth...."* Rom 1:16. We must unplug from the world and plug into God and His gospel.

Recently, I became overwhelmed by a simple truth: the gospel is enough. I began to meditate on this message. I started thinking about the power present in the gospel message, and my own need for that power. In March 2015, while attending a conference held by Andrew Wommack's Association of Related Ministries International (ARMI), I clearly heard the Lord speak to me: *"Heal the sick, cleanse the lepers, raise the dead and cast out demons."* Matt. 10:8. When I heard that message, I was much like the disciples who were told by Jesus to feed the multitudes: What? Then, how? But then, I realized what I heard was not a suggestion but a command. I knew what I was supposed to do, what I was commanded to do and what I wanted to do, but... I realized I fell short. That's when I made a decision to return to and rediscover the gospel message.

Since then, in my spirit, the words, The Gospel is Enough, have ruminated. Those words resonate with me. I know those words are true. I've experienced the gospel's sufficiency. Then, I began meditating on Christ, His ministry and His sufficiency. I thought about Paul, his life and ministry. I remembered my own life and ministry. By God's grace, I've witnessed some amazing things. But, what amazes me the most is the sufficiency of the gospel, and how naturally that sufficiency enters our lives, naturally supernatural.

Heaven's Upgrade for Mankind

I am a prophet. That's my calling. In 1987, God, through an open vision, spoke to me and called me into the ministry. I saw God's glory: it was like 10,000 suns rolled into one, if you can imagine that sight. Such love! And peace. While in that vision, I heard God's voice: He spoke two Scriptures to me. The first Scripture was: *"try the spirits whether they are of God"... "every spirit that confesses not that Jesus Christ is come in the flesh is not of God"... "and every spirit that confesses Jesus Christ is come in the flesh is of God."* I John 4:1-3. Then, *"even as Moses exceeding feared and quaked."* Heb. 12:21. This is my calling. I've sought to fulfill that heavenly vision.

This book is the culmination of that vision. I've learned that the gospel is enough. I've learned its power to bring provision. Healing. Deliverance. And much more. I've experienced the blessing side of the gospel, and its burden side. I've learned how to abound. I've also learned how to be abased. I know what it's like to experience good times, and bad. But, through it all, the gospel has been, and is, enough. I trust that you will partake of its sufficiency as well.

I believe the gospel is enough. Today, in the midst of our technological advances, believers in general, have lost the simple gospel. We have tried to upgrade the gospel. And, while the means by which we share the gospel may have changed, the power of the gospel, and the gospel itself, doesn't need a change. No, the gospel doesn't need an upgrade. The gospel is Mankind's upgrade. Rather than seeking to upgrade the gospel message by our own human reasoning, we need to download the gospel into our spirits. How? By following the simple pattern outlined in Scripture. We can reconnect to the gospel message by faith. Faith? Yes, faith that comes by hearing the gospel message, as it's preached.

Gospel Revelation + Gospel Anointing = Gospel Power

The gospel message requires anointed preachers. The Bible says, "And how shall they preach, except they be sent? as it is written, 'How beautiful are the feet of them that preach the gospel of peace, and bring glad tidings of good things!'" But, that anointing to preach the gospel message doesn't come by accident or chance. No, that anointing comes by hearing (and understanding) the gospel message. That means, to walk in the sufficiency of the gospel, we must know the gospel. Sadly, many don't know the gospel.

Paul the Apostle received the gospel message by revelation. His download came in the desert. And, his understanding of the gospel is paramount: it transformed the Church and turned it from Judaism to Christ. The Early Church relied on Paul. Even Peter was corrected by Paul when he strayed from the gospel. Paul had a deep, deep understanding of the gospel message. Paul's understanding of the gospel was far beyond others. He said, the other disciples "added nothing to him." But, this wasn't braggadocios. No, it was truth. Paul understood the gospel: he spent 17 years learning it, by revelation and study. And, during that quest, he discovered the gospel message.

God confirmed the truth of Paul's gospel by a release of divine power. Paul made a conscious decision to lay aside his own understanding of the Torah, though an expert in the Torah, to embark on a journey of reliance on the sufficiency of the gospel, and its power. Paul came to the realization: the gospel is enough. Paul went from revelation to realization after significant persecution. That persecution drove him back to the simple gospel conveyed to him by Christ while He was in the desert: Christ and Him crucified. That's the gospel. But, there's more.

The Gospel is More Than Enough

Like Paul, we must lay aside the trappings of success and the shames of failure. We must lose ourselves, and lay aside our reputations. We must lay aside our all to follow God's call. God, right now, is on the line with you. His question to you: "Will you give Me your all to follow My call?" He is looking for last day gospel preachers to share His significant message, with power, to a lost and dying generation bound in sin. And, believe me, there has never been a more necessary time for the gospel message. Today, people need the gospel. I need the gospel. You need the gospel. America needs the gospel. Yes, the world needs the gospel. Will you hear God's call?

Isaiah said: *"I heard the voice of the Lord, saying, 'Whom shall I send, and who will go for Us?' Then I said, 'Here am I. Send me!'* And He said, 'Go, and tell this people....'"* Is. 6:9. Go. Tell. Jesus said, *"Go into all the world and preach the gospel*

Like Paul, we must lay aside the trappings of success and the shames of failure.

to the whole creation." Mk. 16:15, HCSB. The gospel is meant to be preached, with power, to those who have never heard it. Millions upon millions. Billions! Billions of hurting men and women, boys and girls, have never heard the gospel message, once. Today, many in the Church don't understand the gospel or its power. We have much to do, for *"this gospel of the kingdom shall be preached in all the world for a witness unto all nations; and then shall the end come."* Matt. 24:14.

God's business is booming. Humanity is hurting. People are dying in sin. Men and women are bound by drugs, alcohol and other forms of addiction. Poverty and economic distress rail against families, communities and nations. Our gospel is needed. There has never been a greater time to be a gospel preacher doing gospel business. Business? Arguably, the business of the gospel is the most important business on planet earth today. Like Jesus, we must say, *"I must be about My Father's business."* Lk. 2:49. We, too, must devote ourselves to God's business: the gospel business. What is the gospel business? Promoting the good news. Proclaiming tidings of peace. The war is over. Satan has lost. God has won. Hallelujah!

Get Ready! The Radical Journey into the Gospel Message

Many today are looking for the return of Christ. And, while this is admirable, we must hear the words of the angels, *"Ye men of Galilee, why stand ye gazing up into heaven?"* Acts 1:11. Or, in my vernacular, what are you doing standing around; it's time to get to work. We must stop looking up and start looking out to touch and transform our world by the gospel. The gospel is enough; it has and can change society. We don't need to add to the gospel or take away from it. We need to preach it. To do that, we must understand it.

My hope is to convey to you, through this book, my understanding of the gospel. I recognize my own frailties in communicating this all-important message, and trust, by God's grace, that He will use His divine graces and downloads in my life to illuminate to you His gospel. That His gospel will enter your life, and radically transform your life and world. That the words on the page of this book, whether in print or electronic form, would enter your life with power: to save, heal, deliver and more.

Get ready! You are about to embark on a radical journey that will permanently and radically change you. Your life, as you know it, is over, and your new life is about to begin. Fasten your seatbelt! We're about to speed things up, and move things forward into higher gears. To paraphrase the gruff air force pilot in the 1998 hit movie, *Armageddon,* "On this mission, you will experience the [best] G[ospel]-Forces in... history...I intend to flip you, spin you, [stretch] your [brains] till your [mind] hurt[s]. ['Your eyes will be sucked into the back of your heads.'] Now load up and enjoy the flight."

Chapter Two

What is the Gospel?

Y ou have probably already heard the term gospel. And, you probably already have a preconceived idea of what the gospel is: Jesus came, died for our sins and redeemed Mankind. Or, what the word gospel means: good news. But, I want to approach this term, gospel, from the perspective of an unlearned person. I want to discover what gospel means by looking, searching and delving into Scripture.

First, the term gospel, as used in the New Testament, comes from the Greek word, **euaggelion,** a noun, which is the subject of the verb, **euaggelizó,** which is comprised of two root words, **eu**, an adverb, which means, well, well done, good or right, and **aggelos,** a noun, which means, an angel or messenger. Or, literally, the term gospel means an angel who announces good and right news that makes one well.

But, understanding the word gospel in its original language, Greek, is not enough. To fully understand the term gospel, we also need to understand it from the perspective of how it's used by those who used this term: Jesus, the Apostles (i.e., the Twelve Apostles of Christ) and the Apostle Paul. By understanding how each used the word gospel, I believe that we can gain insight into the fullness of the meaning of the term gospel.

What Jesus Said About the Gospel

How did Jesus use the term gospel in the New Testament? To answer this question, I want to take a look at places in the New Testament where He used this term. Each passage that follows is in red in the Bible, which means, Jesus spoke these words. As such, they are of special importance in our understanding of the term gospel.

<u>The Gospel of Matthew</u>

"Jesus answered and said unto them, 'Go and shew John again those things which ye do hear and see: the blind receive their sight and the lame walk, lepers are cleansed and the deaf hear, and the dead are raised up, and the poor have good news preached to them.'" Matt. 11:4-5.

"And this gospel of the kingdom shall be preached in all the world for a witness unto all nations; and then shall the end come." Matt. 24:14; See also, Mk. 13:10 *("And the gospel must first be published among all nations.")*.

"Verily I say unto you, 'Wheresoever this gospel shall be preached in the whole world, [there] shall also this, that this woman hath done, be told for a memorial of her.'" Matt. 26:13; See also, Mk. 14:9.

<u>The Gospel of Mark</u>

"Now after that John was put in prison, Jesus came into Galilee, preaching the gospel of the kingdom of God, and saying, the time is fulfilled, and the kingdom of God is at hand: repent ye, and believe the gospel." Mk. 1:14-15; See also, Lk. 7:22.

"And when He had called the people [unto Him] with His disciples also, He said unto them, 'Whosoever will come after Me, let him deny himself, and take up his cross, and follow Me. For whosoever will save his life shall lose it; but whosoever shall lose his life for My sake and the gospel's, the same shall save it.'" Mk. 8:34-35.

"And Jesus answered and said, 'Verily I say unto you, There is no man that hath left house, or brethren, or sisters, or father, or mother, or wife, or children, or lands, for My

sake, and the gospel's, but he shall receive an hundredfold now in this time, houses, and brethren, and sisters, and mothers, and children, and lands, with persecutions; and in the world to come eternal life.'" Mk. 10:29-30.

"And He said unto them, 'Go ye into all the world, and preach the gospel to every creature.'" Mk. 16:15.

The Gospel of Luke

"The Spirit of the Lord [is] upon Me, because He hath anointed Me to preach the gospel to the poor; He hath sent Me to heal the brokenhearted, to preach deliverance to the captives, and recovering of sight to the blind, to set at liberty them that are bruised, to preach the acceptable year of the Lord." Lk. 4:18-19.

In Matthew, Jesus used term gospel, or its variation, three times. In Mark, Jesus used the term gospel, or its variation, six times. In Luke, Jesus used the term gospel, or its variation, four times. In Matthew, Mark and Luke, Jesus used the word gospel sparingly. In John, neither Jesus nor John used the term gospel. The de-emphasis of the word gospel in the four Gospels (Matthew, Mark, Luke & John), was purposeful: to raise attention to that word. Often, for emphasis, author's will use words sparingly.

The word gospel is used 23 times in the 4 Gospels. Jesus used the word gospel 13 times in the Gospels. The authors of the Gospels Matthew, Mark and Luke used the word gospel the remaining 10 times. Neither John nor Jesus used the term, gospel, in the Gospel of John. In Matthew and Mark, the term gospel is primarily used as a noun. In Luke, the word gospel is primarily used as a verb. Matthew's and Mark's teaching is more of the subject matter of the gospel, whereas Luke's emphasis in teaching the gospel was active.

The gospel is both a subject to learn and a function to be done. We learn, then do, the gospel. Then, we do, and learn, the gospel. Our understanding of the gospel should be growing. We must make gospel learning a requirement in our churches or we'll miss the blessing of the gospel. One of my favorite Scriptures in relation to the gospel is in Mark 1:1: *"The beginning of the gospel of Jesus Christ, the Son of God...."* The gospel has a beginning. But, it doesn't have an ending.

Rediscovering the Gospel Jesus Preached

John, the revelator, uses the word gospel once in the five books he wrote: *"And I saw another angel fly in the midst of heaven, having the everlasting gospel to preach unto them that dwell on the earth, and to every nation, and kindred, and tongue, and people, saying with a loud voice, 'Fear God, and give glory to Him; for the hour of His judgment is come: and worship Him that made heaven, and earth, and the sea, and the fountains of waters.'"* Rev. 14:6. Here, John describes the gospel as the everlasting gospel. The gospel will never end.

In Matthew, Mark and Luke, we discover that Jesus Himself preached the gospel:

> *"And Jesus went about all Galilee, teaching in their synagogues, and preaching the gospel of the kingdom, and healing all manner of sickness and all manner of disease among the people."* Matt. 4:23.

> *"And Jesus went about all the cities and villages, teaching in their synagogues, and preaching the gospel of the kingdom, and healing every sickness and every disease among the people."* Matt. 9:35

> *"Now after that John was put in prison, Jesus came into Galilee, preaching the gospel of the kingdom of God..."* Mk. 1:14.

> *"And it came to pass afterward, that He went throughout every city and village, preaching and shewing the glad tidings of the kingdom of God: and the twelve [were] with Him...."* Lk. 8:1.

Preaching the gospel was not an afterthought with Jesus. No, it was a primary purpose. He spent a great deal of time traveling throughout all Israel to preach the gospel to all the Jewish people. His desire was for all Israel to hear the gospel. Matt. 15:24, *GWT* ("I *was sent only to the lost sheep of the nation of Israel.")* And, He faithfully preached all the gospel to all Israel prior to His death. Then, after His resurrection, Jesus commissioned His disciples to take the gospel to the world. Mk. 16:15 (*"Go ye into all the world, and preach the gospel to every creature."*)

Why did Jesus make preaching the gospel a primary focus in His ministry? Because by preaching the gospel, the devil's power is broken. 1 Jn. 3:8(b) (*"For this purpose, the Son of God was manifested, that He might destroy the works of the devil."*). Jesus loves when the gospel is preached, for His kingdom is established. The devil hates when the gospel is preached, for his kingdom is destroyed. That's why the gospel is always confirmed by the healing of the sick and deliverance of the oppressed.

When the gospel is preached, the sick are healed. When the gospel is preached, the bound are delivered. The preaching of the gospel is the cause to the effect of healing and deliverance in the ministry of Jesus and Paul. We need the gospel preached in our churches so that people who are bound and sick can be set free. This is God's will. Why then are so few healed? Why do so many believers suffer under the heavy burden of sin, sickness, disease and oppression? For one reason, the gospel isn't being preached.

How can this be? So many pastors in so many churches across our nation and around the world, week after week, faithfully teach their congregations from the Holy Scriptures. What is it that they are lacking? Why are churches failing to see the lost saved, the sick healed and the oppressed set free? As a pastor, I've asked these and similar questions. I've come to this conclusion: the gospel is sparingly being preached. I've also come to the conclusion that we don't know what the gospel is. Hence, my reason for writing this book.

Christianity 101

We must know what the gospel is, and we must preach the gospel. It isn't enough to teach the gospel. Further, the gospel must be published to all nations. God is waiting for us, His Church, to preach the everlasting gospel. But, we, His people, have focused on teaching the Bible not preaching the gospel. That strategy has not worked. We must go back to basics, Christianity 101: preach the gospel. To do that, we must know the gospel.

I began this Chapter by asking the simple question: What is the gospel? That question has been answered in part. We have learned the following about the gospel:

1) The gospel is good news from supernatural messengers;
2) The gospel brings glad tidings of wellness to those who hear it;
3) The gospel has a beginning, but it doesn't have an ending;
4) The gospel is meant to be preached by anointed preachers;
5) Jesus preached the gospel and was anointed to do so;
6) Jesus anointed and sent His disciples to preach the gospel;
7) The gospel must be preached, published and believed; and
8) When the gospel is preached, the devil's works (sickness, disease, bondage and oppression) are destroyed.

You may have heard or read what I've written above. But, there's more to the gospel. There's so much more. And, as you learn more about the gospel, you are going to realize your need to understand the gospel more. That's where we're going, but we still must answer the question: What is the gospel? Thus far, I've shared everything I've shared to bring you to this point: where you could truly begin to understand that question, and its answer.

Paul's Quest for Gospel Revelation

To answer that question, I must take us beyond where we have been. I must take us into the revelation of the gospel gained by Paul the Apostle. Unlike the 12 Apostles of Christ, Paul did not physically walk with Jesus while Christ was on earth. Paul learned about the gospel by divine revelation. It's that revelation that I want to delve into in the remainder of this Chapter. I want to view the gospel through Paul's eyes.

Paul began as a maniacal murderer. Paul was the least likely of all people to be called to preach the gospel let alone become an Apostle. Paul was a radical, no holds barred, wild-eyed, bloodthirsty Pharisee. Paul met Jesus by divine revelation. Paul, on his way to Damascus, met Jesus. But, Paul did not know who Jesus was. Paul was blinded by the radiance of Christ. Paul heard the gospel, *"I am Jesus whom you are persecuting...."* Acts. 9:5, *NASB*. Paul, stunned by his experience, identified Jesus as Lord.

Then, after being healed, Paul went his way into anonymity, Arabia and Damascus. For three years, he searched and studied the Scriptures. Paul, through the Scriptures, learned of his new-found faith, but he still hadn't learned the gospel. That would take another 14 years in Damascus. Amazingly, Paul emerged from his place of hiddenness to communicate his revelations of the gospel. Paul's burden: to bring his gospel revelation to the Gentiles.

Paul's revelation of the gospel surpassed even the most esteemed Apostles: Peter, James and John. How could this be? A man who persecuted the Church now teaching that same Church its primary message: the gospel? Paul blew the Apostles' minds. Their response: Paul, you preach the gospel to the Gentiles and we'll preach the gospel to the Jews. And, one more thing, Paul, be sure to remember the poor.

Paul's Radical Revelation of the Gospel

What revelation did Paul receive in his 17 years of isolation from much of the rest of the Church? Paul learned the roots of the gospel message. And, those roots run deep; they run all the way back to Abraham. In Galatians 3:3, Paul writes, *"And the Scripture, foreseeing that God would justify the heathen through faith, preached before the gospel unto Abraham, saying, 'In thee shall all nations be blessed.'"* Paul identified the essence of the gospel message: God extended the Abrahamic covenant to everyone, everywhere. How? By justification through faith.

Paul's revelation of the gospel, as revealed in Galatians, consists in his identification of Christ's role in the gospel message. According to Paul, Jesus fulfilled seven distinct roles: He was/is:

1) the Promised Seed,
2) the Promised Heir,
3) the Promise Holder,
4) the Promise Bringer,
5) the Promise Mediator,
6) the Promised Sacrifice, and
7) the Promised Redeemer.

Jesus fulfilled each of these seven distinct roles under Paul's understanding of the gospel. And, Jesus made the gospel available to everyone by fulfilling each one of these roles. The gospel is for everyone, everywhere; no one is excluded because of his/her past, race, gender, income or any other distinguishing mark from a worldly perspective. We must never lose sight of this essential truth. God is no longer working through only one nation, Israel. No! God is calling for everyone, everywhere to come to Him through a simple faith in His Son, Jesus Christ. God's kingdom, through heaven's door, Jesus Christ, has been opened to everyone who chooses to place their faith in Him. And, there's a BIG sign over that door saying, ENTER here.

In Galatians, Paul begins the process of explaining his understanding of the gospel. Paul's understanding of the gospel begins with Abraham. The gospel is designed to bring everyone into Abraham, Jew and Gentile alike. This understanding shocked the conscience of the Jews, especially the ardent students of the Torah, i.e., the Jewish law, the Pharisees and Sadducees. How could the Gentiles find admission into Abraham's covenant without subscribing to the Jewish faith? To Paul, the answer was simple, and it could only be found in Christ.

The Gospel: From Moses to Christ

According to Paul, Jesus was the promised seed, **not** Isaac: Christ was established as the promised seed through the Abrahamic covenant. Further, Abraham's covenant only extends to the promised seed. And, Abraham's other seed, the Jew, cannot gain entrance into the Abrahamic covenant except through the promised seed, Christ. Paul, by his revelation of the gospel, that's contained and revealed in the Torah, brings the Jew down to the same level as Gentiles: Sinners separated from God's covenant.

Paul was hated by the Jews because of that revelation. That's why they tried so hard to kill him: He laid waste their understanding of the Abrahamic Covenant and used the Torah to displace their false understanding of the Torah. Then, he replaced that false understanding with a true understanding of what was contained in the Torah, as revealed through Christ. Paul sets forth a new understanding of the Torah's futility, and the necessity of Christ's faith. And, all are required to come to God through faith in Christ. None are exempt.

Paul's gospel has two different mutually exclusive elements: 1) Moses' Torah was removed and replaced by Christ's faith, and 2) Christ's faith now governs access to God for all humanity. Paul uses the Torah to explain the Torah, and, at the same time, reveals gospel truth contained in the Torah: The law is represented in the Torah by Mount Sinai and Christ's faith by Jerusalem. The law, Mount Sinai, is represented by Hagar, and Christ's faith, Jerusalem, is represented by Sarah. Both are revealed in the Torah by the Torah. Or, the gospel is revealed, by type and shadow, in the Torah.

A New Covenant for All Mankind

Paul's gospel: The Torah is insufficient to make Mankind righteous, and Christ's sacrificial death is sufficient to make Mankind righteous. Grace. But, there's more. The sufficiency of Christ's sacrifice is established through a binding agreement, New Covenant, that was also put into effect by Christ's sacrificial death. Christ's sacrifice is sufficient to make Mankind righteous. Anyone, Jew or Gentile, can enter into Christ's sufficiency by faith in the sufficiency of that sacrifice: the propitiation of Christ's sacrifice is by faith alone. But, there's more.

Christ's death, as the promised seed, caused His estate to pass to those who place their faith in the sufficiency of His sacrifice. Christ, the initiator of the New Covenant by His Sacrificial death, bequeathed His estate, the promise and promised land, to those who place their faith in Him and His sacrifice. Christ, by and through His Will, has established His Testament – the New Testament or New Covenant. Now, Christ, after His resurrection, mediates His Will, aka Testament, to ensure that it's enforced, as He willed. Paul's understanding of the gospel is truly revolutionary.

God, Man's Creator, longed to settle His dispute with Man. What dispute? Man's sin. *"But your wrongs have separated you from your God...."* Is. 59:2, GWT. What sin? *"Your first forefather sinned, And your spokesmen have transgressed against Me."* Is. 43:27. Man ate from the tree of the knowledge of good and evil. Since then, God has sought to resolve that dispute. The prophet Isaiah prophesied of God's desire to end His dispute with Man: *"'Come now, let's settle this,' says the LORD."* Is. 1:18, *NLT.* God offers Man an opportunity to justify himself. *"'Present your case,' says the LORD. 'Set forth your arguments,' says Jacob's King."* Is. 41:21, *NIV.* But, Man had no case. The facts were against us. God was right, Man had sinned. The result: *"You were sold because of your sins."* Is. 50:1, *GWT.* We became slaves to sin.

Christ's sacrificial death is sufficient to make Mankind righteous.

Through ages and generations, God sought for a man to bridge that great divide. *"I looked for someone who might rebuild the wall of righteousness that guards the land. I searched for someone to stand in the gap in the wall so I wouldn't have to destroy the land, but I found no one."* Ezek. 22:30. No one was found. *"He saw that there was no man, and wondered that there was no one to intercede...."* Is. 59:16. All sinned. All placed themselves under the dominion of sin. God loved Man, wanted to redeem Man, but couldn't find a man to bridge the gap between God and Man. That is, until Jesus. Jesus was the Man. Jesus, as a man, was destined to bridge that gap. He was the promised seed – the One.

God's Law of Redemption and Redemptive Process

The Abrahamic covenant established a system of faith, which is separate from and superior to the Torah, whereby Mankind could be justified or made righteous. That covenant made the dispute resolution process possible. How? God needed one Man, Christ, to undo what one man, Adam, had done. But, to undo what Adam had done, Christ needed three things in place at his coming: 1) a sacrificial system, 2) a nation of people and 3) governing authority over that nation. Hence, the process of redemption begins with Abraham. Why? Abraham initiated a new system of exchange between heaven and earth – Faith.

But, faith alone wasn't enough, dominion in the earth was also required: a nation with its own land on earth had to exist where the Abrahamic covenant was practically implemented. That's why the land of Israel is so important to the redemption process. Abraham, by faith, obtained dominion over that land. The LORD told Abram, *"Look off to the north, south, east, and west from where you're living, because I'm going to give you and your descendants all of the land that you see – forever!"* Gen. 13:14, *ISV*. Biblically, the land was promised first. Why? Dominion. To restore Mankind, Abraham's promised seed, Christ, needed dominion in the earth.

God promised Abram the land. Then, God promised Abram his seed would inherit that land. *"And I will establish My covenant between Me and thee and thy seed after thee in their generations for an everlasting covenant, to be a God unto thee, and to thy seed after thee."* Gen. 17:7. Paul's revelation: Christ, not Isaac, was the promised seed. Or, Christ, by birthright, had dominion over the promised land, for He is the promised seed. Christ's dominion over the land meant Christ had authority in the earth like Adam. That authority in the earth gave Christ the right, under law, to redeem Mankind. What law? The law of redemption.

There are two tracks to God: 1) Torah, and 2) Faith. The Torah track had a significant problem: it revealed Mankind's sin but could never justify Mankind. God's dispute with Mankind could never be resolved through the Torah. Even the Jewish people, masters in understanding the Torah, couldn't fulfill its exacting standards. The Torah had an exacting system of rules and procedures for approaching God. No one could fulfill its exacting standards... until Christ was born. Christ's birth, death, life, resurrection and ascension are essential to understanding the gospel message:

1) Jesus was born with sinless blood;
2) Jesus died with His blood still being sinless;
3) Jesus lived a sinless life in the face of overwhelming sin;
4) Jesus' sinless blood, justice demanded, could not die, for death lacked dominion; and
5) Jesus ascended to heaven with His sinless blood as evidence of His dominion over sin.

Mankind was in a desperate place: we were born slaves to sin and became slaves to sin by God's law. But, God had a plan. What plan? To redeem Man. To redeem Mankind, God needed three things in place at Christ's coming:

1) a Man who could redeem,
2) a currency that he could use to redeem Mankind, and
3) a land that that Man could redeem.

Why did God need these three things to redeem Mankind? In the beginning, God gave Adam dominion in and over the earth. But, God placed a special clause in that contract: The redemption clause. The Torah reveals that clause; it's a right of redemption. A man who sold himself into slavery could be redeemed. Land sold to a stranger could be redeemed. Adam, by sin, sold himself into slavery to sin. Adam, by sin, sold the earth to a stranger, Satan. But, a right of redemption existed.

Jesus: The Promised Seed, Promised Land and Promised King

Ruth, a Moabitess woman, married an Israelite. By marriage, she entered the family. But, her husband died, his only brother also died, and her father in law, Elimelech, died. Elimelech owns land in Israel. The land passed to Naomi. Naomi wanted to sell the land. That land could be redeemed. A family member, a kinsmen redeemer, could redeem the land. But, to redeem the land, two conditions had to be fulfilled: the redeemer had to 1) buy the land, and 2) raise up seed. In Ruth, Boaz exercised the right of redemption of the land. Boaz bought the land. Boaz raised up seed for the house of Elimelech: Obed was born. From Obed, Jesse. From Jesse, David. And, David became Israel's king. Jesus is David's descendant.

In Luke, Jesus' lineage on His mother's side is shown. In Matthew, Jesus' lineage on His adopted father's side is shown. On both sides, Jesus is David's seed. Why is this important? Because God promised David: *"When thy days are fulfilled, and thou shalt sleep with thy fathers, I will set up thy seed after thee, that shall proceed out of thy bowels, and I will establish His kingdom. He shall build a house for My Name, and I will establish the throne of His kingdom forever. I will be His Father, and He shall be My Son...."* 2 Sam. 7:12-14(a). Jesus is Abraham's seed, David's seed and God's seed. In the Old Testament, this Scripture is the clearest evidence that Christ is both the Son of God and Son of Man: A New Testament reality.

The Abrahamic covenant contained both a promised land and seed. The Davidic covenant contained both a promised kingdom and seed. Both covenants are everlasting covenants. God further promised David that his seed would build God's house. And, the final promise, which is the greatest promise: That God would be the father of David's seed. Amazing! God connects Abraham, David and Himself by these two covenants with two different men. Why did God make these two covenants with these two men? To reestablish Mankind's dominion in the earth through the promised seed, land, house and kingdom. Jesus has, and is, fulfilling God's promises to Abraham and David.

Christ is the promised redeemer. Christ redeemed Mankind by exercising the right of redemption outlined in the Torah. Christ, to redeem Mankind, required an accepted currency that was not under the dominion of sin. The problem: everything in the earth was under the dominion of sin. Mankind voluntarily submitted to sin's dominion. How? By sinning. But, Christ never sinned. Sin never had dominion over Christ. Christ had something of value on earth that was not under the dominion of sin that could be used to redeem the earth and Mankind. The Torah established a recognized system of exchange, a sacrificial system. Its currency? Blood.

Christ's Authority to Resolve Disputes

Jesus redeemed the earth and Mankind with His own blood. Jesus, as the one who redeemed Man, has authority over the earth and Mankind. Jesus reigns! He is the great arbiter of the New Covenant. He has binding authority over the parties to the dispute: God and Man. God is a party. Man is a party. God has submitted to Christ's decision over Man. Man can submit to Christ's decision. If we submit, He renders God's dispute resolved. This is the gospel. The angels declared the gospel on the eve of Christ's birth: *"Glory to God in the highest, and on earth peace, good will toward men."* Lk. 2:14. This was the inauguration of a new day: Peace!

The Torah failed to resolve God's dispute with Man. Instead, it exacerbated that dispute. So, God replaced the law by fulfilling the law. Now, Christ alone resolves all disputes between God and Man. Jesus Christ, God and Man, has all authority in heaven and earth to resolve all disputes between God and Man. This is truly revolutionary. How so? Christ's work isn't one way. Christ can make binding decisions to resolve any and all disputes between the parties. Think about that for a second. Has that thought sunk in? God has given, and Christ by His sacrificial death has obtained, all authority to judge all disputes between God and Mankind: to bring them to resolution. This is good news.

What about those who doggedly refuse to submit to Christ's authority? If Mankind chooses to not submit to Christ's authority, then God's dispute with Mankind remains and *"[a]ll that is left is a terrifying wait for judgment and a raging fire that will consume God's enemies."* Heb. 10:27, *GWT.* Jesus, either way, as redeemer, has final authority to judge that which He has redeemed: the earth and Mankind. Jesus is Judge, and *"He will not falter or lose heart until justice prevails throughout the earth. Even distant lands beyond the sea will wait for His instruction."* Is. 42:4, *NLT.*

What is the gospel? In a nutshell, the gospel is the good news of the coming of the promised seed, the heir of the promised land, who would establish the promised kingdom and build the promised house by redeeming the earth and justifying Mankind through His own blood by fulfilling the law and placing everyone everywhere, through faith in His sacrificial death, under the Abrahamic covenant: Or, as God said to Abraham, *"in you, shall all families of the earth be blessed."* This is the good news of God's grace toward Mankind.

Chapter Three

The Gospel of Grace

"I am astonished that you are so quickly deserting Him who called you in the grace of Christ and are turning to a different gospel...." Gal. 1:6, ESV.

I magine the gospel message that I've just described as a giant diamond. That diamond is perfect; it's unique and valuable. But, to see the brilliance of that diamond, we must uncover its different facets. Specifically, I want to showcase three different facets of the gospel that are essential to its understanding:

1) the gospel of grace,
2) the gospel of the kingdom, and
3) the gospel of Christ.

I'll also spend time on other facets of the gospel:

1) the gospel of peace,
2) the gospel of the circumcision,
3) the gospel of the uncircumcision, and
4) the gospel of salvation.

In this chapter, I'll share my understanding of the gospel of grace. Your ability to understanding this chapter will enable you to grasp the deeper concepts of the gospel as we move forward. In Chapters Four and Five, I'll spend time sharing my understanding of the gospel of the kingdom and the gospel of Christ. Christ devoted His entire earthly ministry teaching and preaching the gospel of the kingdom, and with remarkable results. We need to understand the gospel of the kingdom. And, the gospel of Christ. Christ is the epitome – the cornerstone and capstone – of the gospel. That facet of the gospel message will contain deeper realms of revelation of the gospel. In Chapters Six and Seven, I'll spend time sharing the difference between the gospel to the circumcision and the gospel to the uncircumcision, and the differences. And, then, will turn to the peace we have with God and the salvation offered.

The Grace Revelation

First, there are not several different gospel messages. No, there's one gospel with several facets. Second, I want to differentiate the term gospel with the terms Gospels. Here, Gospel(s) stand(s) for the four books written by Matthew, Mark, Luke and John. The Church has chosen to call these books of the Bible, the Gospels. When I speak of the gospel, I'm not speaking of one specific book in the Bible. Rather, I'm speaking of the message delivered by several authors in the New and Old Testaments that contained the singular defining message revealed to the Church: the gospel. When I say gospel, that's what I mean. When I say Gospels or Gospel I mean a specific book in the Bible.

What is the gospel of grace? The gospel of grace is a revelation of God's grace. Peter, the Apostle who had the gospel of the circumcision committed to him, called God the God of all grace. 1 Pet. 5:10. The Apostle Paul, who had the gospel of the uncircumcision committed to him, said, *"God is able to make all grace abound toward you; that ye, always having all sufficiency in all things, may abound to every good work...."* 2 Cor. 9:8. Both Peter and Paul understood the gospel of grace.

Peter understood God's grace. Peter failed Jesus miserably. Peter was tempted to deny Christ, and he did three times. Then, Peter saw Jesus on His way to the cross. Jesus locked eyes with Peter just after Peter denied Him. Peter wept bitterly. Peter was broken by this experience. No other experience prepared Peter to understand God's grace like this one. He failed. But, despite Peter's failure, Jesus had a plan for Peter: Peter, by grace, would become a rock.

Paul understood God's grace. Paul was a murderer and blasphemer; he regularly and zealously threatened and persecuted the Early Church. Paul, like Peter, was a proud man. Paul was brilliant: he was chief among his Pharisaical peers. And, he loved it. Until one day, on his way to Damascus, he had a face to face encounter with Christ. Paul was broken by this experience; it forever changed him. Immediately, Paul recognized the depth of his deception, and with these words submitted to Christ: *"Who art Thou, Lord?"* Acts 9:5. Paul received grace.

What is grace? Some have defined grace as unmerited favor. Others have defined grace as God's ability on our behalf. In this chapter, grace is defined as receiving what we don't deserve. Conversely, mercy is not receiving what we do deserve. Neither Peter nor Paul deserved grace. But, they needed it. And, when they received grace, both were changed by it. Grace, unlike anything else, can change the most ardent sinner. Grace can set free those who are bound by guilt and shame. Peter had shame: he denied Christ. Paul had shame: he murdered Christians and blasphemed Christ. But, grace set them both free.

The Joyful Sound of Amazing Grace

One of the most famous songs ever written, *Amazing Grace*, was penned by John Newton, a former slave, former slave trader, poet and minister. In verse, he poetically describes his experience with God's grace:

Amazing grace, how sweet the sound that saved a wretch like me! I once was lost but now am found, was blind but now I see.

'Twas grace that taught my heart to fear, and grace my fears relieved; How precious did that grace appear the hour I first believed!

The Lord has promised good to me, His Word my hope secures;
He will my shield and portion be as long as life endures.

Through many dangers, toils, and snares I have already come;

'Tis grace hath brought me safe thus far, and grace will lead me home.

When we've been there ten thousand years, bright shining as the sun,
We've no less days to sing God's praise than when we'd first begun.

Newton met God's grace, and it changed him. Newton was a slave trader and had also been a slave. He resigned himself to the slavery he was suffering under, and subject to, in Sierra Leone. Newton saw the dark world of slavery, and it changed him. So much so that later in life he joined forces with William Wilberforce to oppose slavery in the British Empire and seek its abolition. Newton wrote Amazing Grace on New Year's Day in 1773.

Since then, it has become one of the most widely recognized hymns in history. Newton's heartfelt song reaches down to the depths of the human spirit, and the inner cry of Mankind for grace. Deep down, we know our own failures. Despite the praise of men, we recognize our own need. We need God's grace. We need something that we don't deserve, that we cannot buy and is offered freely in only one place – the gospel message.

Moments of Grace in America's History

The gospel of grace has changed our nation. America has had several grace awakenings. Americans have been shaken, and changed, by the power of grace. That's one of the reasons we need a renewed understanding of the gospel message today: to obtain grace for the times in which we live. Like our predecessors, we need the gospel message of grace. That message alone has the power to break the chains holding this generation captive to its sins. Whether we acknowledge them or not, our sins have caused us to stumble as a nation. We need God's grace.

The First Great Awakening: In the 1730's and 1740's, America experienced the First Great Awakening. George Whitefield and Jonathan Edwards were considered leaders. Edwards' message,

Sinners in the Hands of an Angry God, was so strong that men and women literally held on to the pews, lest they be dragged into hell. Edwards brought a reverence for God. Whitefield's preaching brought revolution: his booming voice enabled him to preach to 20,000+ people in grass fields across America. Whitefield sparked revival in the hearts of men and women in our nation. That spark led to the American revolution. Their understanding of the message of grace, as shown by Edwards: "There is nothing that keeps wicked Men at any one Moment, out of Hell, but the mere Pleasure of GOD."

The Second Great Awakening: From 1790 to 1820, America experienced a Second Great Awakening. Charles Finney, Francis Asbury, Henry Ward Beecher and Peter Cartwright, among others, led that awakening. Finney, in particular, was instrumental: he brought a message of grace that could save men and women from sin. Finney knew that message and preached it fervently without fear. Through his message, many came to Christ. That message is encapsulated by the following quote by Finney: "Let no one expect to be saved from hell, unless the grace of the Gospel saves him first from sin."

The Third Great Awakening: From 1850 to 1910, America experienced a Third Great Awakening. Possibly the most notable leader within that awakening was D.L. Moody. Moody founded Moody Bible Institute located in Chicago, IL. Moody's message resonated with the hearts of his generation. That message is embodied by this Moody quote: "I find that many Christians are in trouble about the future; they think they will not have grace enough to die by. It's much more important that we should have grace enough to live by."

Grace Awakenings in America's Recent History

America wouldn't be the nation it is today if these, and other, awakenings had not occurred. America experienced the healing grace in the 1940's and 1950's. America's churches experienced charismatic graces in the 1960's and 1970's. Dennis Bennet and

David du Plessis (Mr. Pentecost), in particular, were instrumental in bringing the Holy Spirit's grace to mainline denominations. America's youth experienced grace in the Jesus Movement of the late 1960's and early 1970's. In the 1980's, America experienced more grace, the grace of worship. Maranatha and Integrity Hosanna were instrumental in releasing this grace to the Body of Christ.

In 1991, I prophesied of a coming revival. I published those prophetic words in 1994. My book, *Decade of Destiny*, prophesied of a coming revival, and that war would follow. I experienced the grace offered in that revival. And, it was a mighty outpouring of grace. In 1995, I remember how Wheaton College was visited by God: students openly wept, confessed their sins and prayed for forgiveness. In 1996, revival even took hold of small communities like Smithton, Missouri and propelled them to the national spotlight. In 1997, a million men, Promise Keepers, marched on Washington, D.C. In 1998, I visited Pensacola, Florida where the Brownsville Revival took hold of our nation: hardened sinners were turned to Christ. The fire of revival was present. God showered grace on His people. The prophetic word came to pass.

God has truly shed His grace on America. From 1730 to 2017, grace, that we're often ignorant of as a nation, preserves us still. The Church in America has partaken of that grace. We have been refreshed by grace. Many have been converted because of grace. Grace is in the DNA of America; it's our most precious resource. From that well of grace, billions of men, women and children have drunk. America, by grace, has become the world's #1 superpower. We are it. The world recognizes this fact, and many envy what grace has afforded us. We, as a people, should consider our position, and the necessity of grace.

America has been blessed by grace. But, that grace is also available to other nations, and its people. God has invited everyone to His table to partake of His grace. You are invited. But, this invitation will expire. So, there's urgency in accepting that invitation to partake of God's grace. That's why it's important for us to understand the grace message that's contained in the gospel. The gospel is a gospel of grace.

The Pseudo-grace Movement

The Apostle Paul, in his letter to the Galatians, made a bold declaration: you are *"deserting Him who called you in the grace of Christ and are turning to a different gospel."* Gal 1:6, *ESV.* Paul was astonished that the Galatian believers had departed from the gospel of grace to a different gospel. Even Peter became enamored by this different gospel. Paul plainly states, *"false believers... infiltrated our ranks to spy on the freedom we have in Christ Jesus...."* Gal. 2:4, *NIV.* What did they bring? A different gospel. Paul issues a stern warning to the Galatians regarding this different gospel: *"[I]f any man preach[es] any other gospel unto you than that ye have received, let him be accursed."* Gal. 1:9. And, Paul rebuked Peter.

Paul understood the gospel of grace and set a high value on it. Paul understood what that message brought him: freedom from deception. Paul had been deceived. Unlike the Apostles of Christ, Paul had killed believers in the name of religious zealotry. Paul was zealous. But, his zeal had caused him to do unspeakable things. Paul was stung by the bitter truth: he was deceived. Yes, that truth set him free, but it hurt. And, he was scarred by it. Paul understood how fast deception could grow, and he didn't want deception to steal one of the most valuable things the Galatians had received: the gospel of grace.

What is the gospel of grace? To answer that question, I'd like to take you on a journey of understanding of the grace message. The grace message is vital to the Christian life. Without it, we can easily fall into a different gospel. That being said, many in our day have fallen for a pseudo-grace message. Right now, the Church is struggling with this issue, and asking the question: What is the right message on grace?

Recently, an article by John Burton was published by *Charisma* magazine that's entitled "5 Marks of the False Grace Message." Burton, in his articles, identifies five distinct false messages being spread within the current grace movement:

1) a theology of exemption from the penalties for sin,
2) a worldview that treats sin as temporary troubling but eternally benign,
3) repentance and confession are not needed after salvation,
4) works are renounced as legalistic, and
5) salvation is depicted as easy and permanent.

Michael Brown wrote an article published by *Charisma* magazine entitled, "Confronting the Error of Hyper-Grace." In that article, Brown describes what he believes the message of that Hyper-Grace movement is: "God does not see the sins of His children, since we have already been made righteous by the blood of Jesus and since all of our sins, past, present and future, have already been forgiven." In his article, Brown easily debunks this message. But, no one is named or called to the carpet; it's an ethereal grace movement.

The Grace Revolution: Grace, Grace, Grace

Joseph Prince and Andrew Wommack are leaders who sparked what has been termed the Grace Revolution. And, believe me, the Church does need a grace revolution. But, we need a correct understanding of grace. Neither Brown nor Burton name Prince or Wommack in their confrontation of the hyper-grace message, but it's likely they are speaking of them.[1]

To understand grace, we must understand the gospel. The Church lacks a basic understanding of the gospel. And, that's the reason we don't understand the gospel of grace. But, ignorance of the gospel is no excuse. And, each of us is held accountable for our understanding, or lack thereof, of the gospel. The gospel is a gospel

---

[1] I am a member of Andrew Wommack's ministry association, Association of Related Ministries International (ARMI).

of grace; it's a significant aspect of the gospel. And, as shown, the Church's understanding of that message has changed over the past 200 years. Edwards spoke of God's grace in sparing us from hell. Finney spoke of God's grace in keeping us from sin. Wommack and Prince, like Moody, speak of God's grace to live the Christian life.

Peter tells us to *"grow in the grace and knowledge of our Lord and Savior Jesus Christ."* 2 Pet. 3:18. The Church's collective knowledge of God's grace is, and should be, growing. And we the Church are responsible for understanding what is and was revealed. Remaining in the same place as prior generations

> **We must move from the tombs and monuments of prior generations without forgetting what was revealed to them.**

is not acceptable. We must move from the tombs and monuments of prior generations without forgetting what was revealed to them. Our reflection of His grace, like our faith in His grace, should be ever increasing.

Paul spent much time teaching the Church the gospel of grace. The gospel of grace is reflected to two different groups in two different ways: Jew and Gentile, circumcised and uncircumcised. Peter was called to the circumcision. Paul was called to the uncircumcision. Peter's level of grace extended to the Jew. Paul to the Gentile. So, each ministered the gospel of grace in different ways to their respective audience. Peter wrestled with the grace message: How could Jew and Gentile be the same in God's eyes? Paul didn't; he embraced the grace message: Yes, in God's eyes, both Jew and Gentile are Abraham's seed and heirs of the promise.

Like Peter, some wrestle with the grace message. Like Paul, some embrace it. I prefer to embrace the gospel of grace, for it's an integral part of the gospel. I believe we need more grace, not less. But, for us to receive more grace, we must have an accurate understanding of the gospel. The gospel of grace is one critical facet of the gospel. What I shared in Chapter One is the real gospel: Our identification with Abraham by faith in Christ: His birth, life, death, resurrection and ascension. To the degree that we fail to identify with this message, we have fallen for a different gospel and fallen from grace.

The Real Gospel of Grace and Its Fruits

The gospel of grace begins with this important understanding: *"For by grace are ye saved through faith; and that not of yourselves: it is the gift of God: Not of works, lest any man should boast."* Eph. 2:8-9. Grace opened the door to salvation: *"For the grace of God has appeared, bringing salvation to all people."* Titus 2:11, *ISV.* *"So what makes us think we can escape if we ignore this great salvation that was first announced by the Lord Jesus Himself and then delivered to us by those who heard Him speak?"* Heb 2:3, *NLT.* The gospel of grace says, "Grace is available to save you."

But, salvation is not the only thing grace is designed to bring. In Weymouth's translation of Titus 2:11, it says, *"For the grace of God has displayed itself with healing power to all Mankind...."* Or, grace also brings healing. That means healing is a significant part of the grace message. Healing and grace go hand-in-hand. We need grace for healing, and healing is the result of the work of grace in our lives. Healing grace.

But, there's more. The Greek word for salvation is *sozo,* a verb. Grace brings action. As Paul wrote in Titus, grace brings salvation to all Mankind. That salvation includes miracles of healing. God is a healer. Salvation and healing are God's work, and that work is a work of grace. God grace causes good to happen in our lives. Remember, *"[e]very good and perfect gift descends from above, from The Father of lights with whom there is no change nor a shadow of variation."* James 1:17, *ABPE.* God is unchanging in His work of grace toward us.

My response to the controversy of the "hyper-grace" message and those who oppose that message: *"Each tree is recognized by its own fruit."* Lk. 6:44, *NIV*. Every work is known by its fruit, visible and invisible. Whether the grace revolution is harmful, time will tell. With that being said, I want to propose a different perspective:

1) an absence of grace exists;
2) such absence is notably visible;
3) we need more grace;
4) our failures are the result of the absence and lack of grace;
5) untapped grace is available;
6) we lack grace because we don't know the gospel message; and
7) our failure to preach the gospel message has resulted in a lack of grace.

A Gospel Revolution is Emerging

We need a gospel revolution: ministers and believers who are ready and willing to learn the gospel message, and then preach that message. The gospel message is good news: *"In you [Abraham] shall all nations be blessed."* Gal. 3:8. Specifically, as it relates to this chapter, it's the good news of grace. God's grace has appeared to all Mankind. Christ is the epitome of God's grace. By His grace, Christ solidifies His place in our lives. Or, Christ is revealed in our lives by the grace demonstrated through our lives. That grace brings salvation and healing.

Paul stated, *"But when it pleased God, who separated me from my mother's womb, and called me by His grace, to reveal His Son in me, that I might preach him among the heathen...."* Gal. 1:15-16. The gospel of grace preached by Paul was directly related to Paul's call. God called Paul by grace, committed to him the message of grace, and then, by grace, enabled him to preach that message. Paul, at all times, was required to rely on grace. Paul, in his weakest and darkest moments, was to solely rely on God's grace. Christ's message to Paul: *"My grace is sufficient for you, for My power is made perfect in weakness."* 2 Cor. 12:9.

Christ's message to Paul speaks volumes about the gospel of grace:
1) God's grace is sufficient, 2) God's power is available when we rely on God's grace, and 3) God's grace and power are revealed in our weakest moments. Paul, after years of preaching the gospel of grace, needed that gospel preached to him. Paul, after hearing the gospel of grace, repented for relying

> **We need a gospel revolution: ministers and believers who are ready and willing to learn the gospel message, and then preach that message.**

on his own ability and made a determination to rely on God's grace: he rejoiced in his weaknesses in the midst of great turmoil and torment. Grace.

The Message of Grace in the Gospel

The gospel of grace requires humility: something that's sorely lacking in our day. The gospel of grace requires us to understand our humanity: we're frail and weak. The gospel of grace requires honor: Christ has all power in heaven and earth. Paul committed this gospel of grace to the Church before he was martyred: *"And now I commit you to God and to the message of His grace, which is able to build you up and to give you an inheritance among all who are sanctified."* Acts 20:32, HCSB.

Paul committed the gospel of grace to the Church, and the Church was committed to the gospel of grace: *"And from there they sailed to Antioch, from where they had been committed to the grace of God for the work that they had fulfilled."* Acts 14:26, BLB. That gospel opened the door for all people everywhere to hear of God's grace: *"When they had arrived and gathered the Church together, they began to report all things that God had done with them and how He had opened a door of faith to the Gentiles."* Acts 14:27, BLB.

The grace I speak of in this chapter comes from the Greek word, **charis** or **charisma,** nouns, and it means unmerited grace, favor, blessing, gift, credit and thanks. This gift is different from the gift described in Ephesians 4:8: *"When He ascended up on high, He led captivity captive, and gave gifts unto men."* That gift comes from the greek word, **doma** or **didomi,** and carries the idea of being an abiding endowment from a sovereign. The gospel of grace is an unmerited and free gift: *"For by grace you are saved through faith, and that not of yourselves, for it is the gift of God...."* Eph. 2:8, DRB.

The gospel is God's gift, **doron,** the presentment of a gift, **doma,** to Mankind: *"Thanks be unto God for His unspeakable gift."* 2 Cor. 9:15. That gift was given by an act of grace, **charis**, by God's sovereign will. We didn't earn that gift. No, God gave it. And, He gave it with no strings attached. The gift is available to all who want it. The gospel of grace is the message of good news concerning this gift that has been given to Mankind. When we tell people of God's gift, we're sharing with them the gospel of grace.

Living a Grace-filled Life

The truth is: none of us deserved the grace gift given. We have all failed. We knowingly and willfully sinned against God. That knowing sinfulness enslaved us further to sin. We were bound by invisible chains, made from our sins, to sin. We fashioned our own chains of enslavement. God, by grace, broke those chains. We became free. That freedom came by an act of unmerited favor from God. God, moved by compassion, set us from the chains fashioned by our own sinfulness. Grace.

The gospel of grace: we're no longer slaves to sin, for we have been redeemed. We sold ourselves into slavery: *"Behold, for your iniquities have ye sold yourselves...."* Is. 50:1. And, *"You were sold, but no price was paid. You will be bought back, but without money."* Is. 52:3, GWT. The gospel of grace is the path to freedom from sin, **not** a license to sin. God's grace is sufficient to set us free from enslavement to sin. Further, the gospel of grace teaches us that we have been made sons: *"And because you are sons, God has sent* *the Spirit of His Son into our hearts, crying, 'Abba! Father!'"* Gal. 4:6, *ESV.*

Grace makes us sons of God. We, like Christ, are sons of God. We're not servants, but sons. But, as sons, we serve. Grace frees us from sin and enables us to serve as sons. Further, grace gives us enablements to serve as sons. Like Christ, as sons, we serve by the enabling power of God's grace: *"There are different gifts, but the same Spirit."* 1 Cor. 12:4, *BSB.* Those graces are available to each and every believer: *"Indeed, we have all received grace after grace from His fullness...."* Jn. 1:16, *HCSB.*

The gospel of grace is a message of power: we have 1) power over sin, and 2) power to serve as sons. The gospel of grace is a message of sonship: *"Beloved, now are we the sons of God...."* I Jn. 3:2(a). The gospel of grace is a message of inheritance: *"So you are no longer a bondservant, but a son; and if a son, then an heir of God through Christ."* Gal. 4:7, *WEB.* Grace not only makes each of these things possible; it makes them a living reality for those who are able to receive and walk in that message of grace.

Pure Grace: God's Gift to Mankind

How then do we walk in the gospel of grace? First, we must preach the unadulterated message of the gospel of grace. The grace message is easy to corrupt for utterly human purposes: power, greed, sensuality and selfishness. We corrupt the gospel of grace by: 1) ignoring it, 2) watering it down, or 3) replacing it. In each case, we replace the gospel of grace with another message. When this happens, we lose the power associated with the gospel of grace.

Paul, in Galatians, wrestled with men who sought to replace the gospel of grace with another message: the message of the law. What was the message of the law being preached by those men Paul wrestled with: *"That the Gentiles should live like the Jews."* Gal. 2:14. Paul showed Peter the hypocrisy of this message: Peter, you're living like a Gentile, why do you expect Gentiles to live like Jews? Id. But, that message did not stop with Gentiles being required to live like Jews, it also required Jews to go back to living like Jews. The issue: Neither Jew nor Gentile could keep the requirements of the law; we could not be justified by the law.

Paul confronted this false message being preached by the false brethren. Paul used strong words to rebuke Peter. Paul used strong words to confront the Galatians. Listen to what Paul said: *"I am astonished that you are so quickly deserting the one who called you to live in the grace of Christ and are turning to a different gospel...."* Gal. 1:6, NIV. *"You foolish Galatians! Who has bewitched you?"* Gal. 3:1(a), NIV. *"But even if we (or an angel from heaven) should preach a gospel contrary to the one we preached to you, let him be condemned to hell!"* Gal. 1:8, NET. Paul considered the perversion of the gospel of grace a serious matter. And, we should too!

The Church's ignorance has led us to a place where it's ripe for deception. That deception will likely seek to pervert the gospel message, especially in relation to the gospel of grace. In some corners of the Church today, there's a reintroduction of the law in place of grace. In other corners, there's an open license to sin in the name of grace. In either case, *"How shall we escape if we neglect so great salvation?"* Heb. 2:3, DRB.

License and the Deception of False Grace

Wearing the Christian name badge doesn't make one a Christian. Using Christian lingo doesn't make one a Christian. Undoubtedly, there will be men or women who wore the Jesus pin, or cross, that go to hell. Jesus said, *"Many will say to Me on that day, 'Lord, Lord, did we not prophesy in Your Name, and in Your Name drive out demons and perform many miracles?' Then, I will tell them plainly, 'I never knew you; depart from Me, you workers of lawlessness.'"* Matt. 7:22-23, BSB. Paul understood his responsibility before God: *"Because we understand our fearful responsibility to the Lord, we work hard to persuade others."* 2 Cor. 5:11(a), NLT.

In Paul's day, many were wrecked by the false message being preached by false brethren seeking to turn them from the gospel. Peter, Jesus' disciple, a leading apostle among the twelve Apostles of Christ, was nearly derailed by that false message. Paul rebuked him. Gal 2:11-21. Paul even feared he could be turned: *"But I chastise my body, and bring it into subjection: lest perhaps, when I have preached to others, I myself should become a castaway."* 1 Cor. 9:27, *DRB.* Paul witnessed his own disciples turn: *"Cling to your faith in Christ, and keep your conscience clear. For some people have deliberately violated their consciences; as a result, their faith has been shipwrecked. Hymenaeus and Alexander are two examples. I threw them out and handed them over to Satan so they might learn not to blaspheme God."* 1 Tim. 1:19, 20, *NLT.*

Peter was seduced by a false message designed to lead him from the gospel message: true grace. Paul feared that he could be seduced by a false message that would turn him from the gospel. Paul's own disciples were seduced, left the faith and turned from the gospel. By their example, we should learn, at any cost, how to hold on to the gospel, especially the gospel of grace. We must preach the gospel of grace. We must listen to the gospel of grace. We must know what the gospel of grace is.

The Power of Pure Grace

Today, in our technological age, nothing is more important than rediscovering the gospel, especially the gospel of grace. I've witnessed the power of the gospel of grace in my own life: it has transformed and changed me. I've seen the power of the gospel of grace by way of signs, wonders and miracles. My ministerial friends have walked in the power of grace. I've been walking in the power of grace. That's how I've learned to live: faith in the gospel message.

Like Paul, *"My message and my preaching were [are] not with persuasive words of wisdom, but with a demonstration of the Spirit's power, so that your faith would not rest on men's wisdom, but on God's power."* 1 Cor. 2:4-5, *BSB*. I know that *"God's kingdom is not just talk, it is power."* 1 Cor. 4:20, *GWT*. Power.

Like Paul, *"I am not ashamed of the gospel, because it is the power of God for salvation to everyone who believes, first to the Jew, then to the Greek."* Rom. 1:16, *BSB*. Power. When

The Church's ignorance has led us to a place where it's ripe for deception.

the gospel is preached, it always demonstrates itself through its power. Never forget this.

In 1987, I heard the gospel for the first time; it transformed my life. In 1988, I experienced something that forever changed my life: I heard God speak to me audibly. That experience forever changed me. I was meditating on Act 1:8: *"But ye shall receive power, after that the Holy Ghost is come upon you: and ye shall be witnesses unto Me both in Jerusalem, and in all Judaea, and in Samaria, and unto the uttermost part of the earth."* While meditating on that Scripture, God spoke to me these words, "I said power." When He said this, it shook me to the core. Hearing God's audible voice is like surround sound on supernatural mega-steroids: His voice resonates from everywhere all at once. There's nothing like it.

Power, that's what the gospel, especially the gospel of grace, brings. And, peace. If our message doesn't shake men and women, it's not the gospel. If our message doesn't transform men and women, it's not the gospel of grace. If there's no tangible demonstration of power, it's not the gospel being preached. And, if there's no peace, the gospel isn't being preached. We may be speaking, even preaching, but the gospel isn't going forth. The fruits of the gospel are its power and peace. Anything less is fruitless.

When the kingdom comes, it always comes with power. When the kingdom comes, it always offers peace: *"How beautiful are the feet of those who bring good news!"* Rom. 10:15(b), *NIV.* Now, if someone refuses to receive the gospel message, it doesn't bring them peace. No, it brings them under the weight of its convicting power. Yes, the real gospel brings conviction of sin, righteousness and judgment. That conviction can stir up both contention and controversy. The gospel message is controversial. Paul was beaten and left for dead. I've had friends killed for preaching the gospel. But, God! He raised them from the dead. What did they do? They went back to preach the gospel to those who killed them.

That's the power of the gospel. The gospel of grace is transformative. The gospel of grace is revolutionary. The gospel of grace enables us to move into the next realm of the gospel: the gospel of the kingdom. That's the gospel Jesus preached. He had unprecedented results in preaching the gospel of the kingdom. That's the next facet of the gospel we'll examine.

Chapter Four

The Gospel of the Kingdom

"This gospel of the kingdom shall be preached in the whole world as a testimony to all the nations, and then the end will come." Matt. 24:14, *NASB*.

J esus's message was revolutionary: it was radical. Christ heralded the beginning of a new day: God's kingdom had come to earth. That message caused conflict. From birth, Christ was hunted. Herod, Israel's king, sought to kill Jesus. Why? Herod recognized that Christ would institute a new order and that order would replace him. Christ is king. Ultimately, and ironically, Israel's leaders crucified Christ. What was His crime? The superscription over His head on the cross stated His crime in the Greek, Latin and Hebrew: *"JESUS OF NAZERATH, THE KING OF THE JEWS."* Jn. 19:19.

The gospel of the kingdom is controversial; it has been since its inception. Jesus, of His gospel of the kingdom, said, *"And from the time John the Baptist began preaching until now, the Kingdom of Heaven has been forcefully advancing, and violent people are attacking it."* Matt. 11:12, *NLT*. Violent men and women attacked Jesus because of the gospel of the kingdom. But, Jesus didn't stop. Christ explained to His disciples: *"Don't think that I came to bring peace to earth. I didn't come to bring peace but conflict."* Matt.

10:34, *GWT*. We need to understand that conflict swirls around the gospel of the kingdom.

Kingdoms in Conflict

Why does the gospel of the kingdom bring such conflict? Satan hates this message. He hates it so much that he *"immediately comes and takes away the word [gospel of the kingdom] that is sown in them."* Mk. 4:15, *ESV*. The gospel of the kingdom spells the devil's doom: His kingdom has been and is being destroyed. Jesus declared war on Satan: Christ came to overthrow principalities and powers ruling the earth in secret places. *"And having disarmed the rulers and authorities, He made a public spectacle of them, triumphing over them by the cross."* Col. 2:15, *BSB*. The cross spelled the end. It is finished. The war is over. Jesus won.

The advent of the kingdom brought with it the possibility of transformation: individually and collectively, personally and societally, the gospel changes hearts. Jesus' message transforms: it turns Mankind from Satan's power to God's power. By the gospel, Mankind is literally translated from Satan's kingdom to God's kingdom, instantaneously. The gospel's proclamation causes that transformation: the seed of the kingdom contains sufficient power to immediately and instantaneously stop, reverse and overthrow every satanic power and work. Mankind always overcomes Satan when it hears the gospel of the kingdom and believes it. *"Now thanks be to God, which always causes us to triumph in Christ, and makes manifest the aroma of His knowledge by us in every place."* 2 Cor. 2:14, *AKJV*.

The Manifested Kingdom of God

The gospel of the kingdom is powerful: signs, wonders and miracles always follow its proclamation. Jesus, upon commissioning His disciples, said to them: *"And as ye go, preach, saying, The kingdom of the heavens has come. Heal the sick, cleanse the lepers, raise the dead, cast out demons; freely ye have received, freely give."* Matt. 10:8, *JUB*. The kingdom has come; it's here right now, and we can enter into it. Entrance into God's kingdom always causes its manifestation in our midst. Jesus makes sure of it. *"The disciples spread [the Good News] everywhere. The Lord worked with them. He confirmed His Word by the miraculous signs that accompanied it."* Mk. 16:20, *GWT*.

The gospel's proclamation is powerful, it always causes the sick to be healed, the blind to see, the deaf to hear, the crippled to walk, the maimed to be made whole, the terminally ill to become instantly well, and even the dead are raised. This is the Bible's plain truth, and it's necessary for our day. We need this power. Why do we have so little of it? Because our message doesn't comport to the gospel of the kingdom. We have watered down that message to make it palatable to Mankind: Jesus wants to save you. No! The gospel of the kingdom is much, much more. What is the gospel of the kingdom? Jesus reigns!

Mankind always overcomes Satan when it hears the gospel of the kingdom and believes it.

The Kingdom of Christ Reigns... Now

Jesus' reign began at His immaculate birth. Listen to the wise men that came from the east: *"Where is He who has been born King of the Jews? For we saw His star in the east and have come to worship Him."* Matt. 2:2, *NASB*. Jesus was born King of the Jews. His divine right as King of the Jews is detailed in His genealogy. Matt. 1:1-16. On Joseph's side, His adoptive father, Jesus had divine right. *Id.* On Mary's side, His natural mother, Jesus had divine right. Lk. 3:23-38. Jesus is David's son and Abraham's son. Jesus was king of Israel by virtue of His birth. But Jesus isn't only the Son of Man, He is also the Son of God. As such, Jesus is King of kings by virtue of birth.

Jesus' reign was revealed through His sinless life: He manifested His kingdom's power to triumph over sin and sickness; He loosed men, women and children from bondage to Satan. Jesus never sinned. *"He never sinned, and He never told a lie."* 1 Pet. 2:22. *"God had Christ, who was sinless, take our sin so that we might receive God's approval through Him."* 2 Cor. 5:21, *GWT.* Satan tempted Christ. Christ defeated Satan's temptations. By defeating Satan's temptations, Christ defeated Satan. *"The reason the Son of God appeared was to destroy the devil's work."* I Jn. 3:8, *NIV.* He won! How? By not sinning.

Jesus' reign was sealed by His sacrificial death: He won by allowing hell to perpetrate its injustice against Him, an innocent man, who was not under the dominion of sin. The cross, hell's worst torment, was turned into the instrument of Mankind's salvation. Jesus hanging on the cross was the most unjust act ever committed. Satan crucified Christ. *"None of the rulers of this age understood this, for if they had, they would not have crucified the Lord of glory."* 1 Cor. 2:8. God's wisdom was concealed to them; Satan had no understanding of the purpose of the cross: His injustice would satisfy the demands of justice. By the cross, God was able to execute judgment on Satan and thereby save humanity. What wisdom!

Jesus' reign was proved by His authority over death, hell and the grave. *"I am He that lives, and was dead; and, behold, I am alive for evermore, Amen; and have the keys of hell and of death."* Rev. 1:18, *AKJV.* Jesus, because He committed no sin, had authority to take back His life. *"The Father loves Me because I sacrifice My life so I may take it back again. No one can take My life from Me. I sacrifice it voluntarily. For I have the authority to lay it down when I want to and also to take it up again. For this is what My Father has commanded."* Jn. 10:17-18, *NLT.* That authority stemmed from justice's demand: Christ, an innocent man, was unlawfully executed. That execution proved Satan's lawlessness. Jesus took back His life, and lawfully freed the prisoners bound in Satan's prison. *"I am the LORD, I have called you in righteousness...To bring out prisoners from the dungeon. And those who dwell in darkness from the prison."* Is. 42:7, *NASB.* And again, *"You ascended on high, leading a host of captives in your train...."* Ps. 68:18, *ESV.* Satan intended on keeping Man a prisoner forever. *"He hath made the world as a wilderness, and his cities he hath broken down, of his bound ones he opened not the house."* Is. 14:17, *YLT.* Had Christ not stepped in, Mankind would have been lost forever: no other man could escape the prison house of sin and Satan.

Jesus reigns. Christ's kingdom was established, as prophesied by Daniel: *"In the days of those kings shall the God of heaven set up a kingdom which shall never be destroyed, nor shall its sovereignty be left to another people; but it shall break in pieces and consume all these kingdoms, and it shall stand forever."* Dan. 2:44, *WEB.* Notice: **"in the days of those kings."** What kings? The four kingdoms prophesied by Daniel: 1) the Babylonian kingdom, 2) the Persian-Medes kingdom, 3) the Grecian kingdom and 4) the Roman kingdom. This is historical fact. *"Therefore, because we have received The Kingdom that is not shaken, we shall receive grace by which we shall serve and please God in reverence and in awe."* Heb. 12:28, *ABPE.* Jesus' reign will continue forever; His kingdom is an everlasting kingdom. It has no end.

The Kingdom Message is the Kingdom's Seed

Many believers are waiting for the kingdom to come, someday; they don't recognize that the kingdom has come. Instead, they were taught the kingdom of God will come when Jesus returns. Like ancient Israel, multiplied millions of believers are waiting for the kingdom to come in the future, someday. They have believed a lie. That lie has permeated the Church and kept the Church powerless and in a place of bondage. No! Christ has come; His kingdom is here. This is the gospel of the kingdom: The King has come, and the Kingdom is here. Proclamation of Christ's Kingdom and the triumph of that kingdom is the essential seed. That's the seed we're called to sow into the earth. The sowing of that seed produces powerful results: signs, wonders and miracles. As Paul said, *"God's kingdom is not just talk, it is power."* 1 Cor. 4:20, *GWT.* The gospel of the kingdom is inescapable: *"It is written: 'As surely as I live,' says the Lord, 'every knee will bow before Me; every tongue will acknowledge God.'"* Rom. 14:11, NIV.

Listen to Daniel's interpretation of the dream received by Nebuchadnezzar: *"During the reigns of those kings, the God of heaven will set up a kingdom that will never be destroyed, nor its sovereignty left in the hands of another people. It will shatter and crush all of these kingdoms, and it will stand forever."* Dan. 2:44, ISV. *"This is the stone that you saw cut out from a mountain, but not by humans."* Dan. 2:45, GWT. Now, listen to what Christ said to Peter: *"You are Peter, and I can guarantee that on this rock I will build My Church. And the gates of hell will not overpower it."* Matt. 16:18, GWT. In this Scripture, we see the stone, ***petros*** (Greek) a/k/a Peter, cut from the

Proclamation of Christ's Kingdom and the triumph of that kingdom is the essential seed.

mountain, ***petra*** (Greek), that will lay waste to the kingdoms of this world. Peter, a stone, received revelation from the Father of the Son, the mountain. No wonder Peter says, *"And you are living stones that God is building into His spiritual temple."* 1 Pet. 2:5, NLT. Like Peter, we're living stones cut from the mountain by the Father's revelation of the Son. That kingdom, by proclamation, crushes and destroys every other kingdom of this world.

Peter's Message on the Kingdom of God and Hell's Shaking

Peter proclaimed the gospel of the kingdom on Pentecost: *"So let everyone in Israel know for certain that God has made this Jesus, whom you crucified, to be both Lord and Messiah!"* Acts. 2:36, NLT. Peter proclaimed God's kingdom on Pentecost. The result: *"Stung to the heart by these words, they said to Peter and the rest of the Apostles, 'Brethren, what are we to do?'"* The kingdom has come in power by proclamation. Conviction was present. Listen to Peter's response to their question: *"Peter said to them, 'Repent, and be baptized, every one of you, in the Name of Jesus Christ for the forgiveness of sins, and you will receive the gift of the Holy Spirit. For the promise is to you, and to your children, and to all who are far off, even as many as the Lord our God will call to Himself.'"* Acts 2:38,39.

Peter learned to preach the gospel of the kingdom by listening to the person of Christ. That was and is his primary message. *"Jesus went throughout all of Galilee, teaching in their synagogues, preaching the gospel of the kingdom, and healing all kinds of disease and sickness among the people."* Matt. 4:23, NET. When Christ preached that gospel, tremendous signs, wonders and miracles followed. Jesus spoke of God's kingdom often. In fact, after His resurrection but prior to His ascension, *"He spoke about The Kingdom of God."* Acts. 1:3, ABPE. Think about that for a second: Jesus trained His disciples to walk in His kingdom, spent significant time teaching them about His kingdom and proved, by significant acts, that His kingdom was real, and after all this, spent the last days prior to His ascension teaching them more about His kingdom.

That message, the message of the kingdom, is the message we need today. We need to rediscover what Jesus taught His disciples concerning His kingdom. We should follow Christ's admonition: *"Seek the Kingdom of God above all else, and live righteously, and He will give you everything you need."* Matt. 6:33, NLT. In our day, the gospel of the kingdom must be placed like a battering ram before the Church. Like Jeremiah, the apex of that message gives to the Church *"authority to announce to nations and kingdoms that they will be uprooted and torn down, destroyed and demolished, rebuilt and firmly planted."* Jer. 1:10, NET. A Church with this message at its helm shall not fail, for *"upon this rock I will build My Church, and all the powers of hell will not conquer it."* Matt 16:18, NLT.

The Secret of the Kingdom

Before I begin teaching the gospel of the kingdom, I want to prove to you that it's God's will for us to know about His kingdom. Listen to what Jesus teaches: *"Fear not, little flock; for it is your Father's good pleasure to give you the kingdom."* Lk. 12:32. Christ confronts a common fallacy: God wants to keep us in the dark. No, Mankind lives in the dark because it wants to live in the dark. Or, because *"[t]he god of this age has blinded the minds of unbelievers, so that they cannot see the light of the gospel that displays the glory of Christ...."* 2 Cor. 4:4, *NIV*. But, we can come into the light. We can receive divine revelation of the kingdom of God. We can know what we believe, why we believe what we believe, how what we believe works, why what we believe works and why what we believe matters. We can receive answers to our deepest questions concerning the gospel of the kingdom: who, what, where, when and how.

The Bible contains that revelation. *"The secret of the kingdom of God has been given to you. But to those on the outside, everything is said in parables."* Mk. 4:11, *NIV*. But, that revelation of the kingdom doesn't come in its fullness; rather, it comes in its seed form. Why is that? Because God requires those who want to know the kingdom to have that kingdom seed planted in their hearts. *"Hear then the parable of the sower: When anyone hears the message of the kingdom but doesn't understand it, the evil one comes and snatches away what was sown in his heart. This is the seed sown along the path."* Satan always seeks to steal Mankind's understanding of God's kingdom: he knows how dangerous the kingdom message is to his kingdom.

Hidden Wisdom Ordained by God for Glory

God has, in times past, kept this message hidden from Mankind. Why? Because of the power that's contained in the kingdom message. The kingdom message has explosive power; it can unlock the mysteries of the ages and the powers of the world to come. Col.

1:27; Heb. 6:5. Further, once those secrets are revealed, they become ours. *"The secret things belong to the LORD our God, but the things that are revealed belong to us and to our children forever...."* Deut. 29:29, *ESV.* Understandably, God keeps this kingdom message under lock and key. How? To understand the kingdom message, we must be born again: *"I can guarantee this truth: Mankind cannot see the kingdom of God without being born from above."* Jn. 3:3, *GWT.*

The world doesn't see or believe in God's kingdom. To them, it doesn't exist. And, we who do believe in God's kingdom are considered foolish. In reality, the world is foolish: *"God hath chosen the foolish things of the world to confound the wise...."* 1 Cor. 1:27. *"[B]ecause God's foolishness is wiser than human wisdom...."* 1 Cor. 1:25(a). That's why many, especially wise and learned men and women, don't understand God's kingdom: their own wisdom prevents them from knowing God's wisdom. As such, we cannot understand God's wisdom if we cling to our human wisdom. We cannot understand God's kingdom if we cling to human concepts of how the world works. We can only understand God's kingdom if we lay aside our own wisdom and begin seeking His wisdom, His way. James 1:13-17.

Guiding Principles in Understanding the Gospel

God's way to wisdom is plainly revealed in Scripture. But, that doesn't mean it's easy to receive or easily understood by those who receive it. In regards to entering God's kingdom, Jesus said: *"I can guarantee this truth: No one can enter the kingdom of God without being born of water and the Spirit."* Jn. 3:5, *GWT.* What?! Born of water and the Spirit? Many scholars debate what this section of Scripture means. Some believe "water" represents baptism. Others believe "water" represents God's Word. Still others believe "water" represents the flesh of Man. Still others believe it's the spirit of Man. I've just provided four different beliefs that represent four distinct understandings of what Jesus said in John 3:5. And, there are good arguments for each. So then, to understand what Jesus meant, we need help, for it's not clear, except by revelation.

To understand what Jesus meant in John 3:5, we must understand the first principles of interpretation of Scripture: *"No prophecy in Scripture is a matter of one's own interpretation."* 2 Pet. 1:20. We don't interpret Scripture. No, Scripture interprets itself. What do I mean? I mean that we must learn how to measure what is revealed in Scripture by Scripture. Why? Because *"Scripture cannot be broken...."* Jn. 10:35. What is contained in Scripture is true: *"Your word is truth."* John 17:17, ISV. To accurately interpret Scripture, all Scripture must fit together: *"Be diligent to present yourself approved to God as a workman who does not need to be ashamed, handling accurately the word of truth."* 2 Tim. 2:15, NASB. How do we accurately understand what Scripture teaches? We learn. *"Whom shall He teach knowledge? and whom shall He make to understand doctrine? them that are weaned from the milk, and drawn from the breasts."* Is. 28:10. Here are some guiding principles I've learned and use to understand Scripture:

1) I start from the plain meaning of the text.
2) I look at the context of the text and the plain meaning of the text surrounding that text.
3) I look at each word used in the text, how it's used and how those words are used in the surrounding text.
4) I reference the first place where that word was used in the whole of Scripture, i.e., the law of first reference.
5) If the meaning of the text isn't easily determinable, I let the whole of Scripture determine what the text means.
6) If the meaning of the text isn't easily determinable, I look at the historical and primary language context of the usage of the words in the text.
7) I invite the Holy Spirit to teach me what the text means.

In seeking to instill Biblical insight into the gospel of the kingdom, I'm utilizing the above-referenced protocol to aid in our understanding of Christ's gospel. To start, we must understand what is meant in John 3:3 & 5. To see the kingdom of God, we must be born again. To enter the kingdom of God, we must be born of water and the Spirit. To rightly interpret what Jesus is saying, we must look to other Scripture utilizing the same or similar language. In this case, 1 John 5:6: *"Jesus Christ is the one who came by water and blood – not by the water only, but by the water and the blood."* That strongly leads me to believe that the water spoken of by Christ in John 3:5 means being born in the natural, i.e., having a human body.

Foolish Messages, Demonic Doctrines & False Kingdoms

One of the greatest heresies in the Early Church was a doctrine developed by a group called Gnostics. Gnostics developed a doctrine called Gnosticism, and that doctrine led many believers astray. Essentially, Gnostics taught that all flesh was evil. Because all flesh was evil, Jesus Christ, as God, had to devolve from His divinity to take on human flesh. That act of devolvement meant a number of beings, lesser gods, existed who were below God, but above Christ. Gnosticism is clearly contradictory to Scripture. But, many fell into deception through this foolish teaching, and in the process, fell from the faith.

Today, other religions promote Jesus Christ's goodness but not his divinity. Mormonism is a branch of the resurgence of Gnosticism. Mormons believe Jesus Christ and Lucifer are brothers. Jehovah's Witnesses are a branch of the resurgence of Gnosticism. Jehovah's Witnesses deny Christ's deity and believe Christ was raised as a quickening spirit, not in His resurrected body. The New Age movement is a branch of the resurgence of Gnosticism: they believe they are divine, i.e., God. Further, they believe there are other spirit beings, also gods, who can help them realize their divinity. To them, Christ is the divine force that exists in everything and everyone.

Islam was built, in part, in response to Gnosticism. Muslims believe in one God. Muslims believe Jesus Christ was a prophet. But,

Muslims deny Jesus Christ's divinity. And, Muslims deny Jesus Christ is the Son of God. Islamic teaching states: God has no son. That's one of the major tenets of their faith. Further, they deny the existence of the trinity: Father, Son and Holy Spirit. Mohamed believed Christians were polytheists, belief in many gods, because of the belief in the trinity: three gods, not One God. Muslims are looking to establish, by force, a caliphate, e.g. kingdom, where their Mahdi reigns. The Mahdi is Islam's messiah.

I've identified several different religions that contain significant errors. I've presented those false religions to you for a purpose: to show you how important faith is, and how easy it is to be deceived. What we believe matters. We live in a world that's filled with deception. Satan is called the *"deceiver of the whole world."* Rev. 12:9. Jesus called him the *"father of lies."* Jn. 8:44. No wonder Solomon said, *"Buy the truth and sell it not...."* Prov. 23:13.

What we believe about the gospel is important. That's why Jude, Jesus' brother, said, *"I felt it necessary to write and urge you to contend earnestly for the faith entrusted once for all to the saints."* Jude 1:3. Paul encouraged us to *"fight the good fight of faith."* 1 Tim. 6:12. In *WNT*, 1 Timothy 6:12 states, *"Exert all your strength in the honourable struggle for the faith; lay hold of the Life of the Ages, to which you were called, when you made your noble profession of faith before many witnesses."* I want to encourage you to do the same.

We must contend for the faith delivered to us by those who preceded us. And, we mustn't only learn from their teachings but the lives they lived. Too often, we don't learn from, or respect, those who have preceded us. By honoring our predecessors, we honor God. Further, we protect ourselves from the spirit of deception in this world. The devil has deceived entire nations and generations. Often, we mock and malign the superstitions of prior generations, not realizing we have our own false beliefs. Really?! Yes, really. Here are some examples, to name a few: 1) Evolution, 2) Alien Life, 3)

Overpopulation, and 4) Global Warming. All are deceptions believed by significant numbers of people. We would do well to take heed to Paul's admonition: *"Be not deceived; God is not mocked: for whatsoever a man soweth, that shall he also reap."* Gal. 6:7.

My Revelation of the Kingdom of God

Previously, I spoke about what Jesus meant by His statement: *"I assure you, no one can enter the Kingdom of God without being born of water and the Spirit."* Jn. 3:5, NLT. I believe Jesus meant Man must be born of flesh and Spirit to enter the Kingdom of God. I've explained why I believe what I believe in part. Let me explain my other reasons.

> Prior to 1988, I had a number of supernatural experiences take place in my life. I had an open vision where I saw God's glory. I spoke in tongues. I had numerous dreams. And, I had other supernatural experiences: words of knowledge, prophecies, divine appointments and leadings. I was acutely aware of God's power and presence.
>
> In 1988, I had shared with one of my friends, Kevin Rocca, that God called me into the office of prophet. He being new to the faith, like me, wanted to know if what I said was true. He tested me by asking me a simple question: How did Jesus come? Immediately, I said back to him: *"By water and blood."* When he heard this, immediately, he knew I was God's prophet. He tested my calling by following the Scripture in 1 John 4:4. He wanted to see what my answer would be. He was shocked when I responded like I did. From that point, he knew what I said regarding my calling as a prophet was true. And, I knew what Jesus meant when he said *"by water and blood."* *Decade of Destiny.*

I believe Jesus metaphorically used water to signify flesh in John 3:5. That being said, I don't claim prophetic authority to state with certainty that this is what He meant. Further, there are strong arguments that the water spoken of in John 3:5 is God's Word. Paul referred to the washing of the water by the word. Eph. 5:25. Peter said, *"Being born again, not of corruptible seed, but of incorruptible, by the Word of God, which liveth and abideth forever."* 1 Pet. 1:23. As such, I accept both as reasonable and believe both apply. That means I can authoritatively state that John 3:5 refers to: 1) natural birth, and 2) rebirth by God's Word. In other words, we enter God's Kingdom by natural and spiritual birth, and by God's Word and Spirit.

My reason for explaining how I arrived at my conclusions for John 3:5 are:

1) to show you that reasonable persons can disagree about what Scripture means;
2) to show you my thought process in discerning what Scripture means;
3) to help you think about what you read in Scripture, to discern its true meaning;
4) to show you how to arrive at a reasonable conclusion about what Scripture means; and
5) to provide you a pathway toward an authoritative understanding of Scripture.

As we explore what Jesus meant concerning the Kingdom of God, such a process will prove invaluable. Now, I'm not going to explain line by line my thought process in teaching the gospel of the kingdom. That would be too much work for me, and it would rob you of your own ability to search the Scripture for yourself to see if what I'm saying is true. I don't want to weary myself or incentivize poor work habits. Instead, I want to provide you with an overview of God's kingdom, how it works, and why it works the way it does.

Kingdom Owners, Land Possessors & Hidden Storehouses

In teaching on God's Kingdom, I want to start with in Matthew 13:52: *"'Therefore,' He said to them, 'every student of Scripture instructed in the kingdom of heaven is like a landowner who brings out of his storeroom what is new and what is old.'"* I want to dissect this Scripture. One, to understand God's kingdom, we must become students of Scripture. Two, it's not enough to study Scripture, we must be instructed in God's kingdom. Three, once instructed in God's kingdom, our position changes to that of being a landowner. Four, as landowners, we have a storehouse. Five, that storehouse contains things new and old.

For three years, Jesus preached the gospel of the kingdom; He instructed everyone who would listen about the kingdom of God. Jesus spent a significant amount of time teaching and training the 12 Apostles to walk and work in the kingdom of God. Jesus publicly and privately taught on the kingdom of God. In public, He spoke in parables. In private, He explained those parables. Jesus' entire ministry was dedicated to teaching the kingdom of God. I hope you realize the importance of what I'm saying: Jesus, God in the flesh, instructed 12 men, His Apostles, and then He sent them to do what He did: preach the gospel of the kingdom.

From the beginning of His ministry, that was His plan. Jesus did not consider His ministry effective based on its size. Nor did Jesus dismiss the importance of His work based on the number of people affected. Jesus did not seek to reach everyone during His earthly ministry. Jesus said, *"I was sent only to the lost sheep of Israel."* Matt. 15:24. Were there not others who needed His message? Of course! But, Christ recognized the boundaries that were set for Him by the Father, and He stayed within those boundaries.

Christ's ministry became the most successful when it appeared least successful: on the way to and on the cross. Don't measure your effectiveness as a gospel preacher by false narratives – size and reach aren't always the most important attributes in spreading the gospel message. There are other considerations that must be taken into account, like finding the right soil to sow the seed.

Jesus' message, His gospel, was about the kingdom of God. Jesus taught that message, that gospel, to His twelve Apostles and seventy disciples. Jesus sent His 12 Apostles and 70 disciples forth to preach that gospel. Jesus' apostles and disciples saw their message confirmed through signs, wonders and miracles. Listen to what Jesus told His 12 Apostles, prior to sending them forth: *"Heal the sick, raise the dead, cleanse those with skin diseases, drive out demons. You have received free of charge; give free of charge."* Matt. 10:8, HCSB. The gospel Jesus taught and preached worked.

The Parable of the Kingdom

Jesus' first parable concerning the kingdom of God is the parable of the sower. This parable is fascinating, for in each Gospel where it's referenced, there are slight variations. Mike Murdock, a man who has dedicated his life to the study of wisdom, states, "Wisdom is the study of difference." That means, to gain the wisdom hidden in the parable of the sower, we must study the differences in each parable in each Gospel. The Gospel of John doesn't contain the parable of the sower. So, let's look at the Gospels of Matthew, Mark and Luke.

To unlock the hidden wisdom contained in the parable of the sower, we must understand the parable's purpose, which is revealed in the Gospels of Matthew, Mark and Luke. Specifically, in Matthew 13:11, Mark 4:11 and Luke 8:10, we discover just how important this parable is to understanding the kingdom of God. What is said in those Gospels in regards to the parable of the sower's purpose? Let's look at each Gospel verse relating to understanding the purpose of the parable of the sower.

Matthew	Mark	Luke
"He answered and said unto them, 'Because it is given unto you to know the mysteries of the kingdom of heaven, but to them it is not given.'" Matt. 13:11.	"And He said unto them, 'Unto you it is given to know the mystery of the kingdom of God: but unto them that are without, all these things are done in parables...'" Mk. 4:11.	"And He said, 'Unto you it is given to know the mysteries of the kingdom of God: but to others in parables; that seeing they might not see, and hearing they might not understand.'" Lk. 8:10.

Remember, we're looking at each difference in each verse, and the sameness. By doing this, we can gain clear revelation of the gospel. In this chapter, that's our purpose: to understand the gospel of the kingdom. What is our purpose in understanding the gospel of the kingdom? To preach and walk in the kingdom.

The Parable's Explanation.

Matthew	Mark	Luke
Jesus responded to a question asked by "the disciples" about the parable of the sower.	No mention	No mention

The Parable's Audience. The emphasis is on those to whom He spoke:

Matthew	Mark	Luke
Jesus spoke to "the disciples."	Jesus spoke to "the twelve."	Jesus spoke to "His disciples."

The Parable's Revelation.

Matthew	Mark	Luke
We learn the mysteries of the kingdom of heaven.	We learn the mystery of the kingdom of God.	We learn the mysteries of the kingdom of God.

The Parable's Focus. The Greek word for heaven is **ouranos** and can be either singular or plural, depending on its context, and means heaven(s) or sky(ies). The Greek word for God is **theos** and carries the meaning of the Supreme Being, long before the New Testament was written:

Matthew	Mark	Luke
Matthew points to heaven(s).	Mark points to God.	Luke points to God.

The Parable's Exclusivity. Not everyone will understand this parable. Jesus specifically refers to those who are excluded from knowing its mystery(ies):

Matthew	Mark	Luke
Jesus refers "to them" or, in the Greek, *ekeinos*.	Jesus refers "to them," *ekeinos* "that are without," *exo*.	Jesus refers "to others," or in the Greek, *loipos*, which means the rest, remainder or those left behind.

From these five differences, we can discern the following: Christ is answering a question presented by the 12 Apostles. That question was also in the minds of all those present. Their collective question: "What?!!!" Everyone who heard what Jesus said in regards to the parable of the sower lacked understanding as to what He meant. I also share that same question. I want to know what Jesus meant. I want to walk in the power of the knowing that comes from understanding what He said in the parable of the sower. That's why I've dissected this parable, and Jesus' explanation of it, to answer that collective question: "What?!!!"

> *Jesus is sharing hidden instructions and secrets – secrets of the universe and heaven's governing principles.*

Kingdom Mysteries Revealed by Jesus Christ

In the parable of the sower, Christ is revealing mysteries of the kingdom of heaven and God, and the mystery of the kingdom of God. In the Greek, the word for mystery and mysteries is the same word, **mustérion**, which comes from the root word **mueó**, which means, to learn, instruct or initiate. Literally, Jesus is sharing hidden instructions and secrets – secrets of the universe and heaven's governing principles. And, He is concealing those mysteries revealed. Not everyone has access to those mysteries. Why the secrecy? To prevent abuse. Everything in heaven and earth is governed by the mysteries revealed by Christ in the parables.

God has secrets. God reveals secrets. God conceals secrets. God's kingdom has principles by which it operates. Once understood, those principles and truths release explosive power. Not everyone knows, believes or is willing to be instructed in the principles revealed by Christ. Christ understands and shares His understanding of His kingdom's mysteries. The parable of the sower is key in discerning and understanding what is revealed, and concealed, with regards to Christ's kingdom. Jesus plainly said, *"Do you not understand this parable? Then how will you understand all the parables?"* Mk. 4:13, *BLB*.

In this chapter, I've narrowly focused my attention on the parable of the sower, due to its singular importance in understanding the kingdom of God. According to Jesus, understanding the parable of the sower is essential to understanding the other parables. And, understanding the parables – all of them – is essential to understanding the mystery and mysteries of the kingdom of God and heaven. So, we should pay special attention to the parable of the sower. Understanding that parable is vital to knowing the mysteries of the kingdom of God and heaven.

The Seed, the Soil & the Harvest

In each Gospel, Jesus explains the parable of the sower differently. That parable, on the surface, appears to say the same thing in each Gospel. But as we dig deeper, it becomes obvious that each parable is not the same. To truly understand that parable, we must go beyond what is plainly visible on the surface, into the deeper meaning hidden in the parable. To do that, we must search for answers buried in plain sight in each parable in each Gospel. And, we must lay aside our own prejudices and predispositions concerning what we already know.

Like children, we must approach this parable from the standpoint that we know nothing as we ought to know it. We need divine assistance to learn what Christ clearly communicated. For the sake of time and space, as we identify the differences between this parable in each Gospel, I want to focus on these three things: 1) the seed, 2) the soil and 3) the harvest.

Before we go further, I want to share my simple observations of this parable with you: 1) The seed, once planted, is always capable of growing, 2) the harvest is always determined by the quality and type of the soil not the quality or type of the seed, and 3) the enemy will always seek to rob us of the seed and pollute the soil. We must understand that sowing seed isn't enough. The seed must also be planted in the right soil for it to grow. The only difference between the seed that bears fruit and the seed that doesn't bear fruit is the soil. That's you and me. We are the soil.

But first, I want to share a lesson hidden within what I've just shared for those who are called to preach the gospel as a profession. Many ministers of the gospel never learn how to prepare the soil prior to planting the seed. But, preparation of the soil is essential. The focus in many ministries is on the message rather than the soil. Yes, ensuring that we're sowing the right seed is important, but planting that seed in the right soil is essential to fruitful ministry. We cannot reap a good harvest when we sow seed into bad soil, and believe me, there's plenty of back-breaking, blood-sucking, seed-stealing bad soil. Now, back to the parable.

Matthew	Mark	Luke
Jesus speaks of the word of the kingdom and, by implication, that word is the word of the sower. The emphasis is on the message of the kingdom.	Jesus speaks of the sower sowing the word. The emphasis is on sowing or spreading that word.	Jesus plainly states, "The seed is the Word of God."

Here, the Greek word for word is *logos,* which is derived from the Greek word, *lego,* meaning to speak. Interestingly, **Lego,** a Danish company, sells "toy building bricks," **Lego's**, to children who use them to build structures. In Danish, **lego** means "play well." ***Logos,*** in the New Testament, is primarily used in reference to Christ. Christ and His words are the building blocks for all things, seen and unseen, visible and invisible, in heaven and earth. Indeed, that shows His power over all things, whether in heaven or earth.

The Four Soils of the Kingdom

If you don't remember anything else from this chapter, remember this point: the soil determines the size and scope of the harvest, always. Because the soil determines the size and scope of the harvest, I want to pay close attention to the differences in Christ's description of the various soils in each of the Gospels.

Christ describes four different types of soil: 1) wayside soil, 2) stony soil, 3) thorny soil and 4) good soil. That's it. Christ doesn't describe any other soil type. That means, there's no other soil type. It further means that the only reason for your fruitfulness and breakthrough, or lack thereof, is the soil. Your blessing, or lack thereof, is determined by the soil you are or that you sow into.

Wayside Soil. In each Gospel, wayside comes from the Greek word ***hodos,*** meaning a road, way or path.

Matthew	Mark	Luke
Wayside soil emphasizes those who hear the word of the kingdom, but don't understand it, and as a result, it's stolen from them.	Wayside soil emphasizes the place where the word is sown, i.e., by the wayside.	Wayside soil emphasizes the theft of the word by the devil.

Collectively, wayside soil is: 1) the place where the word is sown, 2) the person into whom the word is sown, and 3) the person robbed of the word by the devil.

Further, in Luke, Jesus states, the seed is "trodden down" prior to it being devoured by the fowl. That begs the question: Who tramples on the seed? To find the answer to this question, I want to look at the Greek word for "trodden down," which is, **katapateó.** That word is derived from two Greek words, **kata** and **pateó.** Interestingly, **pateó** means "I trample." It can also mean spurn. **Kata** means to bring something completely down. Together, **kata** and **pateó** means I completely bring down and trample. Wayside soil represents someone who is their own worst enemy; they spurn and trample down completely under their feet the Word of God.

Often, spite prevents people from hearing the Word of God – in some cases, violently. Not everyone wants to hear the gospel message. Some are and will be opposed to the gospel. Why would someone be opposed to the gospel? For many reasons: some enjoy the evil they do, others profit from their evil acts, and others fear to lose what they gained by committing their evil acts. The gospel is light; it dispels darkness. We must never forget this simple truth: some *"men [love] the darkness rather than light, because their deeds [are] evil."* Jn. 3:19.

The sowing of the gospel always involves a spiritual battle. The battle is always over the growth of the seed. In Mark, Satan is described as coming immediately to take away the seed of the word that's heard. Make no mistake, the word was sown in the hearts of those who heard; they heard the word, understood it, but the devil stole it from them. In Luke, Jesus explains the reason for the devil acting so quickly to steal the seed of the word: *"lest they believe and be saved."* He doesn't want men and women to hear or believe the truth of the gospel.

Stony Soil. In each Gospel, Jesus describes stony soil differently.

Matthew	Mark	Luke
Stony soil means "stony places," not having much earth.	Stony soil means "stony ground," not having much earth.	Stony soil means a "rock" with no mention of earth.

The Greek word for rock in the Gospel of Luke is **petra,** which is a large mass of connected rock. The Greek word for stony places

(Matthew) and stony ground (Mark) is **petródés,** the adjective form of **petra.**

In all three Gospels, we see the seed has grown.

Matthew	Mark	Luke
Jesus describes the growing seed as lacking root: that when the sun comes up over the seed, it's scorched and withers away.	Jesus describes the growing seed as lacking root: that when the sun comes up over the seed, it's scorched and withers away.	Here, we see the heart of the issue: the seed lacked moisture.

In Luke, that lack of moisture causes it to be scorched when the sun comes up. The sun, which is designed to help the seed grow, actually causes it harm, because the seed lacks root and moisture. The reason the seed lacks roots is because of the hardness of the soil; it's rocky.

In explaining the stony places, Jesus shares some very important details:

Matthew	Mark	Luke
Persecution and affliction arise for the word's sake, but he becomes offended *over time*.	Persecution and affliction arise for the word's sake, but he becomes offended *immediately*.	There's "a time of temptation" after the word begins to grow, which is the likely cause of the lack of moisture.

What that means to you and me is, after the word is sown, a time of temptation will come, our walk will become dry, and in the midst of that time of temptation, persecution and affliction will arise. The whole purpose of this is to steal the seed. The question follows: Will we become offended? Or, will we grow?

Thorny Soil. Christ describes the next type of soil as being a thorny place. What are thorny places? Thorny places are places with weed seeds. Weed seeds are sown by the devil. God has His seed, and the devil has his seed. It's critical that we understand this truth. Not all seed is good seed. God's seed is always good seed. The devil's seed is always bad seed. But once sown, the good seed and bad seed grow together – in some cases, intertwined. That's why it's important for us to discern the seed's source. How? By understanding the seed's nature. The seed's nature reveals its source.

Thorny soil is much more difficult to detect than wayside soil or stony soil. Thorny soil is only revealed at harvest time. But by then, it's too late; the damage is already done. Thorny soil blocks the harvest; it chokes the gospel message and prevents the gospel message from bearing fruit in our lives. That blockage is demonic; it's not God's will for us to be blocked in reaping a good harvest. But, it happens. Why? Because we allow the devil to sow his seed into our hearts. What is the devil's seed? Jesus describes the devil's seed: 1) cares of this world, 2) deceitfulness of riches, and 3) the lust for other things. That's the devil's seed, and it chokes the harvest from the gospel seed.

Let's take a look at thorny soil. Thorny soil always has weeds in it. Weeds are demonic seeds that are allowed to grow in our hearts. Jesus describes the thorny soil differently in each Gospel, and each Gospel reveals a different aspect of the thorny soil.

Matthew	Mark	Luke
Thorny soil is comprised of those who hear the word but allow the cares of this world and deceitfulness of riches to choke the word. The result? He is unfruitful.	Thorny soil is the cares of the world, the deceitfulness of riches and lust for other things. The result? He is unfruitful, or the word doesn't bear fruit.	Thorny soil means those who succumb to "cares and riches and pleasures of this life." No fruit is born to perfection, i.e., a hundredfold fruit.

Don't think you won't succumb to the schemes of Satan. Don't think your heart doesn't contain weed seeds. No, we must daily check our hearts to guard against demonic seeds that have been sown into our hearts by the enemy of our souls. Like Adam, we're called to *"till the ground."* Gen. 2:5. In tilling the ground, we must protect the soil of our hearts from demonic seeds. Demonic seeds are words that steer us away from God. Demonic seeds cause us to pursue things for three primary reasons: 1) care or cares, 2) deceitfulness of riches and 3) pleasures of this life. Many have fallen in their pursuit of those things and ended shipwrecked in their faith.

We must guard our hearts against being diverted by the devil's demonic thorny seeds. How? By recognizing weeds at the seed stage. We can recognize the source of the seed, and we can root it out before it can take root. Weed seeds always become thorny ground. Thorny ground chokes us, the soil, from our achieving our full potential. Notice, thorny soil is primarily concerned about this life: cares, riches and pleasures. It's easy to become so earthly minded that we're no heavenly good. Or, we don't accomplish God's will because we're only concerned about what happens in this life. As believers, we must have a kingdom mindset and heavenly vision.

Satan's Ploy: The Pursuit of Worldly Wealth

The kingdom mindset isn't concerned about provision, for God feeds the birds of the air and clothes the grass of the field. The kingdom mindset isn't interested in the accumulation of worldly wealth, for it recognizes that true wealth is found in the kingdom. Kingdom wealth and worldly wealth are not the same. Peter and John had kingdom wealth but lacked money. Hear what they said: *"Silver and gold have I none; but such as I have give I thee: in the Name of Jesus Christ of Nazareth, rise up and walk."* Acts 3:6. That's kingdom wealth: victory over sickness and sin. And, that's something we need, but desperately lack, in our day and age.

Today, many believers equate worldly wealth and kingdom wealth. But, they are not the same. No, worldly wealth and its accumulation can be the result of demonic desires. Or, if we only do what we do to obtain money, we have fallen for Satan's ploy; it's a trap long used by the enemy to divert men and women from the call of God. A powerless Church and powerless believers that don't *"heal the sick, cleanse the lepers, raise the dead and cast out demons"* is the result of weeds and weed seeds. Ah! But the harvest is coming. At harvest time, the weeds and wheat are separated. On which side, do you want to be?

But, the pursuit of worldly wealth isn't the only weed seed that becomes thorny ground. No, the cares of this world are the number one thing with which most believers struggle. That's why Christ made such a point to reveal how much the Father cares for us. Christ sought to assure us of the Father's provision. Yes, God provides. His Name is Jehovah Jireh: "I am your provider." We need to know that in this world today. Some of the most profound Scriptures on cares come from Paul and Peter. Paul said, *"Be careful for nothing, but in everything by prayer and supplication with thanksgiving, let your requests be made known to God."* Phil. 4:6. Peter said, *"Casting all your care upon Him, for He careth for you."* 1 Pet. 5:7. This is contrary to human wisdom, which teaches us to take care of ourselves. But, the kingdom way is different: don't worry, for God cares.

And, when the pursuit of worldly wealth or the weight of worldly cares doesn't ensnare us, the pleasures of this world can. Paul specifically reproved Demas for forsaking him in his hour of need because *"he loved this present world."* 2 Tim. 4:10. Samson was defeated by Delilah, a prostitute, *"for he loved her"* and *"told her all his heart"*: she *"vexed"* and *"afflicted"* him. Today, many are vexed and afflicted by the same heart that seeks the pleasures of this world. James speaks plainly, *"Ye adulterers and adulteresses, know ye not that the friendship of the world is enmity with God? Whosoever therefore will be a friend of the world is the enemy of God."* James 4:4. That's what pursuit of worldly pleasure creates: antagonism and animosity toward God. Don't be deceived.

The gospel cannot bear fruit in a heart weighed down with worldly cares and worries, those consumed with the pursuit of wealth and position and those who seek to live by and in the pleasures of this life. Jesus teaches us, *"For the soul is more important than food, and the body than clothing."* Lk. 12:23, *ABPE.* In order to bear good fruit, we must have our priorities right. That's where most believers fail. Pastors and leaders bear the brunt of this failure, and must learn to guide their flocks away from such error. We must know what we believe and why it's important to avoid the pitfalls Satan has planned for our destruction. After all, Satan is a liar, thief and murderer. Jn. 10:10.

That's the beginning of understanding the parable of the sower:

1) understanding the impact the soil has in bearing fruit;
2) identifying those types of soil that cannot bear fruit;
3) discerning toxic pollutants in the soils that prevent fruitfulness;
4) correcting toxic behaviors that create toxic soil conditions in our hearts; and
5) discovering good soil to plant good seed that will bear good fruit, immediately and over the process of time.

This is my focus here: finding good soil, planting in good seed and bearing one-hundred-fold fruit.

The Good Soil. The last soil in the parable of the sower is the good soil. I think it's important for us to pay special attention to this soil. Why? Because we need to know where to plant our seed. The seed that falls by the wayside does nothing. Seed in stony soil withers and dies. Seed in thorny soil is choked by weeds. Good soil is the only soil that bears fruit. Please hear that. No other soil can bear fruit.

A fruitful life and fruitful ministry of preaching the gospel begins by identifying good soil. And, by preparing the soil to be good soil. That is how important preparation of the soil is in the preaching of the gospel. Yes, the atmosphere the seed is sown in matters. Yes, the soil must be prepared for reception so that we are assured the soil is good. Otherwise, our preaching may fall on deaf ears. As ministers, we don't want that. We want the word to be received and bear fruit,

The Gospels of Matthew, Mark and Luke repeat the same parable taught by Christ: the parable of the sower. That repetition is important. Further, in teaching us about God's kingdom, Christ plainly states that this parable unlocks our understanding of all the other parables. And, the parables teach us the mystery and mysteries of the kingdom of God and heaven. Finally, in the parable of the sower, Jesus teaches us about how God's kingdom works in practical ways by relating to us a simple truth: there are three soils that don't bear fruit: 1) wayside soil, 2) stony soil and 3) thorny soil. That point enables us to discern the one soil that bear fruit and to focus our attention on being, and planting in, good soil that bears. The good ground is the soil that bears fruit.

Matthew	Mark	Luke
Jesus teaches that good ground yields a harvest: a hundredfold, sixtyfold or thirtyfold.	Jesus reverses the order and says good ground yields a harvest: thirtyfold, sixtyfold and a hundredfold.	Jesus says good ground yields "an hundredfold."

In each Gospel, there are subtle nuances to the parable that I want to explore in regards to good soil. My purpose for this exploration is to enable you to understand the following:

1) the type of soil that bears fruit,
2) how that soil bears fruit, and
3) the process by which that soil bears fruit.

Matthew	Mark	Luke
Jesus says about the good ground, "some seed fell into it." Or, by chance, the seed was introduced into the good ground.	Jesus says the seed "sprang up and increased and brought forth fruit." Or, Christ shows us the process by which good ground bears fruit.	Jesus says the seed "fell on good ground, and sprung up, and bare fruit an hundredfold." No process, just production.

In explaining good ground to His disciples, Christ relates the following points:

Matthew	Mark	Luke
The person who is good ground receives the gospel message, hears it and keeps on listening to it, and as a result, understands it.	The person who is good ground hears the word and receives it.	The person who is good ground has an honest and good heart, who after hearing the word, keeps it and brings forth fruit with patience.

Looking closely, we can gain some real insights into what good ground is by listening to what Christ said. Good ground requires:

1) having a good and honest heart,
2) receiving the gospel message,
3) being willing to hear, and keep hearing, that message,
4) desiring to understand and search for understanding of the gospel message,
5) keeping (i.e., doing) the word that's being heard,
6) following the process for bearing fruit, and
7) patiently bringing forth fruit over time.

That's what qualifies us to be considered good ground by Christ. Good ground is the only ground that bears good fruit.

The Mystery of the Kingdom is Hidden in You... the Soil

This is the mystery of the kingdom of God revealed. The kingdom begins as a seed that grows into a harvest. There are only two types of seed: good seed and bad seed. There are only two sources of seed: God and Satan. The good seed is the gospel of the kingdom, God's Word. There are only four types of soil: three are bad, and one is good. The harvest is always determined by the type of soil, not the seed. Satan seeks to steal God's seed. If he cannot steal that seed, he seeks to prevent it from bearing fruit. God's seed always destroys Satan's kingdom. Satan and his kingdom cannot resist the seed that's planted in good soil; he has no defense against it. But, if he can contaminate the soil, he can stop the fulfillment of the seed's potential, the harvest. Our goal as gospel preachers is to cultivate the soil prior to planting the seed to ensure a good and fruitful harvest. Christ's hidden message to us is: prepare the soil.

The gospel of the kingdom is powerful when planted in good soil. God made Adam from the earth. Eve was taken from Adam. Both male and female were made from earth, dirt. That's what we are: soil. But, toxins in the earth will seek to contaminate us. Amazingly, many are consumed by earthly pollution, but few pay any attention to spiritual pollution. Yes, there's spiritual pollution, and the earth is full of it. We call that pollution sin. Sin contaminates, always. Every sin contains its own set of spiritual contaminants. But three, in particular, contaminate the soil of our hearts to block us from bearing fruit: the cares of this world, the deceitfulness of riches and lust for other things. Like Adam, we're called to:

1) "till the ground,"
2) "be fruitful,"
3) "multiply,"
4) "replenish the earth,"
5) "subdue it," and
6) "have dominion."

And, God's mandate to Mankind has not changed.

Heaven is calling. That call is hidden in the gospel of the kingdom. Everything – and I do mean everything – is derived from and hidden within the concepts I've shared in this chapter. You can master these concepts. If you do, your entire life and lineage will be forever changed. Nothing is as powerful as the concepts shared in this chapter: 1) sower, 2) seed, 3) soil and 4) harvest.

Remember these things when you face life's challenges and opportunities. Watch what is planted in you. Solomon said, *"Above all else, guard your heart, for everything you do flows from it."* Prov. 4:23, *NIV*. Now, that's wisdom. Wisdom says, my words are *"life unto those that find them and medicine to all their flesh."* Prov. 4:22, *JUB*. Amen.

Chapter Five

The Gospel of Christ

"Now the birth of Jesus Christ was on this wise: When as His mother Mary was espoused to Joseph, before they came together, she was found with child of the Holy Ghost." Matt. 1:18.

The most significant event in history took place 2,000+ years ago. That event was the birth of Jesus Christ. Today, we celebrate His birth by defining our understanding of time by Him. With the simple letters BC ("Before Christ") or AD ("Anno Domini," i.e., the year of our Lord), we acknowledge the historical significance of Jesus, the Christ. But, Christ is more than a historical figure who once lived. He continues to live. That singular event makes Him unique from a historical standpoint: He is the only man to have defeated death. Yes, Christ was raised from the dead, continues to live today, and He will one-day return. That's what I believe. That's the Christian faith. But, there's more.

Jesus' birth was prophesied by numerous Old Testament prophets. Isaiah described Him as the suffering servant and coming king. In fact, prior to Christ's birth, many Jewish rabbinical scholars believed there were two different Messiah's. Today, we know there's only one, Christ Jesus. That singular revelation is the building block for the Church. Jesus said, *"Blessed art thou, Simon*

Barjona: for flesh and blood hath not revealed it unto thee, but My Father which is in heaven. And I say also unto thee, that thou art Peter, and upon this rock, I will build My Church; and the gates of hell shall not prevail against it." Matt. 18:17-18.

The Revelation of Jesus Christ... Today

Like Peter, we, the Church, need a fresh revelation of the Person of Jesus Christ. That's the only way to truly know Christ... by revelation. Or, for us to know the mystery of Christ, that mystery must be revealed to us. There's no other way to know the mystery of Christ. That revelation of the mystery of Christ is the gospel of Christ. That's the gospel I intend on sharing with you in this chapter: the good news of the person of Jesus Christ. But remember, that mystery can only be understood by revelation. Natural wisdom will not aid in understanding the mystery of Christ. So, with that understanding, we'll move forward.

To help you understand the vastness of this mystery, I'd like to use a natural illustration to aid you in this understanding process. By experience, I know that most men and women are fascinated by the night sky. We look up into the heavens, and we imagine. Our imagination is what limits our ability to understand the vastness of the heavens. The sheer magnitude of the size of our universe is almost overwhelming. So we, as humans, have sought to peer into the depths of space to understand its inexhaustibility. When we look through the Hubble telescope, we catch a glimpse at the vastness of space. When we see images sent back to earth from spacecraft launched into the far reaches of our solar system, and beyond, we stand in awe of what we see – we are amazed!

The mystery of Christ is far vaster than the infinitely finite universe; Christ is infinite.

On September 16, 1977, the National Aeronautics and Space Administration (NASA) launched Voyager 1 into space. On August

25, 2012, Voyager 1 became the first manmade object to enter into Interstellar space. That's the furthest Mankind has traveled from our emerald blue planet. But eventually, Voyager 1's power source will expire. Yet, Mankind's imagination of what is in the universe will remain. Our desire to know is almost unquenchable. We want to know what is out there. Is there life?

When we see the vastness of space, and the deadness of it, we also gain a new appreciation for the majesty of life. Mankind has been to the moon and mars. We have sent manmade rockets into space to explore. What we have found in our explorations are barrenness and desolation. Space is frigid. We cannot survive in the blackness of its expanses. The moon is a barren rock. No life exists. Mars is barren. No life. All the other planets in our solar system are barren, lifeless. We have seen Pluto, Neptune, Uranus, Jupiter and Saturn. All are lifeless. Yet, we're intrigued by the infinitely finite mystery of space.

Today, if we left our planet and began a journey into space at the speed of light, we still couldn't appreciate the vastness of space. Thousands and thousands, millions upon millions of years would go by, and yet, we would still only know a minute piece of our universe. There are galaxies upon galaxies awaiting exploration, known only to the mind of God. When God created all things, He created them in accordance with the majesty of who He is. The Bible declares the universe is measured by the span of God's hand. Is. 40:12. Or, in 35 years, traveling at 38,610 mph or 10.17 miles per second or .0000546 of the speed of light, we have barely escaped our solar system. To help you understand: a bullet travels at 1,126 feet per second. So, Voyager 1 is traveling 47 times faster than a bullet. That's amazing.

But, the vastness of the mystery of space is nothing in comparison to the vastness of the mystery of Christ. Christ is the author of creation; He set the heavens in motion. And, He is the sustainer of the heavens and earth. The mystery of Christ is far vaster than the infinitely finite universe; Christ is infinite. To know Him is to know the infinite. Through Him, we can peer into the depths of the mind of God. How do we know God? By revelation. How do we know the mystery of Christ? By revelation. The Bible teaches: *"From the creation of the world, God's invisible qualities, His eternal power and divine nature, have been clearly observed in what He made."* Rom. 1:20, *GWT*. And, *"The heavens are declaring the glory of God, and their expanse shows the work of His hands."* Ps. 19:1, *ISV*.

Paul's Revelation of Jesus Christ

On the road to Damascus, Paul received a revelation of Jesus Christ. Paul was blinded by Christ's appearance. Later, his eyes were opened and scales fell from his eyes. Acts 9:18. Paul became enthralled by the mystery of Christ – so much so that he invested his life in the pursuit of that mystery. Specifically, Paul made a decision to know Jesus Christ and Him crucified. 1 Cor. 2:2. Paul wanted to know the matchless person of Christ. He said, *"Yes, everything else is worthless when compared with the infinite value of knowing Christ Jesus my Lord. For His sake, I have discarded everything else, counting it all as garbage, so that I could gain Christ."* Phil. 3:8. In the *KJV*, it says Paul counted everything else "dung" in comparison to the revelation of Christ.

The best this world has to offer is dung compared to the knowledge offered in the matchless mystery of the revelation of the person of Christ. And yet, so little attention is paid to that mystery. Life's pursuits are vain when compared to the pursuit of the mystery of Christ. Yet, we invest so much into something worth so little: the things of this life. We pursue wealth or fame or some other vanity, but we ignore the mystery of Christ. The Bible tells us, *"You are just a vapor that appears for a little while and then vanishes away."* James 4:4, *NASB*. That's why we must *"mak[e] the most of the time, because the days are evil."* Eph. 5:16, *HCSB*. We only have a limited time on earth to explore and understand the mystery of the Person of Christ.

By revelation, Paul communicated that great mystery, the gospel of Christ, down through the annuls of time, to the churches. Paul described that mystery as hidden from prior generations but now made known to us. That mystery *"in other ages was not made known unto the sons of men, as it is now revealed unto His holy apostles and prophets by the Spirit...."* Eph. 3:5. Or, Christ's birth opened the floodgates of revelation of the mystery of the person of Christ. Listen to what Paul says in describing the great honor he received in declaring the gospel of Christ: *"Unto me, who am less than the least of all saints, is this grace given, that I should preach among the Gentiles the unsearchable riches of Christ...."* Eph. 3:8. Paul, a murderer and blasphemer, was humbled that God chose him to share in understanding and communicating this mystery to and with His Son's bride, the Church.

The universe is finite, even though it appears infinitely large. The gospel of Christ, on the other hand, is infinite. As such, it cannot be fully comprehended by the human mind, for we're finite beings. When we peer into the gospel of Christ, we need more than learning, teaching, understanding, knowledge or wisdom. In truth, we need revelation, we need the mind of Christ. The gospel of Christ is revealed before it's understood, and it can only be understood by revelation. Why does the gospel of Christ need to be revealed? It has been concealed. Why has the gospel of Christ been concealed? Mankind chose to remain ignorant of what God clearly revealed. Why? Because we loved darkness rather than light. Jn. 3:19. To understand the gospel of Christ, and preach it, we require continual revelation. There's no other way to know the mystery of Christ.

The Son Has Risen

What happens when we understand that mystery? Paul describes the effect on the human heart when the gospel of Christ invades our hearts: *"God wanted His people throughout the world to know the glorious riches of this mystery – which is Christ living in you, giving you the hope of glory."* Col. 1:27, GWT. God's glory shines from the hearts of those who know Christ by revelation. A chain reaction occurs within the human heart when the mystery of Christ is revealed to it, and an explosion of glory is released. The revelation of Christ entering the heart of Man is like a nuclear bomb exploding in the spiritual realm, and explosive glory power is released. That's how powerful the revelation of the mystery of Christ is when it enters our hearts – God's glory is manifested!

Why is that? Because Mankind was created in the image of God. The Bible declares Christ is *"the brightness of His [God's] glory, and the express image of His [God's] person...."* Heb. 1:3. Adam and Eve were made in the image of God. *"God created Man in His own image, in the image of God He created him; male and female He created them."* Gen. 1:27, NASB. But, Mankind fell from that lofty place by committing sin. Sin obscured the revelation of the image of God through Mankind, and Mankind was corrupted. That corruption entered into the world through Mankind's lust. 2 Pet. 1:4. Sin always corrupts. Christ restores Mankind from the corruption that entered into the world through lust. That's how important the revelation of the mystery of Christ is to the Church: it breaks the power of sin and releases the power of the Son into the Church. Rom. 8:2.

The Son is Rising in You

When Mankind sinned, death entered the world. When Christ entered the world, life came back to earth. The Bible describes Christ as "the Life." Christ's life is transmitted to Mankind as He is revealed to us. That transmission has been being played for 2,000+ years. Few have heard the glorious sound of heaven's transmission to earth through the revelation of the mystery of Christ. When that mystery is understood, as it's revealed, divine freedom is the result. Christ sets us free from the bondage of corruption. Not only are we set free by the revelation of Christ, but the whole of creation is set free by the revelation of Christ in us. That's the glorious mystery of the sons of God spoken of in Romans 8:18-23, NASB:

"For I consider that the sufferings of this present time are not worthy to be compared with the glory that is to be revealed to us. For the anxious longing of the creation waits eagerly for the revealing of the sons of God. For the creation was subjected to futility, not willingly, but because of Him who subjected it, in hope that the creation itself also will be set free from its slavery to corruption into the freedom of the glory of the children of God. For we know that the whole creation groans and suffers the pains of childbirth together until now. And not only this, but also we ourselves, having the first fruits of the Spirit, even we ourselves groan within ourselves, waiting eagerly for our adoption as sons, the redemption of our body."

In describing this mystery of the manifestation of the sons of God, Paul plainly states that we, along with all of creation, long for the revelation of the mystery of Christ. We're waiting in earnest longing for the moment of adoption – the redemption of our bodies. Paul states, *"There is a natural body, and there is a spiritual body."* 1 Cor. 15:44. The natural body is weighed down by corruption from original sin. The spiritual body is

Few have heard the glorious sound of heaven's transmission to earth through the revelation of the mystery of Christ.

being built by the things we do in this life. What we do in this life is the seed for our eternity. That includes the revelation we have of the mystery of Christ. Each seed has its own body. 1 Cor. 15:38. Remember what I shared in Chapter Four, the kingdom revolves around these four things: 1) sower, 2) seed, 3) soil and 4) harvest. The mystery of the kingdom and the mystery of Christ are revealed in seed form and grow in us – the soil.

Seed without soil abides alone. Nothing is produced by it. Seed is not enough. There must also be soil. Mankind is important to the purpose and plan of God. We are soil. Jesus is the seed; He is the Word made flesh. Jn. 1:14. Jesus said, *"Very truly I tell you, unless a kernel of wheat falls to the ground and dies, it remains only a single seed. But if it dies, it produces many seeds."* Jn. 12:24, *NIV*. A harvest is coming. That harvest will be the culmination of the manifestation of the seed – Christ. And, that harvest will yield more seed. More seed is always contained within the full manifestation of the culmination of the seed by the harvest. Paul described that revelation as *"the mystery of His will."* Eph. 1:9. That mystery, Paul stated, was *"to usher in the fullness of the times and to bring together in the Messiah all things in heaven and on earth."* Eph. 1:10, *ISV*.

Paul understood that his writings alone were insufficient to communicate the depth of what he was speaking to the churches. Hence, he prayed. Paul knew that only by prayer could believers be enabled to understand the gospel of Christ. Listen to his prayer for the Ephesian believers:

> *"For this cause I bow my knees unto the Father of our Lord Jesus Christ, of whom the whole family in heaven and earth is named, that He would grant you, according to the riches of His glory, to be strengthened with might by His Spirit in the inner man; that Christ may dwell in your hearts by faith; that ye, being rooted and grounded in love, may be able to comprehend with all saints what is the breadth, and length, and depth, and height; and to know the love of Christ, which passeth knowledge, that ye might be filled with all the fulness of God. Now unto Him that is able to do exceeding abundantly above all that we ask or think, according to the power that worketh in us, unto Him be glory in the Church by Christ Jesus throughout all ages, world without end. Amen."* Eph. 3:14-21.

Prior to proceeding further in this chapter, I pray for you what Paul prayed for the Ephesian believers. Now, we're ready to proceed.

The Simplicity of Christ

My desire is to communicate to you the gospel of Christ in its simplicity. I don't want you to be diverted from the simplicity of that gospel. Paul was concerned about Satan's ability to deceive and divert the Church, wholly, and believers, individually, from the gospel of Christ: *"But I am afraid that, as the serpent deceived Eve by his craftiness, your minds will be led astray from the simplicity and purity of devotion to Christ."* 2 Cor. 11:3, *NASB.* I, too, am concerned that you may misunderstand those things that are contained in this book. As such, I pray for a fresh wind of revelation to blow over you – NOW! I know that only Christ, the Anointed One and the anointing that abides in you (1 Jn. 2:20), can keep you from being led astray by the devil.

What is the gospel of Christ? Why is it a mystery? What is the gospel of Christ's relation to the gospel? Why do we need to know the gospel of Christ? What does the gospel of Christ do in us, His Church, if anything? I'll seek to answer these questions and many other questions as we proceed. Before proceeding, I want to ask you to proceed prayerfully. Remain in prayer as you read this chapter, or you may miss the revelation contained in it. I've noticed many believers miss the revelations given because we don't pay attention, prayerfully. Be in prayer, as you proceed.

Paul described his revelation, knowledge and understanding of the mystery of Christ:

> *"If ye have heard of the dispensation of the grace of God which is given me to you-ward: how that by revelation He made known unto me the mystery; (as I wrote afore in few words, whereby, when ye read, ye may understand my knowledge in the mystery of Christ), which in other ages was not made known unto the sons of men, as it is now revealed unto His holy apostles and prophets by the Spirit; that the Gentiles should be fellowheirs, and of the same Body, and partakers of His promise in Christ by the gospel: whereof I was made a minister, according to the gift of the grace of God given unto me by the effectual working of His power."* Eph. 4:2-7.

Paul understood that the revelation of the mystery of the gospel of Christ was His by the grace of God. That grace alone was sufficient to enable him to understand that mystery. That mystery formed a fellowship between all who partook of the mystery of the gospel of

Christ. Or, an understanding heart was given to those who understood, in part, the mystery of Christ. Paul understood, and stated, that no one can fully understand the riches of the revelation of the mystery of Christ; that revelation was simply too vast; it's unsearchable. Eph. 3:9. From that perspective, Paul considered himself, and others who carried that mystery, as stewards: *"One should think about us this way – as servants of Christ and stewards of the mysteries of God."* 1 Cor. 4:1, *NET*.

So then, I am what I am by the grace of God. The revelation I have received of the mystery of the gospel of Christ was given to me by grace. By grace, I'm a steward of that mystery. And you, by partaking of my grace, have become part of the fellowship in that grace and partake of the grace that the mystery of the gospel of Christ brings. Christ communicates grace to impart grace for the purpose of increasing grace by that impartation of grace. The gospel of Christ is the gospel of grace and the gospel of the kingdom.

The Gospel of Christ is LIFE

What happens when we receive revelation of the mystery of the gospel of Christ? We partake of Him. Jesus said, *"I am that bread of life."* Jn. 6:48. And, *"God's bread is the Man who comes from heaven and gives life to the world."* Jn. 6:33, God's Word Translation. The Apostle John, after tasting of that Bread, said, *"We proclaim to you the one who existed from the beginning, whom we have heard and seen. We saw Him with our own eyes and touched Him with our own hands. He is the Word of life."* I Jn. 1:1, *NLT*. Jesus said, *"The words that I speak to you are spirit, and are life."* Jn. 6:63(b), *WEB*. *"Because he who finds them has life, and all healing in His flesh."* Prov. 4:22, *ABPE*.

That's what the gospel brings – life. When we hear the gospel, we're energized by the life that's within it. That's what the true gospel brings. Jesus said, *"I am the way, the truth, and the life: no man cometh unto the Father, but by Me."* Jn. 14:6. But, a false gospel, Satan's gospel (see *Satan and His Gospel* by A.W. Pink), on the other hand, brings death. Where there is an absence of revelation of the mystery of Christ, death becomes normal and sickness becomes natural. Dead men and women walking through the valley of the shadow of death. Jesus described them as *"whited sepulchres, which indeed appear beautiful outward, but are within full of dead men's bones, and of all uncleanness."* Matt 23:27.

What an awful picture of those under the domain of sin and Satan. That's who we once were. But, God *"did rescue us out of the authority of the darkness, and did translate us into the reign of the Son of His love,"* Col. 1:13, YLT. We have been rescued. How were we rescued? By receipt of the revelation of Jesus Christ. That revelation is the gift of God. Peter exclaimed, *"Thou art the Christ, the Son of the living God."* Matt. 16:16. That revelation was the beginning point of the Christ's radical new movement – the Church.

God gives revelation. *"Jesus answered and said unto him [Peter], Blessed art thou, Simon Barjona: for flesh and blood hath not revealed it unto thee, but My Father which is in heaven."* Then, we receive revelation. And, we can only share the revelation we receive. But, even then, it's only by revelation that others can receive the revelation we share. Facts are not enough. No, we need revelation, daily. By that revelation of Christ, God builds His Church. *"And I say also unto thee, that thou art Peter, and upon this rock, I will build My Church; and the gates of hell shall not prevail against it."* Matt. 16:18. On this rock, the revelation of Christ, Christ's Church is built. There's no other way to see Christ's church and kingdom built, or to know the truth of Christ.

The Anointed Purpose of Apostles & Prophets

One of my genuine concerns about the apostolic and prophetic movement today is the trend away from what I've just shared – the revelation of the mystery of Christ. Instead, we have moved to revelations of other things. And, the Bible is chock full of many diverse truths, mysteries and revelations. Yet, the primary purpose of apostles and prophets is to reveal the mystery of Christ to the

Church. Paul declares, that mystery *"was not made known unto the sons of men, as it is now revealed unto His holy apostles and prophets by the Spirit."* Eph. 3:5. Our lack of revelation of the person of Christ is a revelation of our spiritual condition.

Peter received divine revelation that Jesus was the Christ, the Anointed One. *"How God anointed Jesus of Nazareth with the Holy Ghost and with power: who went about doing good, and healing all that were oppressed of the devil; for God was with Him."* Acts 10:38. Jesus,

[T]he primary purpose of apostles and prophets is to reveal the mystery of Christ to the Church.

reading from the Nevi'im (Prophets), states, *"The Spirit of the LORD is upon Me, for He has anointed Me to bring Good News to the poor. He has sent Me to proclaim that captives will be released, that the blind will see, that the oppressed will be set free...."* Lk. 4:18, *NLT.* Jehovah anointed Jesus. And, Jehovah wants to anoint us.

God works by the anointing. God anoints men for a purpose. That anointing is what sets men and women apart for the work to which they are called. Both David and Saul were anointed to be king. Both David and Saul sinned. But David prayed to God, *"Do not reject me! Do not take your Holy Spirit away from me!"* Ps. 51:11, *NET.* *"Saul said to Samuel, 'I have sinned, for I have transgressed the commandment of the LORD and your words, because I feared the people and obeyed their voice. Now therefore, please pardon my sin and return with me, that I may worship the LORD.'"* I Sam. 15:24-25. David was concerned about displeasing God. Saul was concerned with pleasing people. *"The Spirit of the LORD departed from Saul, and an evil spirit from the LORD troubled him."* 1 Sam. 16:14, *ISV.* The anointing is precious and is not to be taken lightly by those who have been anointed.

Jesus is the Anointed One. For a further understanding of Christ as the Anointed One, read *Lord of the Fires* by James Maloney, pg. 77 of 139. The Anointed One is the Messiah of the Jewish people. Jesus is the Savior of all Mankind. In John 3:34, God's Word Translation, it says, *"The man whom God has sent speaks God's message. After all, God gives Him the Spirit without limit."* Jesus was and is God's messenger. In Hebrews 1:1,2, *NTL*, it says, *"Long ago God spoke many times and in many ways to our ancestors through the prophets. And now in these final days, He has spoken to us through His Son. God promised everything to the Son as an inheritance, and through the Son, He created the universe."* Today, Jesus is God's messenger. And, He is still speaking.

The Mystery of Christ Revealed

"Jesus Christ is the same yesterday, today and forever." Heb. 13:8, *WEB*. I want to dig into this bold statement for a brief time. What this statement depicts is the immutability of Christ. Christ is unchangeable. Christ's unchanging nature exalts Him above everything in the universe.

To help you understand the importance of this statement, I want to share with you a little instruction from a Jewish physicist, Albert Einstein. Einstein, the renown physicist, from his understanding of the nature of the universe, developed the famous equation, $E=MC^2$. That equation is significant, in that, it unlocked the power of the atom, via the detonation of a nuclear bomb on July 16, 1945. Ironically, the experimental bomb was given the code name, Trinity. In Einstein's equation, C is a constant; it's the speed of light – 186,282 miles per second. To Einstein, the speed of light was the only constant in the natural universe. Einstein's understanding of the universe matches what the Bible taught nearly 2,000+ years before Einstein unlocked his famous equation: light is constant.

The Bible teaches that Jesus Christ is unchangeable. Christ is constant. Jesus said, *"I am the light of the world. The one who follows Me will never walk in darkness, but will have the light of life."* Jn. 8:12. Christ's understanding of Himself and the early Church's understanding of Christ is in alignment with Einstein's understanding of the constant nature of light. Nearly 2,000 years before Einstein, Christ and His Church correctly understood what Einstein discovered: light is a constant. To unlock heaven's power, we must understand this pivotal truth: Jesus Christ is constant.

As he theorized that light was constant, Einstein began to see how light could be transformed into energy. Einstein's worldview allowed him to take a drastic leap in understanding and see the true nature of light even though he couldn't see light. In fact, Einstein theorized that no one could see light in real time, for no one could move fast enough. Einstein had to imagine what he couldn't see. We, too, need to know what we cannot comprehend, the inexhaustible revelation of Jesus Christ. Paul's describes of the inexhaustible revelation of Christ: *"that He might display in the coming ages the surpassing riches of His grace in kindness towards us in Christ Jesus."* Eph. 2:7, *DBT*. Even ages spent in eternity is insufficient to fully understand Christ.

But, there's a promise. That promise is the promise of revelation. Paul communicates this promise in 1 Corinthians to the believers in Corinth: *"but, according as it hath been written, 'What eye did not see, and ear did not hear, and upon the heart of Man came not up, what God did prepare for those loving Him –' but to us did God reveal them through His Spirit, for the Spirit all things doth search, even the depths of God...."* 1 Cor. 2:9-10. Plainly speaking, God will hold nothing back from His children.

Breaking the Chains of Darkness & Ignorance

God isn't keeping us in the dark. Paul said, *"But if our gospel is hid, it is hid to them that are lost: In whom the god of this world hath blinded the minds of them who believe not, lest the light of the glorious gospel of Christ, who is the image of God, should shine to them."* 2 Cor. 4:3-4, *WBT*. Isaiah describes this darkness that's cast over the whole world: *"On this mountain, He will swallow up the shroud that is over all the peoples, the woven covering that is over all the nations...."* Is. 25:7, *DBT*.

Since the fall of Man, Satan has been spinning a web of deceit to keep Christ concealed from the nations: his intention is to keep Mankind blinded to the revelation of the person of Christ. Why? Because the revelation of Christ shatters the lie keeping Mankind bound in sin. We are no longer slaves, but free, if we chose freedom. *"It is for freedom that Christ has set us free."* Gal. 5:1, BSB. Jesus wants us free; Satan wants us bound. The price

> ***Since the fall of Man, Satan has been spinning a web of deceit to keep Christ concealed from the nations...***

of freedom has been paid, our debt was canceled and the power of sin and sickness has been destroyed. That's the truth that sets us free. *"And you will know the truth, and the truth will set you free."* Jn. 8:32.

Why then are so many bound by sin and sickness? Because, though the price of our debt has been paid and the yoke of bondage has been broken, we can choose to remain under that yoke. For that reason, Paul exhorts us, *"Stand firm, then, and do not be encumbered once more by a yoke of slavery."* Gal. 5:1, BSB. We can be free. Truth sets us free. But, it's only the truth we know that sets us free. To know truth, we must encounter truth as a person – Christ. For us to know Him, we must receive a revelation of who He is. When we receive that revelation, it breaks every bondage. Christ is the stronger one who binds the strongman. Lk. 11:22.

Jesus is the light. Satan is darkness. Light always overcomes darkness. Jesus always overcomes Satan. Ignorance is darkness. An ignorant church is a defeated church. An informed church operating under the spirit of revelation is a victorious church. Men and women fail for want of revelation of the person and work of Jesus Christ. When we receive a revelation of the hidden Christ, we begin to overcome by that revelation, always. *"But thanks be to God! He always leads us triumphantly by the Messiah and through us*

spreads everywhere the fragrance of knowing Him." 2 Cor. 2:14,
ISV. Literally, we're led in triumphant procession by Christ.

The Victory is Yours, Ours... His

Christ's victory has become our victory. We're victorious because
He was victorious. Why then do we so often fail? For one reason, we
lack revelation of Jesus Christ. That absence of revelation invites
defeat. The Apostle John, while on the Island of Patmos, received
the epitome of revelation, The Revelation of Jesus Christ. Rev. 1:1.
Listen to what John says in regards to this revelation, *"Blessed is
the one who reads and those who hear the words of this prophecy
and keep those things that are written in it, for the time is near."*
Rev. 1:3, *ABPE.* The revelation of Jesus Christ came by prophecy to
the Church through John, the Apostle.

When reading John's Revelation, for most, there's confusion. Why
is this? Because few, while reading or listening to John's Revelation,
receive the revelation contained therein: The Revelation of Jesus
Christ. Or, we miss the message in that New Testament prophetic
book because we fail to observe its content, by revelation. I believe
this happens in most of our understanding of Scripture. We fail to
see what is plainly presented in Scripture. That failure keeps men
and women, believers, bound: We don't know what to believe.
Further, we don't seek to know because we don't understand the
importance of knowing. *"My people are destroyed for lack of
knowledge."* Hos. 4:6(a), *NASB.* *"So My people will go into exile
far away because they do not know Me."* Is. 5:13(a), *NLT.*

Daniel saw it a different way: *"[B]ut the people that know their God
shall prevail and succeed."* Dan. 11:32(b), *DRB.* Knowing God is
synonymous with victory. When we know God, we prevail – always.
Knowing Jesus Christ is to know God, *"For He is the Brilliance of
His glory, the Image of His Being, and upholds all things by the
power of His Word...."* Heb. 1:3(a), *ABPE.* Hence, the longing in Paul's
heart to know Christ. That same longing should be in our hearts. *"As*

the hart panteth after the water brooks, so panteth my soul after thee, O God." Ps. 42:1(b).

There is to be a perpetual and continual hunger in our hearts to know Christ. *"How blessed are those who are hungry and thirsty for righteousness, because it is they who will be satisfied!"* Matt. 5:6, *ISV.* Isaiah said, *"Listen to me, you who pursue righteousness, Who seek the LORD: Look to the rock from which you were hewn and to the quarry from which you were dug. Look to Abraham your father and to Sarah who gave birth to you in pain; When he was but one I called him, then I blessed him and multiplied him."* What is the gospel? *"Through you [Abraham] all the people of the world will be blessed."* Gal. 3:8(b); Gen. 22:18.

Why Churches and Believers are Failing

We have missed the gospel: Jesus Christ is the Promised Seed who was given Abraham's promises and promised land, and oversees the distribution of those promises and promised land to all those who put their faith and trust in Him and His completed work on the cross. So, the work of faith begins with a right understanding of the gospel message. I've previously laid a foundation for the work that Christ did. See Chapters One through Four. But, Christ's work has not stopped. No, His work continues to this day. *"For He must reign, till He hath put all enemies under His feet."* 1 Cor. 15:25. Christ's kingdom came and is coming. Satan's kingdom was destroyed and is being destroyed. The gospel is the means by which Satan's kingdom is destroyed and Christ's kingdom is established. *"This is why the Son of God was revealed, to destroy the works of the devil."* 1 Jn. 3:8(b), *BSB.* Christ's revelation spelled and spells Satan's doom.

Why is the Church suffering? Why are so many believers suffering? We don't know Christ. Christ has not been revealed to us. We may know about Jesus, but we don't know Him. Why don't we know Him? *"How then will they call on Him in whom they have not believed? How will they believe in Him whom they have not heard? How will they hear without a preacher? And how will they preach unless they are sent? As it is written: 'How beautiful are the feet of those who preach the Good News of peace, who bring glad tidings of good things!'"* Rom. 8:14-15. Hence, the importance of the preacher of the gospel.

The Good News is God's Business

Why do we need gospel preachers, gospel books and gospel music? So we may know Christ. God exalts and has exalted the gospel preacher. The business of the gospel is the most important business on planet earth today. Like Jesus, we must say, *"did ye not know that I ought to be [occupied] in My Father's business?"* Lk. 2:49, *DBT.* We must be occupied in the business of God. What is the work of God? *"This is the only work God wants from you: Believe in the one He has sent."* Jn. 6:29, *NLT.* The work of God is a work of faith and trust in the person of Jesus Christ. That's it.

The gospel of Jesus Christ is the good news of the person of Jesus Christ. By that good news, we know Him. By knowing Him, we prevail. How do we know Him? By revelation – the revelation of Jesus Christ. John received that revelation while on Patmos. You and I can receive that same revelation wherever we are today. Christ longs to reveal Himself to us. To the world, the gospel of Christ is a mystery concealed. To the Church, the gospel of Christ is a mystery revealed. Christ was revealed, is being revealed and will forevermore be revealed. You and I can partake of that revelation now. How? By the spirit of wisdom and revelation.

Like Paul, *"I pray that the God of our Lord Jesus Christ, the glorious Father, would give you a spirit of wisdom and revelation in the knowledge of Him."* Eph. 1:17, *HCSB.* That revelation of Him will transform your life and world. That's why we need revelation: to know the gospel of Christ. What happens when we receive revelation of the gospel of Christ? The glory of Christ is revealed. *"God wanted His people throughout the world to know the glorious riches of this mystery – which is Christ living in you, giving you the hope of glory."* Col. 1:27, GWT.

Let Your Light Shine

When we know Christ, His glory shines through us. *"For all can see that you are a letter of Christ entrusted to our care, and written not with ink, but with the Spirit of the ever-living God – and not on tablets of stone, but on human hearts as tablets."* 2 Cor. 3:3, WNT. Your heart is God's ink pad. By you, He makes His Son, Jesus the Messiah, known to the world. Your revelation of His Son, Jesus Christ, communicates to everyone the gospel message. That mysterious message is the message with which we have been entrusted. *"So then, men ought to regard us as servants of Christ and stewards of the mysteries of God."* 1 Cor. 4:1, BSB.

Your calling? *"Now it is required of stewards that they be found faithful."* 1 Cor. 4:2, BSB. Are you faithful? Do you want to hear these words? *"Well done, good and faithful slave! You were faithful over a few things; I will put you in charge of many things. Share your master's joy!"* Matt. 25:21, 23. God want you to share in Christ's joy who *"endured the cross, disregarding its shame, and has sat down at the right hand of the throne of God."* Heb. 12:2(b), ISV. You too are called to sit down with Him. *"Together with Christ Jesus He [God] also raised us up and seated us in the heavens,"* Eph. 2:6, HCSB. We're raised with Christ, as Christ is revealed to us, in us and through us.

Peter's observation of the "Nevi'im" (Prophets):

> *"Even the prophets, who prophesied about the grace that was to be yours, carefully researched and investigated this salvation. They tried to find out what era or specific time the Spirit of the Messiah in them kept referring to when He predicted the sufferings of the Messiah and the glories that would follow. It was revealed to them that they were not serving themselves but you in regard to the things that have now been announced to you by those who brought you the good news through the Holy Spirit sent from*

heaven. These are things that even the angels desire to look into." 1 Peter 1:10-12, *ISV.*

The angels are actively excited about and long to look into the mystery of the revelation of Christ. Prophets revealed Christ through their prophecies. We can know Christ through their prophetic writings. We should spend significant time allowing the inexhaustible revelation of the mystery of Christ to be revealed to us, in us and through us.

My prayer for you is simple:

Shine, Jesus, shine,
Fill this land with the Father's glory.
Blaze, Spirit, blaze,
Set our hearts on fire.

Flow, river, flow,
Flood the nations with grace and mercy.
Send forth Your word,
Lord, and let there be light. Amen. [3]

---

[3] Graham Kendrick © 1987 Make My Way Music. International copyright secured. All rights reserved. Used by Permission.

Chapter Six

The Gospel of the Circumcision & Uncircumcision

"In fact, they saw that I had been entrusted with the gospel for the uncircumcised, just as Peter had been entrusted with the gospel for the circumcised." Gal. 2:7, ISV.

Paul was entrusted with the gospel of the uncircumcision. Peter was entrusted with the gospel of the circumcision. Although all Scripture is God-breathed, *"and is profitable for doctrine, for reproof, for correction, for instruction in righteousness"* (1 Tim. 3:16), that doesn't mean we shouldn't listen to whom it was originally written. Paul's writings were primarily to the Gentiles, i.e., the nations. Peter's writings were primarily to the Jewish nation. Through both Peter and Paul, we catch a glimpse of the full gospel of Jesus Christ.

Much of the Church has listened intently to the writings of Paul. At the same time, much of the Church has ignored the writings of Peter. Peter is the overlooked apostle. When we think of Peter, we see an infallible man who often missed God. But, we don't see him as the apostle of the circumcision sent to preach the gospel of the circumcision to the Jewish people. Yet, that's who Peter is: the

Apostle sent to the Jewish people. We miss his importance to our understanding of the mystery of the gospel. But, Peter's understanding of the gospel message is paramount to our understanding of the gospel. The gospel to the Jewish people is different, and yet the same, as it is to the nations.

There's a gospel of the circumcision. There's also a gospel of the uncircumcision. Paul was the Apostle to the uncircumcision. Peter was the Apostle to the circumcision. As Paul received revelation of the gospel of the uncircumcision, Peter received revelation of the gospel of the circumcision. Today, most of the Church focuses on the gospel of the uncircumcision, but we don't seek to understand the gospel of the circumcision. We focus on Paul's writings to the exclusion of Peter's writings. But, I want to understand the gospel through the two lenses provided by God, Paul and Peter.

Through both Peter and Paul, we catch a glimpse of the full gospel of Jesus Christ.

Paul's Gospel: A Message for the Nations

Paul shared his gospel before King Agrippa. Paul was sent to Agrippa by Festus on appeal for the crimes of which he was accused by the Jews. Paul was sent to Festus by Felix. Paul was sent by Felix to Festus. Paul was accused by Tertullus, and the Jews, of being a *"pestilent fellow and a mover of sedition among all the Jews throughout the world, and a ringleader of the sect of the Nazarenes: who also hath gone about to profane the temple: whom we took, and would have judged according to our law."* Acts 24:5,6. Paul was in trouble with the law for having committed no crime. Even the head Centurion, Claudius Lysias, found that Paul *"had nothing laid to his charge worthy of death or of bonds."* Acts 23:29. Paul represented himself throughout his time at trial. From Acts 26:2-28, Paul presented to Agrippa his defense and testimony.

First, Paul answers the accusations laid against him by the Jews. He starts by testifying how he was a Jew among the most orthodox sects among the Pharisees. Paul states to Agrippa that everyone among the Jews knew of his life and beliefs. Then, Paul states, I'm being judged for having hope of the promises presented to our forefathers by the prophets. Specifically, the hope of the resurrection. Hear Paul as he answers the Jews complaint in his own words:

> *"I think myself happy, King Agrippa, because I shall answer for myself this day before thee touching all the things whereof I am accused of the Jews: especially because I know thee to be expert in all customs and questions which are among the Jews: wherefore I beseech thee to hear me patiently. My manner of life from my youth, which was at the first among mine own nation at Jerusalem, know all the Jews; which knew me from the beginning, if they would testify, that after the most straitest sect of our religion I lived a Pharisee. And now I stand and am judged for the hope of the promise made of God unto our fathers: unto which promise our twelve tribes, instantly serving God day and night, hope to come. For which hope's sake, King Agrippa, I am accused of the Jews. Why should it be thought a thing incredible with you, that God should raise the dead?"* Acts 26:2-8.

Then, Paul shares his personal testimony, and states, that he, too, like the Jews, opposed the Name of the Jesus of Nazareth. Paul tells Agrippa that he caused many saints, holy ones, to be cast into prison. He punished entire churches of believers, even to the point of blasphemy. He was a one-man army filled with anger and hatred of the gospel and those who believed it. But, he had a change of heart through an open vision, a revelation of the person of Jesus Christ. In his owns words, Paul states:

> *"I verily thought with myself, that I ought to do many things contrary to the Name of Jesus of Nazareth. Which thing I also did in Jerusalem: and many of the saints did I shut up in prison, having received authority from the chief priests; and when they were put to death, I gave my voice*

against them. And I punished them oft in every synagogue, and compelled them to blaspheme; and being exceedingly mad against them, I persecuted them even unto strange cities. Whereupon as I went to Damascus with authority and commission from the chief priests, At midday, O king, I saw in the way a light from heaven, above the brightness of the sun, shining round about me and them which journeyed with me. And when we were all fallen to the earth, I heard a voice speaking unto me, and saying in the Hebrew tongue, 'Saul, Saul, why persecutest thou Me? It is hard for thee to kick against the pricks.' And I said, 'Who art Thou, Lord?' And He said, 'I am Jesus whom thou persecutest. But rise , and stand upon thy feet: for I have appeared unto thee for this purpose, to make thee a minister and a witness both of these things which thou hast seen, and of those things in the which I will appear unto thee; delivering thee from the people, and from the Gentiles, unto whom now I send thee, to open their eyes, and to turn them from darkness to light, and from the power of Satan unto God, that they may receive forgiveness of sins, and inheritance among them which are sanctified by faith that is in Me.'" Acts 26:9-18.

Then, Paul testifies of his obedience to that vision and his commission by Jesus Christ. Previously, Paul spoke of his own conversion experience, and how he received the gospel. Now, Paul begins to break down the gospel message to Agrippa. Remember, Paul is presenting the gospel in open court before a multitude of witnesses, and before a judge, Agrippa, who is familiar with the Scriptures. Paul seeks to persuade Agrippa by the presentation of the gospel message. Paul, in his own words, presents the gospel of the uncircumcision to Agrippa:

"Whereupon, O King Agrippa, I was not disobedient unto the heavenly vision: but shewed first unto them of Damascus, and at Jerusalem, and throughout all the coasts of Judaea, and then to the Gentiles, that they should repent and turn to God, and do works meet for repentance. For these causes, the Jews caught me in the temple, and went about to kill me. Having therefore obtained help of God, I continue unto this day, witnessing

both to small and great, saying none other things than those which the prophets and Moses did say should come: that Christ should suffer, and that He should be the first that should rise from the dead, and should shew light unto the people, and to the Gentiles." Acts 26:19-23.

Finally, Paul calls for a decision to be made by King Agrippa. Paul states to Agrippa that he knows what Paul has stated in his answer to the accusations made against him is true. Then, Paul reminds Agrippa of his faith in the prophets. Paul, in the midst of his trial, calls for a conversion experience by the judge, Agrippa. And, it works, Agrippa is compelled by Paul's answer, testimony and faith. Agrippa states to Paul that he is almost persuaded by the things Paul has shared. Almost! Listen to Paul compelling call for a decision by Agrippa in his own words:

"And as he thus spake for himself, Festus said with a loud voice, 'Paul, thou art beside thyself; much learning doth make thee mad.' But he said, 'I am not mad, most noble Festus; but speak forth the words of truth and soberness. For the king knoweth of these things, before whom also I speak freely: for I am persuaded that none of these things are hidden from him; for this thing was not done in a corner. King Agrippa, believest thou the prophets? I know that thou believest.' Then Agrippa said unto Paul, 'Almost thou persuadest me to be a Christian.'" Acts 26:24-28.

Paul's Gospel vs. Peter's Gospel

Peter was the Apostle to the circumcision. Peter's message is drastically different than Paul's. Yet, Peter and Paul preached the same gospel but were sent to different audiences. Peter had a hard time understanding Paul's message. 2 Pet. 3:15,16. Yet, Peter recognized Paul's authority, and the authority of the message given to him. In 2 Pet. 3:16, Peter compares Paul's epistles to *"other Scriptures."* Peter's words lend authority to Paul's message.

Paul also lends authority to Peter's message (see Gal. 1:15; Gal. 2:9-10):

1) Paul visits Peter before any other apostle;
2) Paul spends significant time with Peter prior to receiving the full revelation of the gospel;
3) Paul identifies Peter as a pillar in God's house; and
4) Paul submits to Peter's apostolic authority.

But, Paul's greater submission was to the truth of the gospel. Gal. 2:11. Paul recognizes Peter's calling to the Jews. Gal. 2:9.

Peter recognized Paul's calling to the Gentiles. Gal. 2:8. Both respected one another's calling, and authority. Paul recognized Peter's calling to the Jews. Peter was called to the circumcision. Peter's message was uniquely designed for the circumcision; he was an apostle to the circumcision. As Paul was an Apostle to the Gentiles, Peter was an Apostle to the Jews. Peter carried the gospel of the circumcision.

Why is this so important? Because we, Jew and Gentile, are called to be one new man. Paul writes in Ephesians 2:15, *HCBS: "He made of no effect the law consisting of commands and expressed in regulations, so that He might create in Himself one new man from the two, resulting in peace."* And, when Jew and Gentile come together as one new man, the power of the resurrection is released. Paul describes it this way, *"For if their rejection results in reconciliation of the world, what will their acceptance bring but life from the dead?"* Rom. 11:16, *ISV.* The power of the resurrection awaits the spread of the gospel of the circumcision to the Jew. That's the day in which we live.

Peter's Gospel: The Good News is for the Jew

Peter's gospel, the gospel of the circumcision, is important to the advancement of the Church. Truly, the Church cannot move forward on Paul's gospel alone. Both the gospel of the uncircumcision and gospel of the circumcision are vital to the purposes and plans of God. But, Peter's message, his gospel, the gospel of the circumcision, has been lost over the past 2,000+ years. Instead, our attention has been on Paul's revelation of the gospel. Why have we focused our attention there? Because the time of the Gentiles has not yet reached its fullness. Rom 11:25. But, that point is coming. Hence, the necessity of recovering Peter's gospel.

What is the gospel preached by Peter? To understand Peter's message, I want to take us back to the point where Peter preached that message, the Acts of the Apostles. In Acts 2:14-41, for the first time, we hear the gospel preached by Peter, the Apostle. Peter preaches his gospel to those Jews

[W]e, Jew and Gentile, are called to be one new man.

gathered from the four corners of the known world at that time, for they are witnessing an awesome move of God in their midst; it's Jesus' promised outpouring of power by the Holy Spirit. Let's hear Peter's gospel in his own words.

Peter begins by explaining what is taking place amongst those gathered: those who have received the Holy Spirit are not drunk. No, they are being filled by the Holy Spirit. Peter immediately turns their attention to Scripture. Specifically, he speaks of the promised outpouring by Joel, the prophet. It's a fearful message. Peter describes blood and fire and smoke, and states the sun will turn black and the moon into blood. Now imagine for a second that you were in Jerusalem, you see people's heads on fire, a prophetic message comes forth that makes it appear like it's Armageddon and then the minister says, "Who wants to be saved?!" Naturally, you say, "Me!!!"

> *"But Peter, standing up with the eleven, lifted up his voice, and said unto them, 'Ye men of Judaea, and all ye that dwell at Jerusalem, be this known unto you, and hearken to my words: For these are not drunken, as ye suppose, seeing it is but the third hour of the day. But this is that which was spoken by the prophet Joel; And it shall come to pass in the last days, saith God, I will pour out of My Spirit upon all flesh: and your sons and your daughters shall prophesy, and your young men shall see visions, and your old men shall dream dreams: And on My servants and*

on My handmaidens I will pour out in those days of My Spirit; and they shall prophesy: And I will shew wonders in heaven above, and signs in the earth beneath; blood, and fire, and vapour of smoke: The sun shall be turned into darkness, and the moon into blood, before the great and notable day of the Lord come: And it shall come to pass, that whosoever shall call on the Name of the Lord shall be saved.'" Acts 2:14-21.

After explaining what was happening to those Jews gathered in Jerusalem, Peter begins presenting the gospel of the circumcision. That presentation of the gospel starts with a known fact, Jesus of Nazareth was approved of God by miracles, wonders and signs. The gospel of the circumcision hinges on this steady truth: God approves, and disapproves, of men and women who speak in His Name. How does God show His approval? By signs, wonders and miracles. Those acts are a vital part of the gospel message. Then, Peter shifts to the meat of his gospel message. Christ was crucified by the leaders of Israel according to the foreknowledge of God. That by wicked hands all Israel participated in this unjust act, and as a result is responsible for the death of the Messiah. Peter, in essence, said to Israel what Nathan, the prophet, to David: *"Thou art the Man."* 2 Sam. 12:7. Peter goes on and says, But God raised Jesus from the dead, as spoken by David. By the Spirit, Peter likely referenced David, in hopes, that the people would repent.

"Ye men of Israel, hear these words; Jesus of Nazareth, a man approved of God among you by miracles and wonders and signs, which God did by Him in the midst of you, as ye yourselves also know: Him, being delivered by the determinate counsel and foreknowledge of God, ye have taken, and by wicked hands have crucified and slain: Whom God hath raised up, having loosed the pains of death: because it was not possible that He should be holden of it. For David speaketh concerning Him, I foresaw the Lord always before my face, for He is on my right hand, that I should not be moved: Therefore did My heart rejoice, and My tongue was glad; moreover also My flesh shall rest in hope: because Thou wilt not leave My soul in hell, neither

wilt Thou suffer Thine Holy One to see corruption. Thou hast made known to me the ways of life; Thou shalt make me full of joy with Thy countenance. Men and brethren, let me freely speak unto you of the patriarch David, that He is both dead and buried, and His sepulchre is with us unto this day. Therefore being a prophet, and knowing that God had sworn with an oath to him, that of the fruit of His loins, according to the flesh, He would raise up Christ to sit on His throne; He seeing this before spake of the resurrection of Christ, that His soul was not left in hell, neither His flesh did see corruption. This Jesus hath God raised up, whereof we all are witnesses. Therefore being by the right hand of God exalted, and having received of the Father the promise of the Holy Ghost, He hath shed forth this, which ye now see and hear. For David is not ascended into the heavens: but he saith himself, The Lord said unto My Lord, 'Sit Thou on My right hand, until I make Thy foes Thy footstool.' Therefore let all the house of Israel know assuredly, that God hath made the same Jesus, whom ye have crucified, both Lord and Christ." Acts 2:22-36.

On hearing Peter's gospel, the gospel of the circumcision, the hearts of those Jews in Jerusalem were cut to the core. No argument. Just repentance. That repentance opened the door to salvation. God was willing to forgive. Peter's gospel, unlike the former prophets, did not end in judgment, except as to sin. Rather, God offers forgiveness to each man who repents of their singular sin: Israel's rejection of Messiah. That sin still burns in the hearts of Jewish people around the world. But, it's a sin that keeps them from salvation. That's the Jewish people's chief sin and one which all Jewish people must acknowledge before receiving salvation. There's no other way. But, as many as call on Him, are saved from the wicked among Israel. Yes, there are wicked among the Jewish people, as there are wicked among all people. And, Jewish people are called to extricate themselves from the wicked Jews by proclaiming Messiah, Yeshua.

"Now when they heard this, they were pricked in their heart, and said unto Peter and to the rest of the apostles, Men and brethren, what shall we do?" Then Peter said unto them, 'Repent, and be baptized every one of you in the

Name of Jesus Christ for the remission of sins, and ye shall receive the gift of the Holy Ghost. For the promise is unto you, and to your children, and to all that are afar off, even as many as the Lord our God shall call. And with many other words did he testify and exhort, saying, Save yourselves from this untoward generation. Then they that gladly received His word were baptized: and the same day there were added unto them about three thousand souls.'"
Acts 2:37-41.

Peter's Revelation of the Gospel is Hidden in His Three Sermons to the Jews

In the Acts of the Apostles, Peter preaches the gospel of the circumcision on three separate occasions: Acts 2:14-41, Acts 3:11-26 and Acts 4:8-12. We have seen Peter's first and arguably most compelling presentation of the gospel of the circumcision. I want to remind you of the exegetical principle, the law of first reference, I outlined in Chapter Four. Peter's presentation of the gospel on Pentecost is of special significance in understanding the gospel of the circumcision, for it's the place where the gospel of the circumcision was first preached. But, that doesn't mean we should ignore the other two times Peter is shown preaching the gospel of the circumcision. No, they are in Scripture for a reason.

In Acts 3:12-26, Peter is shown preaching the gospel to Jewish people who have just witnessed a great miracle by the hands of Peter and John: the healing of the lame man at the gate of the temple. Peter's message is similar to the first message, but it's not the same. Peter adds to his former message. What does he add? He reminds the people gathered to look to God. He reminds the people of who God is, who Jesus is and what all Israel did: that Israel chose a murderer over the Messiah; that they, the Jewish people, should today choose to make a different choice: to hear the Prophet that God raised up, Jesus of Nazareth, like to Moses. Finally, Peter presents the precursor to Paul's gospel: God wanted to bless the Jewish people through Abraham: to turn them from their iniquities. Let's see what Peter, in his own words, added.

Peter points those who have gathered due to the miracle of healing to the *"God of our fathers,"* the God of Abraham, Isaac and Jacob. Then, Peter points away from himself and John. Peter plainly says God did this miracle. Then, Peter firmly tells them the truth: you killed the Messiah. But, God glorified the Messiah you killed by raising Him from the dead. And, John and I witnessed everything I've just stated. Finally, it's only by faith in the Name of the Messiah that this man stands before you whole. The implication being that you can be made whole too through the same Name of the Messiah – Jesus.

> *"And when Peter saw it, he answered unto the people, 'Ye men of Israel, why marvel ye at this? Or why look ye so earnestly on us, as though by our own power or holiness we had made this man to walk? The God of Abraham, and of Isaac, and of Jacob, the God of our fathers, hath glorified His Son Jesus; whom ye delivered up, and denied Him in the presence of Pilate, when he was determined to let Him go. But ye denied the Holy One and the Just, and desired a murderer to be granted unto you; And killed the Prince of Life, whom God hath raised from the dead; whereof we are witnesses. And His Name through faith in His Name hath made this man strong, whom ye see and know: yea, the faith which is by Him hath given Him this perfect soundness in the presence of you all.'"* Acts 3:12-16.

Peter doesn't blame the Jewish people. No, he restates the common theme in Scripture that Joseph learned in the dungeons of Egypt: *"You thought evil against Me [Jesus]: but God turned it into good, that He might exalt Me [Jesus], as at present you see, and might save many people [all Mankind]."* Israel was ignorant. God used their ignorance to accomplish His divine purpose: the salvation of all Mankind. Finally, Peter plainly points them to the door of salvation: repentance from what they currently believe to the truth about Messiah that was spoken down through the generations by the prophets starting with Moses.

> *"And now, brethren, I wot that through ignorance ye did it, as did also your rulers. But those things, which God before*

had shewed by the mouth of all His prophets, that Christ should suffer, He hath so fulfilled. Repent ye therefore, and be converted, that your sins may be blotted out, when the times of refreshing shall come from the presence of the Lord. And He shall send Jesus Christ, which before was preached unto you: Whom the heaven must receive until the times of restitution of all things, which God hath spoken by the mouth of all His holy prophets since the world began." Acts 3:17-21.

Peter reminds the people of what Moses said: A prophet like me will come to Israel. Further, Peter reminds them that Moses said that the person who wouldn't listen to the words of that coming prophet would be destroyed. Peter plainly tells the people that they are living in the days of the fulfillment of all that was spoken by all the prophets since Samuel. Then, Peter presents the beginning of the message that Paul later had revealed to him: *"[T]he Scripture, foreseeing that God would justify the heathen through faith, preached before the gospel unto Abraham, saying, In thee shall all nations be blessed."* Gal. 3:8. Or, Peter was pointing the Jewish people to the coming gospel of the uncircumcision that would be preached by Paul. Amazing!

"For Moses truly said unto the fathers, 'A prophet shall the Lord your God raise up unto you of your brethren, like unto me; Him shall ye hear in all things whatsoever He shall say unto you. And it shall come to pass, that every soul, which will not hear that prophet, shall be destroyed from among the people.' Yea, and all the prophets from Samuel and those that follow after, as many as have spoken, have likewise foretold of these days. Ye are the children of the prophets, and of the covenant which God made with our fathers, saying unto Abraham, And in thy seed shall all the kindreds of the earth be blessed. Unto you first God, having raised up His Son Jesus, sent Him to bless you, in turning away every one of you from his iniquities." Acts 3:22-26.

In Acts 4:8-12, Peter presents his gospel message for the last recorded instance in the Acts of the Apostles. That message is directed to Israel's leaders. Peter is on trial. Israel's leaders begin to see the writing on the wall. Nothing can stop this Messiah movement. But, they try. Collectively, Israel's leaders conspire to ask "the right question" from this unlearned fisherman: 1) By what power was this miracle done? and 2) By what name? That question is the exact question needed. Peter's faith is strong. Peter responds: Jesus! Then, Peter proceeds to quote David from the Psalms: *"The stone which the builders rejected, that has become the head of the building."* Ps. 118:22, *ABPE*. Peter finalizes his message, and says, *"Salvation comes in no other Name."* Acts 4:12. Aghast at Peter's bold response, and his wisdom, Israel's leaders are forced to set him and John free. Peter's gospel convinces the Jewish people, shakes the religious establishment and prepares the way for Paul's gospel. Not bad!

Restoring the Whole Gospel to the Church

I hope you are beginning to see the continuity of the gospel message as preached by Peter and Paul. Both are twin pillars of the gospel and stand before the Church for all time to present the full gospel. And, that's the gospel we need today. But, recovering the full gospel requires us to relearn those things we have been taught. Much of what we have been taught are the religious traditions of men and not the gospel. The gospel is sacred; it's the message of Christ to both the circumcision and uncircumcision. That gospel is the engine that moves the Church forward into the ages to come. We need that full gospel today.

But, that gospel has been muddied by numerous men and women throughout decades and centuries. We have neglected the necessity of understanding the gospel we preach. We have not searched for the gospel earnestly, as Paul did, for we think we know it. Nor have we recognized our fatal flaws, as Peter did, prior to being endued with power from on high to preach that gospel. Beloved, we must earnestly seek to recover the gospel: its message, ministry, motivation and maturation. Who better to teach us than these twin apostles – Peter and Paul? Saints, we have much to learn.

The Importance of Mark's Gospel to the Church Today

Possibly the most compelling gospel preached by Peter was written by John who surname was Mark. Acts 15:27. The Gospel of Mark was written by John Mark. (Most scholars don't believe the gospel of Mark was written by John Mark. But, it's acknowledged that it's the earliest of the four gospels, which lends credibility to my belief that it was written by John Mark who received it from the Peter). From Acts 13:13-14, we see John Mark as an inexperienced gospel preacher who left Paul and Barnabas on their first missionary journey. Barnabas wanted to take John Mark with them on their

> *The gospel is the engine that moves the Church forward into the ages to come.*

second missionary journey. Paul wanted to leave him behind. Paul and Barnabas separated over John Mark. Acts 15:36-41. Later, Paul instructed the churches to receive John Mark. Col. 4:10. That implies Paul instructed them to not receive him. In Paul's final letter to Timothy, his son in the faith, he states, John Mark is *"profitable to me for the ministry."* 2 Tim. 4:11. The difference? Peter. As Timothy was Paul's son in the faith, John Mark was Peter's son in the faith. 1 Pet. 5:13. Peter mentored John Mark. During that mentorship, Peter likely downloaded to John Mark the Gospel of Mark.

The Gospel of Mark begins: *"The beginning of the gospel of Jesus Christ, the Son of God...."* Mk. 1:1. There are three books of beginning in the Bible: Genesis, John and Mark. In Genesis, we see the beginning of creation. In John, we see the beginning of all things. In Mark, we see the beginning of the gospel. The gospel has a beginning. For something to have a beginning, that means it must not have existed prior to its beginning, or it wouldn't have had a beginning. The gospel does have a beginning. We see that beginning in the Gospel of Mark. Hence, its special place of importance to the gospel preacher. The Gospel of Mark is the training manual for the gospel preacher to preach the full gospel.

Mark's Gospel: The Church's Miracle Manual

In the Gospel of Mark, we see the preeminence of Christ's miracles in the spread of the gospel message. Without miracles, and, in this case, without the manual of miracles, which the Gospel of Mark is, we fail to truly understand the relevance of the gospel message. The gospel message is relevant because all of Mankind needs it. Everyone. No exceptions. And, for such a message to have such universal application and relevance, it must be shown not just known. Miracles show the relevance of the gospel message to hurting humanity.

Miracles demonstrate the reality of the gospel message. Without them, our gospel is unheard. With them, the world beats a pathway to our door. To needy humanity looking for bread, light and water, the gospel brings all those things and much more. The gospel brings life, freedom and peace. That's what the gospel has brought to all who have embraced it. When we embrace the full gospel of both the circumcision and uncircumcision, we're raised into the new man prophesied by Paul in Ephesians. We become who we were made to be, and, in that, creation joins us in jubilant celebration.

I want to encourage you to *"receive instruction"* in the gospel message. Prov. 1:3. *"Buy the truth, and sell it not; also wisdom, and instruction, and understanding."* Prov. 23:23. The gospel preacher must be taught to preach the gospel. Yes, revelation is essential, but so is instruction. There's a foolish notion in some parts of the Church where it's claimed that instruction isn't necessary for the revelatory offices of apostle and prophet. I don't agree. Nor does the Scripture. Receive instruction. Learn. Grow in your understanding. That's why God gave us a mind: to learn. And, with all your getting, get understanding, Prov. 4:7; receive instruction in the gospel message by anointed messengers of the gospel. Rom. 10:15. The gospel is vital; it is enough.

I hope you are beginning to feel overwhelmed by your lack of knowledge of the gospel. Why? Because our own pride is often the greatest hindrance to the gospel. We place ourselves and our needs above those of the kingdom. That hinders the gospel. In spite of his flaws, Peter laid it all down to follow Jesus: He preached the gospel. Paul did the same. Paul found that nothing in this life could compare to the matchless wisdom awaiting him in the person of Jesus Christ. Do you feel the same? If not, then there's a hole in your life. That hole can only be filled by the missing piece: the gospel. May your heart be filled with the gospel.

I hope that I've sparked in you an awakened consciousness of the gospel. I hope you are beginning to understand the gospel's simplicity and complexity. We have much to learn. God has much to teach us about the true nature of the gospel. Are you ready? Before we can move into the next phase of our understanding, the gospel's power – yes, there's power in the true gospel, and I want to awaken you to the gospel's power – there are two more facets of the gospel that I want to discuss: the gospel of salvation and the gospel of peace.

Chapter Seven

The Gospel of Salvation & the Gospel of Peace

"You, too, have heard the word of truth, the gospel of your salvation. When you believed in the Messiah, you were sealed with the promised Holy Spirit...." Eph. 1:13, *ISV.*

"And your feet shod with the preparation of the gospel of peace...." Eph. 6:15.

T he gospel brings salvation. *"For the grace of God that bringeth salvation hath appeared to all men,"* Tit. 2:11. That salvation is more than an eternal home in heaven. Yes, it's also fuel for living life in the here and now on earth. The gospel is sufficient; it is enough. But, we have not understood how great the salvation we have received is. We have neglected the gospel. To that, the writer of Hebrews states, *"How shall we escape, if we neglect so great salvation; which at the first began to be spoken by the Lord, and was confirmed unto us by them that heard Him...."* Heb. 2:3. Piercingly, he asks the same question of us today. What is your response?

For most, there is no response. *"Instead, you must worship Christ as Lord of your life. And if someone asks about your Christian hope, always be ready to explain it."* 1 Pet. 3:15, *NLT.* We must be prepared to answer questions concerning salvation, always and everywhere. This is essential instruction for believers. But, many believers remain uninformed in how to share the essentials of salvation. For this to change, we must be prepared to answer some basic questions about salvation; we must be able to present the gospel of salvation.

Salvation – God's Gift to Mankind

What is the gospel of salvation? To answer that question, I want to take a look at the word salvation in the Greek language. The word salvation in the Greek language in Ephesians 1:13 is *sótéria.* That word, in addition to meaning salvation, also means deliverance,

preservation, prosperity,

God's great gift to Mankind is salvation. welfare and safety. That word is derived from the root word, *sótér.* That word is a noun and is used in reference to a person, always. And, it's derived from another Greek word, a verb, *sózó,* which means: I save, heal, preserve, rescue. Jesus is not passive when it comes to salvation. No, He brought and is actively bringing salvation to Mankind.

God's great gift to Mankind is salvation. Many have diminished this gift by not understanding or appreciating its importance. Yes, many have been negligent concerning their own salvation, and through that negligence have abused the privileges obtained by that gift. To that abuse, we are warned: *"How shall we escape, if we neglect so great salvation; which at the first began to be spoken by the Lord, and was confirmed unto us by them that heard Him...."* Heb. 2:3. As such, we need a sure guide to keep us on the path of salvation. And, that's who Christ is, our eternal guide to the place of salvation.

Christ: The Captain of Mankind's Salvation

God has exalted Jesus Christ above all and has given Him a Name which is above every other name. Eph. 1:21. Further, God has instructed us to follow Him in the way of salvation. In Hebrews, He is described as the *"Captain of their salvation."* Heb. 2:10. As Captain, He has gone before us. Jesus knows the troubled waters of life that lay ahead. He warns us to enable us to avoid those troubled waters and avoid the swales of sin, sickness and Satan. He is Savior. Gabriel speaking to Joseph said, *"And she [Mary] shall bring forth a son, and thou shalt call His Name JESUS: for He shall save His people from their sins."* Matt. 1:21.

Many have preached against sin. Some have preached about Mankind's redemption from sin. But, few have preached about the salvation we have received from sin. Listen to Peter's message on the day Pentecost regarding the salvation offered by and through Christ: *"Unto you first God, having raised up His Son Jesus, sent Him to bless you, in turning away every one of you from his iniquities."* Acts 3:26. Paul's mission from Christ given on the road to Damascus was similar: *"You will open their eyes and turn them from darkness to light and from Satan's control to God's. Then they will receive forgiveness for their sins and a share among God's people who are made holy by believing in Me."* Acts 26:18, GWT.

Unless we understand the depths of our own depravity, we can never truly understand just how great the gift of salvation is that we have received. At one point, we were all under Satan's control. But the gospel of salvation broke the bonds and shackles to which we were held. The gospel of salvation includes the gospel of healing, the gospel of deliverance, the gospel of prosperity, the gospel of safety and the gospel of peace. There's an eternal Shalom over the people of God: His Name is Jesus. That's the Name in which we should place our faith and trust.

Healing and Salvation are Forever Linked

The gospel of healing is part and parcel of the gospel of salvation. Jesus taught us this by exposing the lie of their difference. In the Gospel of Mark, we're told the story of the paralytic man (In the Gospels of Matthew and Luke, this same story is also told; see Matt. 9:2-6; Lk. 5:18-25.) Here is what it says:

"And they come unto Him, bringing one sick of the palsy, which was borne of four. And when they could not come nigh unto Him for the press, they uncovered the roof where he was: and when they had broken it up, they let down the bed wherein the sick of the palsy lay. When Jesus saw their faith, He said unto the sick of the palsy, 'Son, thy sins be forgiven thee.' But there was certain of the scribes sitting there, and reasoning in their hearts, Why doth this man thus speak blasphemies? who can forgive sins but God only? And immediately when Jesus perceived in His spirit that they so reasoned within themselves, He said unto them, Why reason ye these things in your hearts? Whether is it easier to say to the sick of the palsy, 'Thy sins be forgiven thee;' or to say, 'Arise, and take up thy bed, and walk?' But that ye may know that the Son of Man hath power on earth to forgive sins, (He saith to the sick of the palsy,) I say unto thee, 'Arise, and take up thy bed, and go thy way into thine house.'" Mark 2:3-11.

Jesus healed many paralytic people. Why then is this healing so important? It's identified in three of the four Gospels. What makes it important? For one simple reason, Jesus connects the forgiveness of sin and the healing of sickness. And in His question to the Pharisees and Sadducees, He shows their similarity, *"Which is easier: to say to this paralyzed man, 'Your sins are forgiven,' or to say, 'Get up, take your mat and walk?'"* Mk. 2:9, NIV. That question cuts across the theological spectrum of healing. Healing and forgiveness originate from the one and same source – the cross.

Healing is always God's will. Always. There's no person, who approaches God, in faith believing, that He will not heal. God never says, "No," to our request for healing. I'm not going to teach much on this because there are many good books that discuss God's will to heal and the ministry of healing.[4] Further, it's always His will to

---

[4] I have spent a significant amount of time reading and studying on the subject of healing, and here are some good resources to help you in understanding the healing message: 1) A.A. Allen, *God's Guarantee to Heal You,* 2) F.F. Bosworth, *Christ the Healer,* 3) T.L. Osborn, *Healing the Sick,* 4) T.J. McCrossan, *Bodily Healing and the Atonement,* 5) Bill Johnson and Randy Clark, *The Essential Guide to Healing,* 6) Andrew Murray, *Divine Healing,* 7) Charles S. Price, *The Real Faith for Healing,* and 8) John Eckhardt, *Prayers That Bring Healing.*

heal now. *"For God says, 'At just the right time, I heard you. On the day of salvation, I helped you.' Indeed, the 'right time' is now. Today is the day of salvation."* 2 Cor. 6:2, *NLT*. You mean it's God's will to heal me right now? Yes! And, the only thing that prevents it is your inability to believe it.

I myself have struggled with this concept. I know it's a principle, but have struggled to apply it in my own life. I don't condemn myself or others if they are not healed. Nor do I condemn those who visit doctor's offices seeking medical attention. I believe this is good wisdom. Nevertheless, I don't ever want to lose what is clearly revealed in Scripture: healing is God's will, always, just as salvation is God's will, always. Imagine for a second that you told someone that if they only waited long enough, God might forgive them of their sin. We would easily recognize the error of such a statement. But, we apply the same flawed logic to healing. If you only wait and pray, and wait and pray, God may heal you. No. Such is false teaching clothed with false humility.

The gospel of healing is for everyone. Everyone can be healed. It's God's will for all to be healed. *"He [Jesus] healed all the sick among them...."* Matt. 12:15, *NLT*. Jesus is the very expression of God's will. Heb. 1:3. Jesus did not make people sick. No, He made them well. That's who He is, a healer. *"God anointed Jesus of Nazareth with the Holy Ghost and with power: who went about doing good, and healing all that were oppressed of the devil; for God was with Him."* Acts 10:38. In truth, healing is the children's bread; it's part of our provision in this life. Matt. 15:26. Christ has already made provision for your healing; His sacrifice is sufficient. That's the good news of healing, and it's for you.

The Believer's Authority to Trample Satan's Kingdom

The gospel of deliverance is part and parcel of the gospel of salvation. God doesn't want anyone to be oppressed or possessed by the devil. And, the gospel of deliverance is more important today than ever. Millions of people subject themselves to demonic activity by participating in gross sin, including occultism. Yes, demons are real. Yes, demons have power. But, Jesus made this point blatantly clear to His disciples and to us, *"I have given you authority to trample on snakes and scorpions and to overcome all the power of the enemy; nothing will harm you."* Lk. 10:19, *NIV.*

We have authority over the activity of the enemy. And, demons are powerless against us. That means we can stop demons and their activities on earth. The size of the demon is unimportant. The number of demons is unimportant. The power level of demons is unimportant. We all have authority to shut down, stop and restrict all demonic activity. Why then do demons not flee when we command them to flee? Listen to what Scripture teaches: *"[T]he disciples came to Jesus privately and asked, 'Why couldn't we drive it out?' He told them, 'Because of your lack of faith...'"* Matt. 17:19-20. In Mark 9:29, Jesus tells His disciples, *"This kind can come forth by nothing, but by prayer and fasting."* Mk. 9:29. In Luke 9:19, Jesus confronts the wickedness of an entire generation: *"'You unbelieving and perverse generation,' Jesus replied, 'how long shall I stay with you and put up with you?'"* Lk. 9:41. Group unbelief, wickedness and perversion can hinder deliverance. But, it cannot stop it, if the believer is "prayed up."

The gospel of deliverance begins with and ends on the cross. Jesus *"gave Himself for our sins, that He might deliver us from this present evil world, according to the will of God and our Father...."* Gal. 1:4. Notice, deliverance is God's will. When is it God's will to deliver us from demonic activity? To help you, I'll ask you some simple questions: 1) When is it God's will to save us? and 2) When is it God's will to heal us? That's right! Now is the answer. Deliverance is for each and every person who places their faith in the completed work of Christ on the cross. Christ died to free us from the devil's bondages. Listen to Paul: *"It is for freedom that Christ has set us free. Stand firm, then, and do not let yourselves be burdened again by a yoke of slavery."* Gal. 5:1, *NIV.*

I've personally experienced Christ's delivering power. I know what it's like to be bound in my mind. At times, I felt like a mental paraplegic. When I was first saved, I experienced terrible demonic attacks. Demons appeared at night in dreams. In the dreams, I tried to rebuke them. But, I couldn't speak. I was oppressed. I had uncontrollable thoughts and severe imaginations caused by demonic activity. I did not know how to stop it. I prayed and prayed and prayed and prayed. Nothing seemed to work. Then, I went to a meeting and received a 30+ minute prophetic word. Immediately, I was set free. Later, I received other deliverance as my soul was healed from deep hurts caused during my life. God healed me. It was supernatural. Deliverance. Freedom.

Deliverance is God's will.[5] You can be delivered from alcohol, drugs, pornography or other types of vices, addictions or demonic activity. Christ will free you from anything that's binding you. Christ knows your hurts and pain, and how the devil gained access to your life. And, He wants to close the door to the devil and kick him out. Let Him do it! You can receive freedom today. You don't need twelve steps. There's one step, the step of faith. And, you can take that step right now. Receive freedom from the devil's yokes of bondage in your life. In the Name of Jesus Christ of Nazareth, I loose you...NOW!

The Believer's Authority to Prosper in Every Area

The gospel of prosperity is part and parcel of the gospel of salvation. God's will is for His people to prosper. This has been His will from the beginning. Remember what God said to Abraham, *"Surely blessing I will bless thee, and multiplying I will multiply thee."*

---

[5] I have spent a significant amount of time reading and studying on the subject of deliverance, and here are some good resources to help you in understanding the healing message: 1) Francis Frangipane, *The Three Battle Grounds*, 2) Francis Frangipane, *Holiness, Truth and the Presence of God*, 3) Frank Hammond, *Pigs in the Parlor*, 4) Gary Greenwald, *Seductions Exposed*, 5) Randy Clark, *The Biblical Guidebook to Deliverance*, 6) Peter J. Horrobin, *Healing Through Deliverance*, 7) Francis McNutt, *Deliverance from Evil Spirits*, 8) John Eckhardt, *Prayers that Rout Demons*, and 9) Don Nori, *Breaking Demonic Strongholds*.

Heb. 6:14. As Abraham's seed, God also says that to you. You are blessed. God will bless you. Part of that blessing is to prosper you financially. *"Your fruit baskets and breadboards will be blessed."* Deut. 28:5, NLT. *"The LORD will guarantee a blessing on everything you do and will fill your storehouses with grain. The LORD your God will bless you in the land He is giving you."* Deut. 28:8, NLT.

What is the foundation for that prosperity? The cross. *"You know the generous grace of our Lord Jesus Christ. Though He was rich, yet for your sakes He became poor, so that by His poverty, He could make you rich."* 2 Cor. 8:9, NLT. That's why Paul could say, *"God is able to multiply every favor toward you that you may always have whatever is sufficient for you in all things and that you may superabound in every good work...."* 2 Cor. 9:8, ABPE. *"And my God will supply all your needs according to His riches in glory in Christ Jesus."* Phil. 4:19, NASB. It's upon this foundation that we obtain prosperity.

Knowing that it's God's will to prosper us is vital to our success in this life. God wants us to be successful in this life. That success is measured by what we accomplish in this life. But, that success is decided on the basis of the cross and covenant we have with God through Jesus Christ. Our prosperity is not governed by anything else, including our ability to keep God's law. We function and operate under God's grace. But, that grace isn't a license to sin. Rather, it's a grace to be set free from sin.

Sin is always antithetical to prosperity. God's blessing moves us from our sin. Peter said, God *"sent Him [Jesus] to bless you, in turning away every one of you from his iniquities."* Acts 3:26. We will never truly prosper by living in sin. Asaph, in Psalm 73, meditates on the picture he sees: the wicked appear to prosper, and the righteous appear to suffer. He is so moved by this thought that he states, *"I was envious at the foolish when I saw the prosperity of the wicked."* Ps. 73:3. Then he says, *"Verily, I have cleansed my heart in vain, and washed my hands in innocency."* Ps. 73:13.

Finally, he realizes the place he is in and comes to his senses: *"So foolish was I, and ignorant. I was as a beast before thee."* Ps. 73:22.

Oftentimes, believers think that living godly is fruitless and pointless. That lie is predicated on things that happen in their lives. Believers suffer and blame God. But, blaming God doesn't satisfy them. No, they begin to envy the wicked, saying, "God allows those living wickedly to prosper, including the prideful and arrogant; they have it good." Then, believers fall into sin under the weight of the lie they have believed. Yes, the wicked may prosper for a season. Yes, the wicked may appear to get away with their wickedness for a season. But, that season comes to an end, and when that end comes, it concludes with their utter destruction.

David saw this and said, *"Do not emulate the wicked neither envy the workers of evil. Because they dry up quickly like straw and they wither like green grass. Hope in God and do good, dwell in the land and seek faithfulness. Hope in Lord Jehovah and He will give you the requests of your heart."* Ps. 37:1-4, *ABPE*. In several translations it says, *"Delight yourself in the LORD; And He will give you the desires of your heart."* Ps. 37:4, *NASB*. That's the path to prosperity. We can walk that path. That's our decision. God gave us His Word so we could understand His ways, and then walk in those ways with Him. That's prosperity.

Prosperity is found in honest living. Prosperity is found by faithful men and women. Prosperity is found by those who are generous to God and others. Giving is one of the cornerstones of the Christian faith. *"For God so loved the world, that He gave...."* Jn. 3:16. That giving did not end on the cross. No, it began on the cross and continues today. Life is a gift. Marriage is a gift. Children are gifts. Jobs, skills and talents are gifts. So, is the income we receive. All are gifts. Yes, we work. But, we work to give, not to live. Eph. 4:28. Our provision is sure in the Father, as sons. Jesus said, *"I tell you to stop worrying about what you will eat, drink or wear. Isn't life more than food and the body more than clothes?"* Matt. 6:25, *GWT*. Instead, we are to *"Seek the Kingdom of God above all else, and live righteously, and He will give you everything you need."* Matt. 6:33. *NLT*. Prosperity is about more than having a job, it's about having a life.

Angels are Watching Over and Protecting You

The gospel of protection and safety is also found in the gospel. Accidents are not God's will. There's nothing good about suffering from accidents. But, accidents can and do happen. That's why we need to remember the gospel of our protection. Protection from harm is God's will. God has an angelic assurance policy issued on each of us, which states, *"[H]e will order His angels to protect you wherever you go."* Ps. 91:11, *NLT*. And, *"The LORD's angel camps around the LORD's loyal followers and delivers them."* Ps. 34:7, *NET*. In one translation it says, God's angel *"surrounds His [God's] worshippers."* Ps. 34:7, *ABPE*.

Why then do so many believers suffer harm from accidents? Because of neglect. We don't know the gospel also contains a protection policy. That policy is in effect today if you are a believer and choose to believe the gospel. Jesus experienced that kind of protection. *"All the people in the synagogue were furious when they heard this. They got up, drove Him out of the town, and took Him to the brow of the hill on which the town was built, in order to throw Him off the cliff. But He walked right through the crowd and went on His way."* Lk. 4:28-30, *NIV*. The people wanted to kill Jesus, but He walked away unharmed. Angels were watching over Him. Angels are also watching over you, if you believe the gospel.

God's salvation to Mankind is meant to bring us into all these things and more. That's the good news that Jesus Christ came to share with us. We can be made whole by Him. We can walk free in this life with Him. Sin cannot hinder us. Satan cannot stop us. God is for us. Knowing that should bring peace into your heart. God's gift to the prayerful believer is a *"peace, which goes beyond anything we can imagine [that] will guard your thoughts and emotions through Christ Jesus."* Phil. 4:7, *GWT.* That peace is the gospel of peace. The gospel of peace is the promise of God to the believer; we have been fitted to walk in that kind of peace, daily.

Peace is Your Portion in Life

The gospel of peace is the good news that the war is over. Mankind and God are no longer at war. God has chosen to embrace those who were once His enemies and call them His sons. All who hear this message of peace, and embrace it, can become God's sons. There are no exceptions or

> *God has chosen to embrace those who were once His enemies and call them His sons.*

exclusions. That's the good news proclaimed by the angels at Christ's birth to the shepherds: *"Glory to God in the highest, and on earth peace, good will toward men."* Lk. 2:14. Today, that same peace is being proclaimed in the gospel of peace. That's the gospel we're called to bring to the world – the good news of peace.

Paul describes our mission and mandate this way: *"For shoes, put on the peace that comes from the Good News so that you will be fully prepared."* Eph. 6:15, *NLT.* Paul describes how the world sees these messengers of peace: *"How beautiful are the feet of them that preach the gospel of peace, and bring glad tidings of good things!"* Rom. 10:15. The gospel message is a message of peace, and the gospel of peace prepares the hearts of men and women to receive the gospel message. Where peace is proclaimed, men will listen. Where war is promoted, men will run, duck and take cover. That's why we have failed as the Church: we are not preaching the good news of peace. But, that can change.

The good news of peace is still available to the Church. Our warfare is no longer with men and women. Eph. 6:12. We cannot represent God by presenting Him as an angry God. He isn't angry. He has forgiven our sin, and He has made provision for the forgiveness of our sin. That provision is part of the gospel message. And, that message is the message we're called to proclaim to the world. Why then is this message not being preached? Because we don't know it. We have failed to peer into the Scriptures to learn what the gospel is. We don't know why Jesus really came. We know bits and pieces of God's Word. But, we have missed the full measure of that word by not understanding the basic precepts in it – the gospel is good news. The good news is the war is over, and peace has begun. That's the message I bring to you – the good news of peace.

But, for us to preach the gospel of peace, we must have peace in our own hearts. That's why Paul stated plainly and simply to the Colossians: *"Let the peace of Christ rule in your hearts, since as members of one Body you were called to peace. And be thankful."* Col. 3:15, *NIV*. Our calling is a calling to proclaim peace among the nations. If and when we do that, we'll see the greatest harvest of souls the world has ever known. Until then, we'll see wars and rumors of wars. That's why the gospel of peace is so important, and must be preached and published to the ends of the earth. And, that's why God is looking for and raising up an army prepared with the message of the good news of peace.

Blessed are the Peacemakers

If we want to be in God's army, we cannot be hell-bent on war. No, we must be about the Father's business of proclaiming peace. That message will resonate in the hearts of men and women. That message will pull multitudes into the Church. That message will bring salvation to the nations. That message will emerge as the predominant message in the end times. By the way, Satan hates the gospel of peace. Why? *"The God of peace will quickly crush Satan under your feet."* Rom. 16:20, *NET*. When the intent of God – peace – is proclaimed to humanity, we gravitate toward that. Most people want to live in peace. God wants that too.

The great commission starts with "go." So, *"go in peace."* Lk. 7:50. But, it doesn't end there. The great commission is to end in peace,

peace in the hearts of hurting humanity and peace in the world. The Prince of Peace, Jesus Christ, has sent us to proclaim the gospel of peace to a war-torn world ravaged by sin and Satan. Watch the nightly news and you will see men and women in need of peace from this sin-soaked age. Yes, they long for peace: peace on the streets of the City of Chicago ravaged by gun violence; peace in communities across America ravaged by police brutality and judicial incompetence; peace in the middle east ravaged by radical Islamic extremism. Peace.

America's wars have turned a peace-loving people into a nation of war mongers. We no longer know the gospel of peace, nor do we proclaim it. That's why we've lost the trust of the nations. We have turned toward tyranny in the name of Christ. But, Christ is not the tyrant we have made Him to be to a hurting world. No, He reaches down to the helpless, the hopeless, and picks them up; He lifts them. We can be like Him, seeking to lift lost humanity from the ravages of sin and Satan by presenting the gospel. We are the answer. You are the answer. Now, you have the answer – the gospel. Go and share it.

Chapter Eight

The Power of the Gospel

"I am not ashamed of the gospel, because it is the power of God for salvation to everyone who believes, first to the Jew, then to the Greek." Rom. 1:16, *BSB*.

I believe in the necessity of the power of God. We cannot reach a world hardened by sin without that power. That's why, prior to leaving His apostles and disciples, Christ told them to *"tarry ye in the city of Jerusalem, until ye be endued with power from on high."* Lk. 24:49. Wait for power from on high, then witness. That's the pattern Christ set for the Church. Yet today, we witness without power and we think that's the pattern. It's not.

I Said... POWER

In 1988, while attending college at the University of Iowa in Iowa City, Iowa, I was quietly lying on my bed meditating on Act 1:8. *"But ye shall receive power, after that the Holy Ghost is come upon you: and ye shall be witnesses unto me both in Jerusalem, and in all Judea, and in Samaria, and unto the uttermost parts of the earth,"* I heard the audible voice of God speak to me. God said, "I said POWER!" His voice reverberated in me, as if it was coming from all directions – inside and outside of me, all at once. Startling, to say the least!

My understanding of the gospel, and God's intention for the gospel, was transformed that day. I understood that God intended His message to be preached with power. That power was an important part of the gospel message. That power had been lost by much of the Church and was desperately needed. Power. I had witnessed a powerless Church that rarely spoke of the gospel outside of the sacred zone of "the Church." But, I wanted the power. That's what I needed, and that's what we need.

From Human Wisdom to God's Power

Paul identified this very real need for God's power in his epistle to the Corinthian believers when He said, *"When I came to you, I was weak. I was afraid and very nervous. I didn't speak my message with persuasive intellectual arguments. I spoke my message with a show of spiritual power so that your faith would not be based on human wisdom but on God's power."* Paul didn't rely on his intellectual ability, which was considerable, to persuade people to believe the gospel. Rather, he relied on God's power. 1 Cor. 2:4-5.

I heard the audible voice of God speak to me. God said, "I said POWER!"

Today, the opposite is true. Most believers have been taught to rely on their own wisdom and wit to persuade people to believe the gospel. That's why so many believers are afraid to share the good news. What if they aren't persuasive enough? What if they don't say exactly the right thing? What if? What if? What if? That's the land in which we dwell – the land of "What if?" And to spread the good news, we must leave the land of "What if" and move to the land of "it is." Jesus said, *"It is finished."* Jn. 19:30. He didn't say, "I am finished." He wasn't. He isn't. Not yet.

God's power is available to believers today. We can receive power from on high, just like the Early Church did. And, it isn't just about speaking in tongues. That's a sign of the power, it's not the power itself. The power is the power of God to do the following: *"Heal the* sick, cleanse the lepers, raise the dead, cast out demons...." Matt. 10:8(a). The gospel is free. The power of the gospel is free. We cannot purchase it.

God Has More Power Than Money Can Buy

Simon the Sorcerer learned that lesson the hard way. Listen to the rebuke of Peter, *"Your money perish with you, because you have thought that the gift of God may be purchased with money."* Act 8:20, *AKJV*. Peter didn't mince words with Simon. Peter didn't seek to become politically correct in what he said to Simon. Peter rebuked Simon. Possibly, Peter saw some of himself in Simon, being a Simon, as well.

God's power is His gift to a Church that's sold out to Him. On his way to the gate of the temple called Beautiful, Peter said this to the lame man who was begging at the gate: *"Silver and gold I have none, but what I have, that I give to thee; in the Name of Jesus Christ of Nazareth, rise up and be walking."* Acts 3:6, YLT. Today, we have silver and gold, but we lack power. That's the problem with much of the Church: we choose "the gold standard" rather than "the God standard." But, today, we need the God standard.

Walking in the GOD STANDARD

God has a plumb line He uses to measure His people. Listen to what God said to the prophet Amos: *"And the LORD asked me, 'What do you see, Amos?' 'A plumb line,' I replied. Then the Lord said, 'Look, I am setting a plumb line among My people Israel; I will spare them no longer.'"* Amos 7:8, NIV. God's power is that plumb line in the Church. God uses His plumb line to measure us according to His scales. And, His scales are different from ours. The God standard is higher than the gold standard and more valuable.

Peter boldly declared on the day of Pentecost, *"Ye men of Israel, hear these words; Jesus of Nazareth, a man approved of God among you by miracles and wonders and signs, which God did by Him in the midst of you, as ye yourselves also know...."* Acts 2:22.

God confirms the gospel message. God also confirms the gospel messenger. Is it possible that our lack of power is a lack of confirmation? Is God withholding His approval from us? If so, what does that mean? I think we have some serious questions to ask and answer.

Yes, power is essential to the gospel message, it's incomplete without it. And, an incomplete message steals truth from those who hear it. The truth of the gospel message is essential, and an absence of power associated with the gospel message misrepresents the gospel. Clearly, we don't want to misrepresent the gospel message. No, we want to preach, prophesy and proclaim the full gospel message. But to do that, we must regain the power associated with the gospel message. And, how do we do that?

By recognizing it. Unless we recognize God's power as being an essential element of the gospel message, we'll continue to misrepresent that message by our lack of power. And, we must forsake this apostate message in which the Church has walked for far too long. No, we must choose to walk in the power of the gospel by seeking to regain the power that the Church has lost. Recognizing that we lack that power enables us to start seeking it. Seeking God's power is essential to receive it. We cannot receive what we do not seek. Lk. 11:9,10.

The Gospel: God-approved Message & Messenger

We need God's power for it's His stamp of approval on our message. God approves His message by "power moves." That's how we know someone is sent; they have God's approval and their message is confirmed by God's power. If we don't have the approval of God by miracles, signs and wonders, then we need to question the calling we claim to have to preach the gospel. In Proverbs 25:14, *ABPE*, it says, *"As when there are clouds and wind without rain, so is a man that boasts of false gifts."* A false gift brings ruin; it's like a cloud without rain.

Jude, Jesus' brother, makes it clear how God views those who boast of false gifts in the Church. *"These are spots in your feasts of charity, when they feast with you, feeding themselves without fear: clouds they are without water, carried about of winds; trees whose fruit withereth, without fruit, twice dead, plucked up by the roots; raging waves of the sea, foaming out their own shame; wandering stars, to whom is reserved the blackness of darkness for ever."* Jude 1:12-13. Strong words against masquerading gifts. Paul says this about men and women claiming to be apostles: *"But I am not surprised! Even Satan disguises himself as an angel of light."* 2 Cor. 11:14, *NLT.* Satan puts on a disguise when coming to the Church; he sends men and women with false gifts, false anointings and false messages. We must recognize this reality.

God's message carries God's anointing and God's approval by miracles, signs and wonders. In Proverbs 18:16, NET, it says, *"A person's gift makes room for him, and leads him before important people."* God gives gifts to men. *"Having ascended on high, He led captive captivity, and gave gifts to men. And He gave some indeed to be apostles, and some prophets, and some evangelists, and some shepherds and teachers...."* Eph. 4:8, 11, *BLB.* God's inherent approval is on those gifts He gives that are harnessed under His power and yield fruit to the praise of His Name. We want God's stamp of approval on our ministries, churches, families and lives. To have that stamp of approval, we must have His power.

Paul's Example to Future Apostles & Ministers

Paul said to the Corinthians:

> *"But when I came to you, my brethren, I did not proclaim to you by magnificent speech, neither by scholarship, the Gospel of the mystery of God. Neither did I judge myself as knowing anything among you, except Yeshua the Messiah, even Him as He was crucified. And I was with you in much fear and in trembling. And my message and my preaching were not in the persuasiveness of the words of philosophy, but in the demonstration of the Spirit and power, that your*

faith would not be in the wisdom of men, but in the power of God." 1 Cor. 2:1-5, *ABPE.*

Paul based his ministry to the Corinthians believers entirely on the demonstration of God's power. Of the Corinthians, Paul said, *"Even if others think I am not an apostle, I certainly am to you. You yourselves are proof that I am the Lord's apostle."* 1 Cor. 9:2, *NLT.* Paul went further, *"The true marks of an apostle – signs, wonders and miracles – were performed among you with great perseverance."* 2 Cor. 12:12, *BSB.* Paul boasted to the Corinthians, *"Since you want proof that Christ is speaking through me, that's what you'll get. Christ is not weak in dealing with you. Instead, He makes His power felt among you."* 2 Cor. 13:3, *GWT.* Paul understood *"the Kingdom of God is not just a lot of talk; it is living by God's power."* 1 Cor. 4:20, *NLT.* Today, we have a lot of talk.

The Proof of the Pudding is in the Eating

Preaching is essential to the Church, but preaching doesn't validate the message of the Church. Power is essential to demonstrate the validity of the message preached. Where there is no power, the message remains invalidated; it's not God approved. And, an invalidated message remains in doubt. When he was standing on Mount Carmel watching the prophets of Baal, Elijah wasn't wringing his hands wondering what God would do. No, Elijah knew what God would do. God would confirm Elijah's message with power. And, that's exactly what happened. Immediately, God's people, who were torn between two opinions, said on confirmation by God's power, *"The Lord, He is the God; the Lord, He is the God."* 1 Kgs. 18:39.

When the gospel is confirmed by demonstrations of power, doubt is removed, faith is restored and revelation illuminates our lives. We're removed from the theoretical into the practical. We learn what the gospel really means by seeing its power manifested in the lives of those in genuine need. We witness the hope of the gospel arise in the hearts of people. People by the droves line up to receive what they have witnessed. Humanity is restored to broken people and the pride of Mankind is humbled. God's power humbles us.

When cancers dissolve, tumorous growths disappear, terminal illnesses die, broken limbs are mended, maimed men and women are made whole, blind men and women see, the true glory of the gospel is revealed. The good news manifests itself and spreads like wildfire. Men and women will travel for hundreds, thousands of miles to receive healing

> **Where there is no power, the message remains invalidated; it's not God approved.**

from a terminal disease. Others will travel that same distance to witness the power of the gospel message. Jesus said it plainly, *"Except ye see signs and wonders, ye will not believe."* Jn. 4:48.

Whatever Happened to God's Power?

Today, we have a famine of power in the Church. We have not paid the price necessary to receive power from on high. Yes, we have wonderful services. Yes, we have some miracles. Yes, some receive healing. But, more do not. Many walk away from healing services, sick. Many walk away from gospel meetings, wondering, "Why did I not receive my healing?" And, rather than confront that issue, we shy away from it. We use trite answers, like: "You didn't have enough faith." But, is that true? I'm not so sure. I believe we must investigate our lack of power.

In his book *Whatever Happened to the Power of God?* Dr. Michael L. Brown slaughters sacred cows on the altars of examination. He poses numerous questions, like: "Why are the seriously ill seldom healed? Why do people fall in the Spirit, yet remain unchanged? Why can believers speak in tongues and wage spiritual warfare without impacting society?" I believe these and other questions must be asked and answered.

Self-examination is Essential

Examining what we believe is not doubt. No, Paul said, *"Test yourselves to discover whether you are true believers: put your own selves under examination. Or do you not know that Jesus Christ is within you, unless you are insincere?"* 2 Cor. 13:5. In one translation it says, *"unless indeed you are disqualified."* Or, *"if ye be not in some respect disapproved of?"* Insincere, disqualified and/or disapproved of. What is the measuring stick affirmed by Scripture to determine our state of faith on the examination table? God's tangible and demonstrable power. That's it.

The gospel always comes with power. The gospel is a gospel of power. The gospel must be confirmed by power. And, where there's an absence of power, the gospel is not fully manifested. The gospel requires full power to be fully apprehended. That means we cannot understand the gospel at 10% power levels, 25% power levels, 50% power levels, even 99% power levels. No, anything short of 100% causes the gospel to be misrepresented. And, we cannot afford to misrepresent the gospel to a hurting needy world in our day. Too many have done this before. We must be different. It's my hope and fervent prayer that this book will change this lack of gospel power in gospel believing churches.

Regaining Our Godly Heritage of Power

How do we connect with the power of the gospel? How can we – you and I – walk in God's power? By understanding the gospel message. The gospel message contains gospel power. What is the gospel message? Galatians 3:8, *"And the Scripture, foreseeing that God would justify the heathen through faith, preached before the gospel unto Abraham, saying, 'In thee [Abraham] shall all nations be blessed.'"* That's the cornerstone of the gospel message, as I've previously shared. To determine if our gospel message is genuine, it must be measured against that cornerstone. How? By viewing our gospel through the lens of Abraham.

Isaiah said, *"Look to Abraham your father and to Sarah who gave birth to you in pain; when he was but one I called him, then I blessed him and multiplied him."* Is. 51:2, *NASB*. The gospel begins with Abraham. The Scripture says of Abraham, *"Without weakening in his faith, he acknowledged the decrepitness of his body (since he was about a hundred years old) and the lifelessness of Sarah's womb."* Rom. 4:19, *BSB*. Abraham recognized the impossibility of having progeny by Sarah: *"Humanly speaking, it is impossible. But not with God. Everything is possible with God."* Mk. 10:27. Abraham saw beyond his ability to God's ability. That's faith.

Walking in Our Father Abraham's Faith

Faith doesn't deny reality; it recognizes that only God can and will overcome reality and supersede it. By faith, we go beyond our own human ability into a place called grace. Grace is God's ability working in and through us that enables us to accomplish that which is impossible. Faith doesn't deny there's a mountain, it speaks to the mountain and recognizes that God moves mountains. But, faith isn't enough. We need action. Miracles don't happen by chance. No, they happen by choice. Our decisions make miracles possible. God makes them happen. But, He only makes miracles happen when faith is applied, i.e., a working faith.

Faith is God's gift. That gift comes as we listen to God. *"Consequently, faith results from listening, and listening results through the word of the Messiah."* Rom. 10:17, *ISV*. Faith results from listening. Or, as it states in the *King James Version*, *"by hearing."* We hear, then we believe. What we hear is what produces faith in our hearts. But, hearing comes by listening to the words of the Messiah. When we hear from Christ, then and only then can we have a genuine faith. And, genuine faith is what is required for miracles to happen. God's power is the result of right believing, and right believing is a result of right hearing of the right words.

A Church Without God's Power is in Error

That's why Paul said what he said about the gospel being the power of God unto salvation. Paul correctly understood the basis for receiving from God: working faith. Faith that works is a genuine faith. When faith doesn't work, it's not genuine. When faith doesn't work, the problem is in our understanding of what we have heard. And, that means we need to unravel what we have been and are hearing in our hearts. Bias regarding God's Word is the single greatest threat to walking in the genuine power of God. We think we know. When we think we know something, but that something we know doesn't work, that means what we know about that something is wrong in some way. And, that means we have to go back to discern our error.

> *Bias regarding God's Word is the single greatest threat to walking in the genuine power of God.*

Jesus said to the Sadducees, *"You are in error, through ignorance of the Scriptures and of the power of God."* Matt. 22:29. What they believed regarding God's Word was erroneous, for they did not understand what the Scriptures clearly communicated. The Scriptures are God's instruction manual on all things. Now, we often misunderstand what is clearly stated in them. Often, we approach God's Word with our own preconceived ideas of what is being said. I'd like to illustrate this point by discussing a correct understanding of one of the most famous passages on faith in the Bible, Mark 11:22-24, which says:

> *"And Jesus answering saith unto them, 'Have faith in God. For verily I say unto you, that whosoever shall say unto this mountain, Be thou removed, and be thou cast into the sea; and shall not doubt in his heart, but shall believe that those things which he saith shall come to pass; he shall have whatsoever he saith. Therefore I say unto you, What things soever ye desire, when ye pray, believe that ye receive them, and ye shall have them.'"*

The Lesson of the Fig Tree

Jesus was instructing His disciples on faith. That instruction was based on an illustration He used of a physical fig tree. Let's read about the fig tree to understand what Jesus said regarding faith. Mark 11:12-14 says:

> "And on the morrow, when they were come from Bethany, He was hungry: And seeing a fig tree afar off having leaves, He came, if haply He might find any thing thereon: and when He came to it, He found nothing but leaves; for the time of figs was not yet. And Jesus answered and said unto it, 'No man eat fruit of thee hereafter for ever.' And His disciples heard it."

Most ministers have glossed over what is happening here by not hearing what Jesus is actually saying. For that reason, I want to point out what He did say, and what the Scriptures say about what He said. To start, Jesus was hungry. Then, Jesus saw a fig tree. He went to the fig tree to see if there was fruit on the fig tree. Instead, there are only leaves on the fig tree. The Scripture even states that it wasn't time for the figs to be there. But still, Jesus expected figs.

Didn't Jesus know what time it was? Yes, Jesus knew the time. But, more importantly, Jesus knew the Father. And, Christ's faith in the Father was greater than His faith in the season. Christ expected figs, for He was hungry, and He knew that the Father had made provision for His hunger. But, the fig tree spoke to Jesus something that was opposite to what Christ knew. What did the fig tree say? It said, "this isn't the right time for figs." And, that was true. But, it wasn't the truth. The truth: God made provision for His Son. That provision: the fig tree. The fig tree was lying to Jesus about the nature of His Father. Jesus became upset by the fig tree's lie, and, as a result, he cursed the fig tree.

What happened? In Mark 11:19-21, we find out. It says:

> "And when even was come, He went out of the city. And in the morning, as they passed by, they saw the fig tree dried

up from the roots. And Peter calling to remembrance saith unto Him, 'Master, behold, the fig tree which Thou cursedst is withered away.'"

Peter saw the results of Jesus faith. But, it wasn't just about faith. No, it was about much more. What does this story reveal? It reveals many things. But, one that I'd like to point out is a simple truth understood by the entirety of Scripture. That truth: Christ could not have cursed the fig tree if it had been obedient. Christ's faith in cursing the fig tree rested in His understanding of the nature of His Father. The Father is Jehovah Jireh; He is my provider. The fig tree was disobedient to the Father, and from that place of disobedience, lied to Jesus about the Father's nature. What did it say? Your Father didn't provide for you when you were hungry. Jesus answered the fig tree. He cursed it. Why? Because it was lying; it was disobedient to the Father's command to provide for His Son. That disobedience resulted in the curse.

In context, this story teaches us about genuine faith. Jesus explained the principles of faith to His disciples. But, for many years, the Body of Christ has tried to misappropriate Mark 11:22-24. How? By not understanding the message of faith, as taught by Christ. Christ's faith was predicated on the Father's nature. And, it was predicated on a clear understanding of Scripture: a curse always rests on the lying and disobedient. While what the fig tree said was factually correct, it isn't the right time for me to have figs, that didn't mean God couldn't require more from it. And, He did. God required that fig tree to feed His Son. It didn't. That disobedience to the Father's command is why Jesus cursed it.

The Context for Real Faith

Everything that Jesus said about faith is hinged on this understanding. Further, Jesus was also speaking about Israel's disobedience. Israel was disobedient to God's command. What was that command? *"You will be My kingdom of priests and My holy nation."* Ex. 19:6, *GWT.* That was God's intent for Israel. And, when

Christ came, that's what He expected. But, when He went into the temple in Jerusalem, that's not what He saw. What did He see? In Mark 11:15-18, we see. It says:

> "And they come to Jerusalem: and Jesus went into the temple, and began to cast out them that sold and bought in the temple, and overthrew the tables of the moneychangers, and the seats of them that sold doves; And would not suffer that any man should carry any vessel through the temple. And He taught, saying unto them, 'Is it not written, My house shall be called of all nations the house of prayer? but ye have made it a den of thieves.' And the scribes and chief priests heard it, and sought how they might destroy Him: for they feared Him, because all the people was astonished at His doctrine."

Jesus expected the temple at Jerusalem to be filled with the joyful sound of prayer. He expected the temple to be a house of prayer for the nations of the world. He expected them to be praying for the salvation of the world. But, what Israel said to Christ is what the fig tree said to Christ: "It isn't the right time." What Israel said was: "Jesus, it isn't the right time. We are waiting for the Messiah to come." Israel, instead of being about the Father's business, as expected, they were waiting on God. Or, they only had leaves, no figs. Christ was looking for the fruit of prayer in God's temple. Was that a reasonable expectation? Yes. Why was there no fruit? Israel believed a lie: the time isn't right. We too, believers and leaders in churches, have believed that same lie. Many are patiently waiting for "the rapture." That's sin.

Please understand: Jesus is looking for fruit. Jesus asked, "When the Son of Man comes, will He find faith on earth?" Lk. 18:8. Jesus' expectation is clearly spelled out in the Scripture: "At harvest time, He sent a servant to the tenants to collect his share of the fruit of the vineyard." Mk. 12:2, BSB. Jesus expects fruit. He said, "'I AM THE LIVING GOD, the True Vine, and My Father is the vine dresser.'" Jn. 15:1, ABPE. "Herein is My Father glorified, that ye bear much fruit; so shall ye be My disciples." Jn. 15:8. God is glorified when we bear fruit; He expects it. In James 5:7, we discover, *"Behold, the husbandman waiteth for the precious fruit of the earth, and hath long patience for it, until He receive the early and latter rain."* God is waiting for us to bear fruit prior to Christ's second coming. Israel had it wrong, and we have it wrong. And, that's leading to fruitlessness.

Faith is the Fruit of the Gospel Message

God expects the fruit of the gospel to pervade the earth. God expects the fruit of the gospel to pervade our nation. God expects fruit. He is waiting for it with bated breath. He longs to see fruit. Jesus told this parable in reference to the Father's desire for fruit:

> *"A man had a fig tree planted in his vineyard, and he came seeking fruit on it and found none. And he said to the vinedresser, 'Look, for three years now I have come seeking fruit on this fig tree, and I find none. Cut it down. Why should it use up the ground?' And he answered him, 'Sir, let it alone this year also, until I dig around it and put on manure. Then if it should bear fruit next year, well and good; but if not, you can cut it down.'"* Lk. 13:6-9, ESV.

There are many typologies in this passage. One is: we see a specific reference to three years. Often, the three years represent the third day of the Church, the day in which we are right now. You can read about this topic further in my book, *The Third Reformation is Coming*. The third day is the day in which Christ's return is expected. But in this parable, we find the gardener requests more time when he reports that the fig tree isn't bearing any fruit to the owner of the vineyard. The gardener requests one more year after the three years he has already used to nourish the fig tree. Sometimes, there's a last and final chance.

There are many lessons of faith from the fig tree found in Mark. One is: Christ doesn't tolerate disobedience, even from something that could easily be considered good cause. The fig tree had a good excuse: it isn't the right time for figs. Jesus didn't accept that one. Nor does He tolerate lies about His Father's nature. God has already made provision for His people, but, often, we live outside that provision, due to our own disobedience. Then, we blame God. Jesus is longsuffering, but He does expect the fruit from the gospel message to be manifested in the lives of His followers. That's you and me. Fruit.

Walking in Obedience to Christ's Commands

Recently, in March 2015, while at an ARMI meeting in Colorado, God spoke to me. Barry Bennett was speaking about the Apostles' response to Jesus' command in Mk. 6:37, which was: *"You feed them."* Mk. 6:7, *NLT*. Their response to Jesus: "With what?" Barry started elaborating about how he would have responded to Jesus, had he received this command. While he was speaking, God spoke to me: *"Heal the sick, cleanse the lepers, raise the dead, cast out devils: freely ye have received, freely give."* Matt. 10:8. When I heard those words, I reacted in much the same way as the disciples reacted: Me? Then, I realized this wasn't a request or suggestion. Rather, it was a command.

Our powerlessness isn't Christ's problem. No, He has already made provision. Nor does Christ change His command on viewing our situation, e.g. the excuses we present. Yes, Christ does expect fruit from His Church. Yes, we're the ones who are commanded to carry the gospel message in power. Yes, we can often feel grossly inadequate. And, we should. But, that recognition of our own inadequacy is meant to do something in us – humble us. That humility opens the door for demonstration of the gospel in power.

Grace is available to help the humble. Our humility is an essential element of the gospel's power. We cannot walk in demonstrations of power with pride in our hearts. Pride repudiates the gospel's message. Pride says, "We don't need all those miracles to get the job done." To that, I say, "Hooey!" We need the power of the gospel to demonstrate and validate the reality of the gospel. How do we validate the gospel? By healing the sick, cleansing the lepers, raising the dead, and casting out demons. Simple.

Faithlessness is one reason we lack power. Our unbelief can hinder manifestation of the gospel's power. Pride is another reason for our powerlessness. Prayerlessness is another. Sinfulness is another. Division is another. *"We must learn to lay aside those sins that so easily beset us,"* Heb. 12:1, and *"press toward the mark of the prize of the high calling of God in Christ Jesus."* Phil. 3:14 Recognition of our calling to do the miraculous and supernatural is essential to moving forward in the supernatural work of spreading the gospel. We must understand that the gospel's power is a necessary and unavoidable part of sharing the gospel message.

Unlocking the Gospel Message by God's Power

Faith unlocks God's power. Prayer unlocks God's power. Holiness unlocks God's power. Unity unlocks God's power. And, preaching the cross unlocks God's power. In fact, preaching the cross is the essential element of the gospel's power. That's why we need a fresh understanding of what Christ did on the cross. *"The message of the cross is foolish to those who are headed for destruction! But we who are being saved know it is the very power of God."* 1 Cor. 1:18, *NLT*. The gospel revolves around and is powered by Christ's work on the cross. That's why we must focus our attention on Christ's sacrificial work on the cross. Paul said, *"For I determined not to know any thing among you, save Jesus Christ, and Him crucified."* 1 Cor. 2:2.

Are you acquainted with the message of the cross? Do you understand that message? Do you know what Jesus actually accomplished by and through the cross? Do you believe it? Is your conversation centered on and around that message? If not, then you are missing the cornerstone that transforms lifeless preaching into powerful preaching. Further, we must move beyond a surface level understanding of the work of the cross to a transformational understanding of the work of the cross. Until our understanding of the work of the cross radically and completely transforms us, we don't know it. And, if we don't see the power of the cross manifested as we're preaching the cross, we don't know it.

Preaching the Cross and Walking in Power

For the remainder of this chapter, I want to focus my attention on walking in God's power. I've witnessed and experienced God's power at several pivotal moments in my life. My life has been changed by that power. That's why I believe it's essential to walk in the power of the gospel. I'm not alone in needing that power. Many are awaiting gospel power to be raised above the turmoil of life and into the place of peace offered by Christ. Christ's gospel is a gospel of peace; it brings peace into the lives of those who hear it. That peace fuels the gospel message by placing us above the wages of sin and sickness and the works of Satan. Paul said, *"The God of peace will quickly crush Satan under your feet."* Rom. 16:20, *NET.*

Peace comes as we understand and walk in the truth of the gospel. The good news of peace is hidden within the message of the cross. That good news is that we, Mankind, now have been made righteous with God through faith in Jesus Christ. Christ offered Himself for our sins to bring us into that place of peace. *"Now that we have God's approval by faith, we have peace with God because of what our Lord Jesus Christ has done."* Rom. 5:1, *GWT.* That peace came by what Christ did on the cross. *"God was also pleased to bring everything on earth and in heaven back to Himself through Christ. He did this by making peace through Christ's blood sacrificed on the cross."* Col. 1:20. *GWT.*

When we work for peace, we're recognized as God's sons. *"How blessed are those who make peace, because it is they who will be called God's children!"* Matt. 5:1, *ISV.* In the *WNT*, it says, *"Blessed are the peacemakers, for it is they who will be recognized as sons of God."* Are we searching and seeking to live in the place of peace? "For the Scriptures [Ps. 34:14,15] say, 'If you want to enjoy life and see many happy days, keep your tongue from speaking evil and your lips from telling lies. Turn away from evil and do good. Search for peace, and work to maintain it." 1 Pet. 3:10,11. There, in that place of peace, we'll discover God's blessing: the power of the gospel. How? By the blessedness of Christ's work on the cross.

Recovering the Message of the Cross

There are numerous main Scriptures that reveal what Christ accomplished on the cross.[6] In them is identified the completeness of what Christ accomplished on the cross. Each Scripture releases a demonstrable work accomplished by Christ's sacrifice on the cross. In 1 Corinthians 1:17,18, *NIV*, Paul writes, *"For Christ did not send me to baptize, but to preach the gospel – not with wisdom and eloquence, lest the cross of Christ be emptied of its power. For the message of the cross is foolishness to those who are perishing, but to us who are being saved it is the power of God."* The message of the cross contains power. That message releases specific evidence of Christ's work on the cross into the lives of those who believe in what Christ did on the cross.

What is that evidence?

Forgiveness of Sins. *"He is the payment for our sins, and not only for our sins, but also for the sins of the whole world."* 1 Jn. 2:2. That payment came through this blood. *"He is so rich in kindness and grace that He purchased our freedom with the blood of His Son and forgave our sins."* Eph. 1:7, *NLT*. Or, *"In Him, we have redemption through His blood, the forgiveness of sins, in accordance with the riches of God's grace."* Eph. 1:7, *NIV*. *"In whom we have redemption through His blood, even the forgiveness of sins...."* Col. 1:14.

Healing of Sicknesses. *"When evening came, many who were demon-possessed were brought to Him, and He drove out the spirits with a word and healed all the sick. This was to fulfill what was spoken through the prophet Isaiah: 'He took up our infirmities*

---

[6] Matt. 8:16-17; Rom. 5:15-21; 15:3; 1 Cor. 1:17-18; 10:16,17, 2 Cor. 5:14-15, 21; 8:9; Gal. 1:4; 2:20; 3:13-14; Col. 1:20-22; 2:13-15; 1 Pet. 1:18-19; 2:22-24 and many others.

and bore our diseases.'" Matt. 8:16-17, *NIV.* Notice, He healed **all** the sick. That means, no one was left out. All means all. *"He personally carried our sins in His body on the cross so that we can be dead to sin and live for what is right. By His wounds, you are healed."* 1 Pet. 2:24. The link between healing and the cross is of paramount importance to the gospel message.

Deliverance from Demons. Jesus set people free from demons to show the efficacy of the cross. In Matthew 8:16-17, Jesus *"drove out the spirits"* that it might be fulfilled that *"He took up our infirmities and bore our diseases."* Christ worked His work on earth from the completed work that was to be accomplished on the cross. *"And having disarmed the powers and authorities, He made a public spectacle of them, triumphing over them by the cross."* Col. 2:15, *NIV.* *"He has delivered us from the domain of darkness and transferred us to the kingdom of His beloved Son...."* Col. 1:13, *ESV.* Christ accomplished His mission to destroy the works of the devil. 1 Jn. 3:8. Delivered those who were bound in captivity by the devil. Eph. 4:8. Took us as the spoils of war from the demonic jail cell of sin where we were held captive. Col. 2:15. Then, He translated all us, all who believe in Him, into His kingdom. Col. 1:13. By the cross, Jesus defeated Satan. And, we have become the recipients of His victory by faith in what He did on the cross. *"See, I have given you authority to tread on snakes and scorpions, and over all the power of the enemy. Nothing will harm you."* Lk. 10:19, *NLT.* *"These miraculous signs will accompany those who believe: They will cast out demons in My Name...."* Mk. 16:17, *NLT.*

Peace of Heart and Mind. Today, many people are tormented in their minds. That torment is often caused by fear. *"There is no fear in love; but perfect love casteth out fear: because fear hath torment."* 1 Jn. 4:18, *WBT.* Fear torments. Sometimes, it's bitterness of soul from events in this life that cause torment in people's minds. *"In her deep anguish, Hannah prayed to the LORD, weeping bitterly."* 1 Sam. 1:10, *NIV.* Hannah was tormented because she couldn't have children. How did she handle this disappointment? She prayed. Then, through a backslidden minister, God spoke to her. She received her answer from God. We can be wounded by things that happen in this life. *"A cry was heard in Ramah – weeping and great mourning. Rachel weeps for her children, refusing to be comforted, for they are dead."* Matt. 2:18, NLT. Here, those women who suffered loss refused to be comforted due to anguish of soul.

We can also be wounded by the attacks of the devil. Satan is a destroyer: he comes to steal, kill and destroy. Jn. 10:10(a). But, Jesus came to bring life, abundant life. Jn. 10:10(b). That means a mind freed from tormenting thoughts, nightmares or other visual imaginations. *"Once you were alienated and hostile in your minds because of your evil actions."* Col. 1:21, HCSB. The imagination is God's gift, but it can often rage out of control if we fail to exercise control over it. *"For we overthrow arrogant 'reckonings,' and every stronghold that towers high in defiance of the knowledge of God, and we carry off every thought as if into slavery – into subjection to Christ...."* 2 Cor. 10:5, WNT. Jesus went to the cross to give us back control over our own minds. Paul declared, *"we have the mind of Christ."* 1 Cor. 2:16, YLT. By the cross, we have regained our minds and our peace. Jesus Himself has become our peace. Eph. 2:14-17. That's how we received the gospel of peace.

Prosperity and Wealth in Life. Possibly one of the most misunderstood subject in the Bible is of the divine grace to prosper. God wants His people to prosper. *"Let the LORD be magnified, which hath pleasure in the prosperity of His servant."* Ps. 35:27. *"Beloved, I wish above all things that thou mayest prosper and be in health, even as thy soul prospereth."* 3 Jn. 1:2. *"But remember the LORD your God is the one who makes you wealthy. He's confirming the promise which He swore to your ancestors. It's still in effect today."* Deut. 8:18, GWT. That prosperity is found through the completed work of Christ on the cross. *"You know the generous grace of our Lord Jesus Christ. Though He was rich, yet for your sakes He became poor, so that by His poverty He could make you* *rich."* 2 Cor. 8:9. Grace, when received, enables us to walk in prosperity. That means natural wealth and abundance. *"And God is able to make all grace abound to you, so that having all sufficiency in all things at all times, you may abound in every good work."* 2 Cor. 9:8, *ESV*. Grace in action by the work of the cross releases supernatural wealth into our lives, i.e., prosperity.

Sanctification in Spirit, Soul and Body. Holiness is accessible to believers today by the completed work of Christ on the cross. *"Yet now He has reconciled you to Himself through the death of Christ in His physical body. As a result, He has brought you into His own presence, and you are holy and blameless as you stand before Him without a single fault."* Col. 1:22, *NLT*. We have been sanctified by Christ's death on the cross. *"For God's will was for us to be made holy by the sacrifice of the body of Jesus Christ, once for all time."* Heb. 10:10, *NLT*. *"For by one offering, He has perfected in perpetuity the sanctified."* Heb. 10:14, *DBT*. We're sanctified. *"[Y]ou are chosen people, a royal priesthood, a holy nation, people who belong to God. You were chosen to tell about the excellent qualities of God, who called you out of darkness into His marvelous light."* 1 Pet. 2:9, *GWT*. God *"is able to keep you from falling, and to present you faultless before the presence of His glory with exceeding joy...."* Jude 1:24. Holiness happens as we believe in what Christ did on the cross. *"It is because of Him that you are in Christ Jesus, who has been become for us wisdom from God: our righteousness, holiness and redemption."* 1 Cor. 1:30, *BSB*. Now, by His work on the cross, we're able to overcome sin, and live healthy, happy and holy lives. That's His will.

Righteousness and Justice in Our Personal and Business Relationships. *"For God made Christ, who never sinned, to be the offering for our sin, so that we could be made right with God through Christ."* Righteousness revolves around Christ's work on the cross. Paul describes what David foresaw: *"Blessed are those whose transgressions are forgiven, whose sins are covered. Blessed is the one whose sin the Lord will never count against* *them."* Rom. 4:7,8, *NIV;* Ps. 32:1,2. Through Christ's work on the cross, propitiation was made for our sin. *"He is the propitiation for our sins, and not for ours only but also for the sins of the whole world."* 1 Jn. 2:2, *ESV.* In Romans 5:14-21, we see that righteousness now reigns by what Christ did on the cross. We have received *"the gift of righteousness."* Rom. 5:17. That gift means we have access to justice for every wrong suffered. God is just; it's His nature. He demands justice. The Scripture says, *"People die once, and after that, they are judged."* Heb. 9:27, *GWT.* But, God's justice and judgment aren't just for the future. Now, He judges and metes out justice. How? By the work of the cross. On the cross, sin is punished, injustice is vanquished and judgment is rendered.

Redemption from Curses and Release of Blessings. Curses are real. Blessings are real. For centuries and millennium, people held power over others by using curses or blessings. *"Now come and put a curse on these people, because they are too powerful for me. Perhaps then I will be able to defeat them and drive them out of the land. For I know that whoever you bless is blessed, and whoever you curse is cursed."* Num. 22:6, *NIV.* Balaam cursed people for money. Balaam was known for having this power. And, it worked.

Today, many don't believe in curses. But, they are real, and we need to know about them. In Christ, we have been redeemed from any and every curse. *"Christ paid the price to free us from the curse that God's laws bring by becoming cursed instead of us. Scripture says, 'Everyone who is hung on a tree is cursed.'"* Gal. 3:13, *GWT.* Every curse is rooted in disobedience.

Christ was obedient unto death on the cross. Phil. 2:8, Heb. 5:8. Obedience always brings blessing. *"If you are willing and obedient, you will eat the best from the land."* Is. 1:19, *GWT.* Having a heart that desires to obey is a blessing from God. *"God raised up His servant and sent Him first to you, to bless you by turning each one of you from your iniquities."* Acts 3:26, *NET.* We are redeemed from the curse by Christ's work on the cross. We receive the blessing of a right heart to obey God. And, that right heart from God releases God's blessings into our lives.

Blessings and curses originate from the heart of Man. James 3:8-12. Jesus said, *"Evil thoughts, murder, adultery, [other] sexual sins, stealing, lying, and cursing come from within."* Matt. 15:19, GWT. Paul said, *"Bless those who persecute you; bless and do not curse."* Rom. 12:14, NIV.

Daily Manifesting the Power of Christ

I've identified several areas where God's power is manifested in our lives. That power is tangible: it's evidence can be seen by others. When we walk in a right understanding of Christ's work on the cross, that understanding releases the power of the cross to work in our lives on our behalf. Believers often fail to appropriate what Christ did. Their lives lack the redemptive power of the cross. That power is not only available to some. No, it's available to all. We can receive power to walk a

Never underestimate your power to shape history by your actions in Christ rooted in the cross.

victorious life. We can receive power to overcome every demonic attack. We can receive power to break chains and curses over people's lives. We can bless people by turning them from their sins to Christ's completed work on the cross. That's the power we wield.

Where do we start? We start by witnessing to our families. Then, our friends. Then, our neighbors. Then, our coworkers. Then, acquaintances. We must always walk out our faith, daily. When we do, power is manifested in our lives, homes and churches: healing flows and sickness leaves, sins are forgiven and hearts are yielded, relationships are restored and justice is done, blessings are released and curses broken, and those we touch are delivered from every work of the devil and God's work emerges in their lives.

Never underestimate your power to shape history by your actions in Christ rooted in the cross. Your witness matters. Your life matters. Your knowledge of what Christ did is vital to your future, and the future of others. I want to repeat what Jesus said to His disciples as He sent them to Jerusalem: *"But you will receive power when the Holy Spirit comes on you; and you will be My witnesses in Jerusalem...."* Acts 1:8, *NIV.* Receive that power, NOW! And, watch what He does through you and your life.

Chapter Nine

The Gospel Must be Preached

"And this gospel of the kingdom will be preached in all the world as a testimony to all nations, and then the end will come." Matt. 24:14, *BSB*.

There is something about the proclamation of the gospel message that releases its power into the lives of those who hear and believe it. The gospel was meant to be preached. Why? Because God has chosen preaching as the primary method for people to obtain faith. God chose preaching because Mankind chose to rebel in pursuit of knowledge. God chose a foolish act – preaching – to undo the foolish act – eating the forbidden fruit – Man had chosen in its quest for wisdom. Mankind wanted the wisdom that was rooted in disobedience and rebellion. The wisdom of sin.

But, sin is foolish. Sin always brings death. It always brings a curse. It always destroys. Since Adam and Eve took that first bite into the forbidden fruit of the tree of the knowledge of good and evil, Mankind has made its quest to pursue knowledge. We have sought to understand, to know, to reason and to gain knowledge and wisdom. And, we fail to recognize the wisdom we lost when Mankind fell. Our fall from grace has caused us to misunderstand everything in creation and has made us susceptible to deception.

Deception: Satan's Number One Weapon

The number one weapon our adversary uses against us is deception. Satan seeks to keep us from knowing the truth. Why? Because in the truth is hidden freedom. Freedom, which is the longing of every human soul, cannot be found unless truth is first received. But, to know truth, we must have truth. And, due to our sin, we lacked the ability to discern right from wrong, we couldn't understand truth. Through the centuries, Mankind gradually lost truth. We wrestled with, avoided and finally ignored truth. We didn't want to hear the truth. Our hearts became hardened and we fell into deeper sin.

Paul describes this descent into darkness in the first chapter of Romans:

> "Yes, they knew God, but they wouldn't worship Him as God or even give Him thanks. And they began to think up foolish ideas of what God was like. As a result, their minds became dark and confused. Claiming to be wise, they instead became utter fools. And instead of worshiping the glorious, ever-living God, they worshiped idols made to look like mere people and birds and animals and reptiles. So God abandoned them to do whatever shameful things their hearts desired. As a result, they did vile and degrading things with each other's bodies. They traded the truth about God for a lie." Romans 1:21-25, NLT.

Mankind traded truth for a lie. When we did that, we became foolish. That foolishness can only be corrected by the proclamation of the gospel. Paul states, "And because, in the wisdom of God, the world did not know God by wisdom, God was willing that by the insanity of preaching He would give life to those who believe." 1 Cor. 1:21, ABPE. Preaching is foolish in the world's eyes. How is it possible that by preaching the blind see, the deaf hear, the lame walk, sick are healed, drug addicts and alcoholics are freed, pornographers and pedophiles are delivered, the demonized are loosed and the dead are raised? That and much more happens when the gospel is preached.

Why Preaching the Gospel is Important

Teaching isn't enough. Even teaching on the Bible isn't good enough. Yes, Bible teaching is good, but it's not enough. No, preaching is required. And, that's where much of the Church has fallen short in its delivery of the gospel message: we haven't preached it. Many pastors and ministers have taught, presented, prayed, sermonized, and even eulogized the gospel, but they haven't done what they were called to do: preach the gospel. The gospel must be preached: it must be proclaimed: it must be shouted from the housetops. *"What I tell you in the darkness, speak in the light; and what you hear in the ear, proclaim upon the housetops!"* Matt. 10:27, BLB. And, to do that, one must be willing to appear foolish.

The preacher is a fool to those in the world. Yes, he can even appear to be the king of fools among those initiated in the world's practices of deception. *"My servant is truly blind, My messenger is truly deaf. My covenant partner, the servant of the LORD, is truly blind."* Is. 42:19, NET. Often, preachers are derided; they are accused and maligned, mocked and abused. The world will accuse the gospel preacher: "All that preacher wants is your money!" But, God chose preaching of the gospel as the primary means by which His ministers are to receive their sustenance. The gospel preacher survives by the preaching of the gospel. But...

Channel Flipping, Sin Surfing & Gimmicks in the Church

Many gospel preachers rely on gimmicks now instead of the gospel. We have great productions but weak souls. In many churches, the gospel has taken a backseat. Music, theater, dramas, socials, classes, and a host of other good ideas have sought to replace gospel preaching. In fact, most people can't remember what they heard in the church from week to week. How can a message on Sunday transform society if it can't even be remembered until Monday? But, that's what we have today. And, it's our fault. We have chosen what we currently have: a powerless, gospel-less, sin-soaked generation of wayward believers waiting for the next wave.

We have sin surfers: men and women who go from church to church and sin to sin, they are never changing, darkened black souls who always harangue the rest of the church by their deeds of darkness. In his day, Jude saw this type of misconduct was "coming to a church near you," and warned us, stating:

> "When these people eat with you in your fellowship meals commemorating the Lord's love, they are like dangerous reefs that can shipwreck you. They are like shameless shepherds who care only for themselves. They are like clouds blowing over the land without giving any rain. They are like trees in autumn that are doubly dead, for they bear no fruit and have been pulled up by the roots. They are like wild waves of the sea, churning up the foam of their shameful deeds. They are like wandering stars, doomed forever to blackest darkness." Jude 1:12-13, NLT.

I, too, warn you. "[I]t is appointed for people to die once – and after this, judgment...." Heb. 9:27, HCSB. There is and should be a sobriety in the preaching of the gospel message. God is good and the gospel is good news and it can be fun, but the gospel is also serious business. Souls are dying, leaving this earth and ending in a living eternal hell. There's a heaven to gain and a hell to shun. The gospel alone is our salvation from that hell. The gospel is what enables us to move forward in

We have sin surfers: men and women who go from church to church and sin to sin, they are never changing, darkened black souls who always harangue the rest of the church by their deeds of darkness.

life with full assurance of our eternal future. Your eternity hangs in the balance, as does that of your children, parents, relatives, friends and, yes, the world itself. The gospel is the sole cure for Man's sin. We freely offer that cure to a sin-soaked and sick world. How? Through preaching.

Taking the Family Business Seriously

God established the methods of distributing the cure for Man's terminal illness – sin. Preaching is one of those methods. Preaching isn't the sole means of reaching men and women with the cure for their sin, but it's a primary means of distribution of the cure. The other primary means of distributing the cure is publishing. Preaching. Publishing. Those are the two methods God has established for spreading the cure. In both methods, the cure for Man's sin is contained within the gospel. When the gospel is heard, the cure is released to those who place their faith in the gospel they have heard. That gospel message, once heard, enters the heart, and upon belief, fills the heart. We accept or reject the cure by choosing to believe or deny the gospel.

In this chapter, I want to provide a solid Biblical foundation on why the gospel must be preached, why the preaching of the gospel is vital to God's business on earth and why the gospel ministry must be funded by believers. You may have never considered that God has a business He is running on earth. Yes, God has a business address on earth, and it's called the local church. God has elevated the local church as the primary place where His business is conducted on earth. Men and women are saved by and through God's business being conducted in the local church. When we attend a local church, and the gospel message is preached, powerful things begin to happen in our lives.

Few ministers, including pastors, truly understand just how important their calling into the gospel business is. Fewer still take the gospel business as seriously as worldly businessmen and women take their earthly businesses. And lastly, very few, maybe only a handful, truly appreciate or are ready to account for the real value of their business in the gospel. God is a good businessman, and He wants His sons and daughters educated in the business of the gospel. We are to learn how to conduct gospel business the right way. There's a right way to conduct gospel business and it's not by selling doves as in Jesus' day or Jesus pins as in our day. No, there's a right way to do gospel business and many wrong ways of doing gospel business.

Being Trained in the Family Business

Are you ready to learn the family business? At the age of twelve, Jesus was ready to work in the gospel business: *"'Why is it that you have been searching for Me?' He replied; 'did you not know that it is My duty to be engaged upon My Father's business?'"* Lk. 2:49, WNT. Yes, at that age, Jesus was ready to start working in His Father's business. Jesus was entrepreneurial: He went into the real "Shark Tank" – the temple – where the doctors of the law were engaged in discussions concerning the law amongst themselves, and they were confounded by this Nazarene's wisdom in God's business. But, Jesus submitted to Joseph and Mary and first learned the Carpenter's trade as Joseph's apprentice.

Joseph was a businessman: He knew the Carpenter's trade. Further, I imagine, as a Carpenter, Joseph had customers for His Carpentry business. Joseph earned his living and supported his family by his Carpentry trade. And, for a period of time, so did Jesus. Jesus, through Joseph, learned how to be a Carpenter. That became Jesus' trade prior to the beginning of His gospel business. After Joseph passed away, as the eldest son, Jesus likely supported His brothers and sisters. The Father entrusted Joseph with Jesus' training in business. God used Joseph's training of Jesus to prepare him for His work in the gospel business.

We need training to do God's business. I believe the reason why the Church experiences so little gospel fruit is we don't truly understand the gospel business. The gospel business, according to Jesus, is a lot like being a farmer. What does a farmer do? He prepares soil to receive seed. He plants his seed in good soil. He waters that seed. He guards that seed. And, he reaps a harvest from that seed which he uses to support his family and farm. Farmers know the business of farming is hard work; they start from that premise.

Gospel business is just as difficult as farming, if not more so. And ministers, including pastors, invest a great deal to preach the gospel. There are many costs associated with preaching, of which many believers are unaware, including the initial seed capital. Every business, including gospel business, requires capital. Funding is one of the primary hardships that gospel preachers face. Paul said, *"the Lord has commanded that those who preach the gospel should receive their living from the gospel."* 1 Cor. 9:14, *NIV.* For many ministers, including pastors, who freely give their time and energy to those to whom they minister, they rarely receive adequate compensation. Often, they are forgotten. And, as their lives near the finish line, they live in abject poverty. Awful!

The Church's Need: Gospel Preachers & Gospel Preaching

For that reason, the gospel preacher has become rare. Few believers want to be gospel preachers, due to the noticeable lack of provision. Fewer still heed that calling. Many gospel preachers have left the gospel business because they were unable to support their family. The Church, more than she knows, misses gospel preachers: the loss of the value of those gospel preachers to the Church is incalculable. That's why the gospel business is suffering around the world: few are willing to support the gospel business. We have too many competing interests. And, the gospel business suffers. That's why churches are struggling: we lack gospel preachers.

The Church, by and large, has good teachers. But, we lack good, soul-stirring, preachers. And, preaching is a primary method the gospel message is meant to be delivered in the gospel business. Teaching is good. Preaching is better. Preaching releases men and women from the shackles of darkness and bondage to corruption and leads them into a new life in Christ. Hearts are circumcised and minds altered from destructive thought patterns. Teaching cannot do what preaching can. And, preaching cannot do what teaching can. Each is important. But, the gospel preacher is necessary for the cure offered through the gospel message to be administered. By preaching, we receive the gospel message, and that message saves, heals, delivers, blesses, prospers and redeems us.

Recovering Gospel Preachers and Preaching

Why does the Church lack gospel preachers? Because we don't support them. Why don't churches, especially pastors, support gospel preachers? For the same reason, they don't support prophets. Pastors often fail to recognize the value of the gospel preacher, as they fail to recognize the value of the prophet. Prophets are important to church growth. Gospel preachers are important to church growth. But, pastors are often content with keeping the sheep they have happy.

Pastors have a tough job keeping the local church afloat because believers often don't support it. The local church is to be supported by the tithe. Less than 20 percent of believers' tithe. Some ministers even preach against tithing, and believers with itching ears follow that erroneous teaching. Fewer believers give offerings.

In the same way, pastors and churches are to be supported by the believers' tithe, gospel preachers and prophets are to be supported by the church's tithe. But, many churches, like many believers, don't tithe. I do not have a percentage of churches that tithe beyond the four walls of their own church or ministry. That failure is the primary reason why the church, as a whole, lacks gospel preachers. And, the church's lack of gospel preachers is the primary reason we are not reaching our world with the gospel message.

How can we remedy this situation? By putting our money where our mouths are. We must learn to support God's work. That means, we must be willing to tithe, individually, and it means pastors and churches must be willing to tithe, corporately. Where do churches tithe? To gospel preachers, prophets, apostles and other anointed ministers. The absence of these ministries should concern us. The absence of signs, wonders and miracles should concern us. We're losing an entire generation because we don't know how to do God's business, God's way. Instead, we invest in things that don't bring any value to the Father's gospel business. That's a tragedy.

My Life and the Gospel Business

Please hear me: I have been in ministry for 25+ years. In 1991, I began my journey as a minister and prophet by writing down the prophetic words that God gave to me and publishing them in my first book, *Decade of Destiny.* That book has proven to be an extremely accurate prophetic word to the Church in America. I have also ministered prophetically to individuals. I found pastors were afraid of the prophetic call on my life and avoided it. They wanted me to bless their people, but on my own dime. Foolish. In 1998, I ministered briefly as an itinerant minister in the Dallas/Fort Worth area. Then, I traveled to Florida, North Carolina and Virginia. I ministered at different cities in each state. People gave, but too little to make a life.

In 1999, I founded the local church I now pastor, All Nations Worship Center in Elgin, Illinois. From the local church, I began to learn and grow the gospel business. When I founded All Nations Worship Center, I began supporting various ministries in the manner described. We have given $250,000+ to 50+ ministries during our 17 years of existence. I've experienced the ups and downs of being a pastor. I've seen our churches income go from $20,000+ to $130,000 and down to $40,000 to $50,000. I've experienced the hardships that pastors often go through in silence, as I've experienced the hardships that itinerant ministers often go through in silence. Most churches don't want to talk about money. Most believers don't want to hear about money, unless they're told they're going to be receiving some in the near future. But, we must talk about this issue, especially in relation to understanding the gospel business.

From 1991 to 2016, I've owned and operated several businesses. I've also worked as an employee in several different businesses. I've worked in multi-million dollar businesses, small businesses and even in government businesses. I've owned small businesses and was a shareholder of a $100-million-dollar international business. In every business, I was expected to produce for that business. In owning a small business, I was required to have a business plan to obtain funding for that business. I learned what it takes to make a business successful. I've also learned what it takes to make a gospel business successful. I'm not perfect, but I've acquired much knowledge and wisdom concerning the what's, how's, where's, when's and why's of worldly business and gospel business. Both are important.

Change is Key to the Church's Future Success

I've also experienced the dark side of both. I know what it's like to lose everything, multiple times. Life doesn't always work as we plan. But, as I've learned along the way, God does have a plan. We, too, should also have a plan. And, we should learn how to work that plan. That means we should look for mentoring and gain training to fulfill the plans we make so that we can fulfill God's plans for our lives. Mentoring and training are vital to our success, whether in worldly business or gospel business. By them, we can avoid much heartache and hardship that comes with not knowing what we're doing. And when we start in business, most people don't know what they're doing. Whether in business or ministry, we should all start by learning and being a learner.

When asked what his profession is, Mike Murdock, a man of tremendous wisdom, says, "I'm a learner." He has spent and continues to spend His life learning. I'm a learner. I, too, have learned much regarding doing business. I've learned how gospel business is meant to be conducted to bring pleasure to the Father' heart. Believe me, God is not happy with many who are involved in His gospel business. The failures that I've mentioned and others I have not mentioned have caused him disappointment. I'd like that to change. I'd like to see the restoration of the gospel preacher to the Church. I'd like to see the atmosphere of revival burning brightly in churches across our nation and around the world. But for that to happen, we must change.

Relearning How to Preach the Gospel

Change? Yes, we must change how we conduct gospel business, and we must support the work of the gospel preacher. We must learn why the preaching of the gospel is so important from a Scriptural foundation, what the preaching of the gospel is designed to bring into the church and how the gospel business should be conducted. To do that, I want to briefly walk with you through the business of preaching the gospel, how the gospel is meant to be preached and what should

> *In this age of such tremendous knowledge, I'm shocked by the ignorance of believers, in general, to the basic truths in God's Word, even among ministers.*

happen when the gospel is being preached and gospel business is being conducted. To start, I want to look at Romans 10:14-15, *WEB*, which says,

> "How then will they call on Him in whom they have not believed? How will they believe in Him whom they have not heard? How will they hear without a preacher? And how will they preach unless they are sent? As it is written: 'How beautiful are the feet of those who preach the good news of peace, who bring glad tidings of good things!'"

Paul makes it clear why the gospel preacher is vital: Unless a person hears the gospel, they cannot believe in the one who is the subject of the gospel message, Jesus Christ. In fact, apart from the gospel preacher, people won't even know their need to call on Christ; they will remain ignorant of Him. In this age of such tremendous knowledge, I'm shocked by the ignorance of believers, in general, to the basic truths in God's Word, even among ministers. When there is no gospel preacher, people will not call on God. When there is no gospel preacher, people will not hear the gospel message. When there is no gospel preacher, there is no peace. Isaiah plainly states,

"There is no peace for the wicked...." Is. 57:21, *NLT.* When there is no gospel preacher, good things are absent from the lives of God's people: we never learn of God's benefits for those who serve Him. For that reason, God has exalted the gospel preacher.

The gospel preacher is vital for the salvation of the lost, and the salvation of the saved. In Romans 10:1-17, we see how lost men and women are saved by the preaching of the gospel. Clearly, this section of Scripture is speaking of those who are lost coming to the saving knowledge of Jesus Christ. But in 1 Corinthians 1:17-24, we see how vital the gospel preacher is to the saved, for He states, *"The message of the cross is foolish to those who are headed for destruction! But we who are being saved know it is the very power of God."* We believers need to hear the gospel preached to partake in its power. 1 Cor. 1:24. The gospel is *"the power of God unto salvation to everyone that believes...."* Rom. 1:16.

The Gospel Preacher is Called to Preach

But, for someone to be a gospel preacher, they must be called to preach the gospel. Being a gospel preacher is different from sharing the gospel with friends and family. I remember when I was in college at the University of Iowa and I heard someone who was called to preach the gospel preaching to crowds of several hundred students. I was amazed as I saw how students became enthralled at the preaching of the gospel. One, in particular, was able to attract significant crowds as he spoke. Conviction came. Salvation came. Transformation came. God moved. I spent hours listening to the gospel being preached in those open-air meetings. I loved it.

Feeling the call, I tried to do the same thing. I failed miserably. Few listened. I knew Jesus saved. I knew the Holy Spirit came. I knew God was real. But, I didn't have much else to say. And, I wasn't called to preach the gospel like the person I saw. I had a different message and a different people I was called to. I learned. I grew. And eventually, I had something to say, and I found the people to whom I was called to preach. I even had my own pulpit built. I still use that pulpit today. And, God has honored my attempt to fulfill His call. I've learned that I'm not sent to everyone. I'm sent to some. You, gospel preacher, are one of the ones to whom I've been sent. I was sent to declare to you the importance of your mission and assignment. Don't ignore it!

The Apostle Paul: Staying the Couse of the Gospel's Mission

The Apostle Paul, after significant failure in his first missionary journey, was required to make a decision, a determination of how he would preach the gospel. That decision involved going back to gospel basics: Christ and Him crucified. Why was Paul failing in his first missionary journey assignment? Remember, Paul had been sent out by church leaders in Antioch. Paul argued persuasively that Jesus is the Christ. But, Paul's arguments didn't persuade the Jews; instead, they sought to kill Him. Paul was driven from Damascus, Salamis and Iconium. Then, Paul entered Lystra: he was martyred. Acts 14:19. Paul finds his way to Corinth after being beaten, driven out of cities, stoned to death and mocked. In Corinth, he makes the decision to stop trying to persuade the Jews: *"from henceforth I will go unto the Gentiles."* Acts 18:6. Then, he hears Jesus: *"Be not afraid, but speak, and hold not thy peace...for I have much people in this city."* Acts 18:9-10.

Think about this for a second, Paul almost missed his assignment, even though called by Christ Himself. How? By preaching to the Jews and ignoring the Gentiles. Paul's assignment was to the Gentiles, not the Jews. Paul saw little fruit on his first missionary journey, until he came to Corinth: *"Even though I may not be an apostle to others, surely I am to you! For you are the seal of My apostleship in the Lord."* 1 Cor. 9:11. Paul saw the Corinthians and his work in Corinth as the seal of the apostolic work to which he was called. Although called as an apostle, Paul did not experience the full fruits of being an apostle until he went to Corinth. There, he entered into the power and position of the apostolic call. How? By his decision to stop arguing in the name of the gospel and to start demonstrating the gospel by means of the power of God. Paul preached the gospel: *"not with the wisdom of words, lest the cross of Christ should be made of none effect"* (1 Cor. 1:17), *"but in demonstration of the Spirit and power: that your faith should not stand in the wisdom of men, but in the power of God"* (1 Cor. 2:5). We, too, can miss our calling. We can try to do things in our own wisdom and strength. We can try to preach the gospel in our own wisdom. But, it will fall on deaf ears. No, the gospel must be preached by the demonstration of the Spirit and power.

So, the gospel must be preached. As the gospel is preached, arguments will not persuade people of the gospel's efficacy or relevance. No, it requires power to do the gospel justice. And, that power is hidden in the gospel's message: Christ and Him crucified. But, mere information cannot save men and women. No, revelation of the gospel must be experienced by the demonstration of its power. *"I am not ashamed of the gospel, because it is the power of God for salvation to everyone who believes, first to the Jew, then to the Greek."* Rom. 1:16, BSB.

The Anointed Gospel and Gospel Preacher

In the late 19th Century, Charles S. Price, a well-known evangelist and extremely well educated and eloquent man, visited his alma mater, where he was invited on a particular day to teach. While teaching, he demonstrated the difference between oratory eloquence that evoked emotional outburst and gospel preaching that brought genuine conviction. He demonstrated to students present that day how he, by just reciting the alphabet, could move them to tears. He started, a... b... c... d... Shortly, many could be heard crying. But, that was emotion. No gospel was preached. Conviction was not present. Then, he preached the gospel. Sobs could be heard. Conviction was present. But, it was in the power of the Spirit not the wisdom of men.

God is looking for gospel preachers. The gospel preachers He chooses are not the most eloquent men and women on earth. God isn't looking for human wisdom to bring the gospel to Mankind. Rather, He is seeking those who are willing to let Him do the work of convincing; He is looking for those who are willing to rely on His power, not their wisdom. *"For consider your calling, brothers: not many of you were wise according to worldly standards, not many were powerful, not many were of noble birth. But God chose what is foolish in the world to shame the wise; God chose what is weak in the world to shame the strong...."* 1 Cor. 1:26,27, *ESV*. Andrew Wommack shares an extremely funny story that illustrates what I'm trying to share with you:

> *"One day, Wommack received a letter from a man sharing his testimony of salvation. In that letter, the man stated that he enjoyed watching Wommack's television program: not to hear the gospel but because the program was so boring that it put him to sleep. For years, the man had suffered from insomnia; he couldn't sleep through the night. Eventually, after listening to Wommack preach the gospel a number of times, the man accepted Christ. Wommack shared this tongue in cheek story at a Gospel Seminar event I attended in the Chicago, Illinois area to show that it wasn't his eloquent preaching that produced results but the gospel message."*

We must always understand that the gospel is what produces eternal fruit. Our eloquence and ability to share the gospel aren't what brings men and women to salvation. No, the gospel's ability to bring men and women to salvation is hidden in the gospel's self-actualizing power. The real gospel has power to bring salvation. False gospels don't have real power to bring men and women to salvation. That's how we discern the difference between salvation's power manifested in the lives of those who hear and believe the gospel. The real gospel always has real power that leads to genuine salvation. Don't accept any substitute. We don't need a "watered down" gospel. We need the full gospel. Believers, yes, the world itself, is looking to hear the full gospel message, as described herein. We must preach it.

Plundering Hell and Populating Heaven

Jesus plainly said, *"This gospel of the kingdom shall be preached in the whole world as a testimony to all the nations, and then the end will come."* Matt. 24:14, *NASB.* And, *"[t]he gospel must first be preached to all the nations."* Mk. 13:10, *NASB.* The full gospel must be preached. That gospel will be preached to all the world before the second coming. Needless to say, the gospel, as described herein, hasn't been preached to all the world, yet. Many peoples around the world sit in the darkness of ignorance to the gospel message. That must change. Christ cannot come until the gospel is fully preached to the whole world. We have lots of work. Let's get busy. *"Go into all the world and preach the gospel to every creature."* Mk. 16:15, *BSB.* When? Now. How? By any means necessary. For how long? Until Christ returns.

You have been called to preach the gospel. You are reading this book because of that call. You are being positioned with power to preach the full gospel. No longer will the Church sit in the darkness of ignorance as to what the gospel is, why it's important and other trivial matters that hinder it from being preached to a world dying to hear its glorious message. You are anointed. You have been appointed. Heaven is behind you. Hell is before you. As the famous evangelist Reinhard Bonnke states, "We must plunder hell to populate heaven!" That's our mission. Our mandate is clear. The call unequivocal. Preach the gospel! Now, go do it. Amen.

Chapter Ten

The Gospel Must be Published

"And the gospel must first be published among all nations."
Mk. 13:10.

"The Lord gave the word: great was the company of those that published it." Ps. 68:11, *KJV.* In the *ESV: "The Lord giveth the word: the women that publish the tidings are a great host."*

On June 1, 1980, Ted Turner launched CNN. CNN stands for Cable News Network. Prior to that date, the news was heard only at certain times on certain television stations. Much has changed.

Today, we have 24-hour news. And, there's an appetite to digest the news taking place around the world. Much in popular culture revolves around the news. And, many of the icons in our world today are news commentators. News commentators don't just proclaim the news but present their opinion of the news. Spin. Oftentimes, that news circulates on cycles within minutes, especially if it's new or breaking news. Who can forget the news cycle on September 11, 2001, where that horrible event was shown over and over and over again. That event was witnessed multiple times across the world on a steady stream of that news cycle phenomenon. And, it has grown.

With the advent of that 24 news cycle, our world rapidly changed. And, it continues to change today. Much of what is taking place in our world is being driven by the news cycle. This has caused men and women to live in a state of constant fear. *"People will faint from terror, apprehensive of what is coming on the world, for the heavenly bodies will be shaken."* Matt. 21:26, NIV.

Johannes Gutenberg, Gospel Publishing and the Renaissance

In the 14th century, when Johannes Gutenberg and other Germans created what was known as moveable type for printing presses, that advance transformed nations. A revolution began. That revolution in printing made books affordable and available to the masses. Prior to that time, books were extremely expensive to produce, and they could only be produced one by one. With the advent of printing, knowledge increased across the globe. Education became one of the most desirable byproducts of the printing revolution. Schools were opened. Universities began. Mankind was transformed by ease of access to knowledge brought by that innovation, for books were produced where prior knowledge from previous generations could be shared with, read by and understood by future generations. And, we're the better for it.

Gutenberg's major life project was publishing the Bible. That act transformed the consciousness of Mankind to God's Word, and with it, Mankind's conscience was revived. Prior to that, Mankind was afflicted by what was known as the Dark Ages. The Dark Ages were an age of ignorance. That ignorance caused Mankind to ascribe everything to superstition. The world and how it functioned was unknown. Even basic laws that were previously understood by prior generations were lost to the masses in the mire of history. Mankind was ignorant and suffered from that ignorance. Gutenberg's army of presses, even in their simple form, waged war on Mankind's ignorance, specifically of the Bible. Nearly everything we have today came from Gutenberg's publishing of the Bible.

Mankind's access to the Bible due to Gutenberg's presses enabled men and women to read it. And, they read it often. The Bible is and was the most popular book ever published. Mankind inherently understands its difference from every other book produced in history. The masses readily understood the Bible's relevance to their lives, and they read it. From reading it, the masses began to apply the Bible's principles to their lives. Much of the United States Constitution was derived from the knowledge gained by the principles made available in Bibles printed on printing presses. And, that knowledge revolutionized our nation.

Daniel Webster[7], possibly the greatest legal scholar in American history, considered the Constitution a miracle from God. Further, he believed in and encouraged gospel publishing. In his own words, Webster said:

> "If religious books are not widely circulated among the masses in this country, I do not know what is going to become of us as a nation. If truth be not diffused, then error will be. If God and His Word are not known and received, the devil and his works will gain the ascendency. If the evangelical volume does not reach every hamlet, the pages of a corrupt and licentious literature will. If the power of the gospel is not felt throughout the length and breadth of this land, anarchy and misrule, degradation and misery, corruption and darkness will reign without mitigation or end.

> "If we abide by the principles taught in the Bible, our country will go on prospering and to prosper; but if we and our posterity neglect its instructions and authority, no man can tell how sudden a catastrophe may

---

[7] Daniel Webster is highly regarded as one of the greatest lawyers in American history. He argued 223 cases before the United States Supreme Court, and won approximately 50% of those cases. And, that was at a time when judges more closely held to the rule of law, did not substitute their judgment for valid laws and truly sought to interpret laws rather than making law from the bench, as is often done today. Webster said of the Constitution, "I regard it (the Constitution) as the work of the purest patriots and wisest statesman that ever existed, aided by the smiles of a benign Providence; it almost appears a "Divine interposition in our behalf... the hand that destroys our Constitution rends our Union asunder forever."

overwhelm us and bury all our glory in profound obscurity."

Publishing and Exporting Gospel Truth

Freedom entered the world through those truths contained in the Bible. The publishing of that truth expanded freedom to the four corners of the earth. America has freedom and is a free nation due to those principles. The Bible led to that revolution. Gospel seeds, via gospel publishing, were sown across our nation, and that message inspired men and women to desire freedom. That's the moral compass on which America was founded. And, it's that moral compass we have lost, in part, as a nation.

Today, America is no longer #1 exporter of Bibles. In 2012, China, a communist nation, became the #1 exporter of Bibles in the world. Is it any wonder why China is the world's #1 exporter at $2.27 trillion dollars in 2015? And, America has slipped to #3 at $1.598 trillion. We no longer value the Bible as we once did. But, the Chinese do. No wonder China is leading America: we have failed to understand or appreciate the value of what our forbearers gave us by way of an abundance of principles and precepts founded on God's Word.

The Bible's demand in China outweighs its production. In China, 50+ million desire to have Bibles. Yet, of that number, only approximately four million are able to get a Bible, annually. A famine of the Word of God exists in China, but not in America. We have plenty of Bibles, but oftentimes, we don't value or read it. In America, there's an abundance of Bibles, but little hunger for God's word. By God's grace, we can drive to a local Dollar Tree or other dollar store and buy a full copy of the Bible for $1.00. In China, the Bible is valued and desired by the masses. In America, it's neglected by the masses. America has enjoyed the truths in the Bible for 150+ years, but in the last 50+ years, we have neglected its precepts and warnings. Instead, we have placed our own opinions above its eternal truths. How sad!

I'm grateful for the publishing of Bibles in China, and I'm grateful that Bibles are exported by China to the world. I'm grateful for the hunger for the Bibles in China by the Chinese people. Yet, I'm deeply concerned by the absence of that same hunger in America.

In Jesus' day, the Jews had the Torah; they knew who they worshiped, "for salvation is of the Jews." Jn. 4:22. But, in the midst of their knowledge of Torah, many Jews had lost their hunger for God. God came to the Jews in human form, and they rejected Him. Listen to what Jesus said of the Jewish people, *"O Jerusalem, Jerusalem, the city that kills the prophets and stones God's messengers! How often I have wanted to gather your children together as a hen protects her chicks beneath her wings, but you wouldn't let Me."* Lk. 13:34, *NLT*. Today, America is rejecting Jesus by disregarding and disrespecting His words. Let's change that. How? By publishing the gospel.

Raising an Army of Gospel Publishers

Jesus said, *"the gospel must be published."* Mk. 13:10. In reviewing the word for published, I discovered that the Greek word for publish is **kérussó,** which means, proclaim, herald, preach. Since the time of *Homer*, that word carried the following meaning, according to *Thayer's Greek Lexicon:* "to be a herald; to officiate as herald; to proclaim after the manner of a herald." Or, that Greek word was always understood to be a message conveyed with formality, gravity and an authority that must be heard and obeyed. Further, that Greek word carries with it the inference of an authoritative document brought by an official messenger that the messenger was meant to deliver publicly. The gospel must be preached. The gospel must be proclaimed, publicly. The gospel must be published; it is essential to the health of our world.

The gospel is and always was meant to be delivered publicly by those who believe its message. Jesus said, *"I tell you the truth, everyone who acknowledges Me publicly here on earth, the Son of Man will also acknowledge in the presence of God's angels."*

Lk. 12:8, *NLT*. The gospel is not a private matter; it's a public matter of great importance to the public. The preaching, publishing and proclamation of the gospel message is vital to society's health, as Webster stated. Like Webster, the Founding Fathers understood this truth and acted on it. Today, we don't. Oftentimes, we think the gospel is meant to be a private matter of faith, and that the public demonstration of faith is optional. It isn't. Public proclamation of the gospel, including publishing, is the #1 most important thing to the health of any and every society. A society that's sick no longer values the publishing and public proclamation of the gospel

Publishing of the gospel is and has always been our world's greatest need. That need is so great that Scripture tells us God has recruited a great army or men and women to publish it. Ps. 68:11. In fact, the majority of publishers of the great gospel message recruited by God into that great gospel army are not men, but women. According to Scripture, women are uniquely qualified to proclaim the gospel message by publishing. Or, more and more widely read gospel books will be written and published by women than men. And, as I survey the Church world, that certainly seems to be the case. Sarah Young's book, *Jesus Calling*, is currently the bestselling book, selling 10+ million copies, according to the Evangelical Christian Publisher's Association list by the Christian Book Expo. This is still far behind the J.K. Rowling's series of books, *Harry Potter*, which was 450+ million books sold, and *Goosebumps*, which sold 350+ million books. That's almost one billion books sold based on occult practices. More gospel publishing is needed. And, better Christian authors are needed. We need more gospel.

Communicating the Gospel in Print

Christ longs for great Christian evangelists to arise and communicate the gospel to this generation. Fiction is especially popular among younger audiences. Movies are first written, and then shot, edited and produced for distribution. Writing is key. Publishing is key. Hollywood is always seeking a good story. And, before it was Hollywood, it was <u>Holy</u>-wood, a place for the proclamation of the gospel through film.

Who can forget the story of Moses in *The Ten Commandments* (1956) or *Ben-Hur* (1959) played by Charlton Hesston? Both were epic stories that contained a Christ-centered message of faith in the power of the gospel to transform the lives of the most embittered of men and women. We must learn to communicate the gospel through the message of stories, as Christ did. Jesus' parables hooked Jewish audiences: men and women, boys and girls would sit for hours, even days, to hear the gospel stories shared by Christ. Both young and old longed to hear Christ's stories and to understand their meaning.

Irrespective of who publishes the gospel message, it's vital that the gospel message is published. The publishing of that message can make a difference in our world today. We mustn't shirk our responsibility by failing to publish the good news of the gospel of peace proclaimed by Christ to a lost and hurting world. We can invade this world with gospel truth and thereby change our society for generations to come. People long to hear good news; they want to receive the blessing.

Fear has gripped the hearts of many people, including believers, in our world today, and many people want freedom from their fears. We can bring them that freedom. A generation of Calebs and Joshuas are needed to say to this generation: *"Fear thou not; for I am with thee: be not dismayed; for I am thy God: I will strengthen thee; yea, I will help thee; yea, I will uphold thee with the right hand of my righteousness."* Is. 41:10. The Bible teaches us to not be afraid; to *"fear not."*

How I Entered Gospel Publishing

Since the early 1990's, I've been involved in the publishing industry. I published my first book, *Decade of Destiny,* in 1994. From that experience, I learned a great deal about publishing. I'm still learning about publishing. In the 1990's, publishing was very costly for the average person, it cost several thousand dollars. Today, publishing is inexpensive, you can self-publish your book for less than $1,000. And, your book can be made available worldwide in an instant. Amazing! Further, not only can you self-publish your book, you can also promote your book on well-known sites like *Amazon.com* and *BarnesandNoble.com*. In fact, Amazon allows individuals to self-publish their books on their kindle device as an e-book. Then, the author can set their own price for that book. In all of history, it has never been easier to publish. Therefore, publish the gospel. Learn to write. Find a good editor. Communicate the message that God has placed in your heart. People need to hear your message.

We're no longer living in an Industrial Age or Agricultural Age. Today, we live in an Information Age. Because we live in an Information Age, a transformation in society has occurred. That transformation has made it possible to publish the gospel around the world, in both print and digital formats. Language is no longer a barrier to publishing the gospel in other nations. Books can be translated into numerous languages, even by computer software applications. Do not think your part in the spreading of the gospel is insignificant. No, your part is vital.

The gospel must be published to all nations. We must look for ways to publish the gospel. And, we should look to make the gospel message easier to understand to the hearer. Every available avenue should be used to publish the gospel: that *"publisheth peace; that announceth glad tidings of good, that publisheth salvation, that saith unto Zion, thy God reigneth!"* Is. 52:7, *DBT*. That's our message. Let's speak it. Let's proclaim it. Let's publish it.

Publishing the Gospel in You to the World

The gospel message must be published to all the world: whether in books, magazines, blogs, Twitter posts, Facebook, Instagram or other social media outlets. God is looking for men and women, willing vessels, in this great task of gospel publishing. Are you willing? Are you ready? Do you have a desire to write? Publish? To proclaim good news? Then, you have been called for such a time as this. Esther 4:14. You are anointed to declare the good news to lost souls. Lk. 4:18.

Christ has sent us into the world to bring men and women back from the depths of hell, into the heights of heaven. Jesus said, *"Peace be with you! As the Father has sent Me, I am sending you."* Jn. 20:21, *NIV.* God anoints His gospel messengers with fire from His altar: *"He sends His angels like the winds, His servants like flames of fire."* Heb. 1:7, *NLT.* To carry the fire, angels walk in the midst of stones of fire that are located on the mountain of God. Ezek. 28:14. Stay in the heavenly fires by preaching and publishing the gospel message in and to the Mountain of God, His Church.

The gospel is waiting for you to proclaim its good news to a lost world in the way you were designed to speak it. Don't hold back any longer! Rise up, man of God, woman of God! Proclaim the good news. Speak it. Preach it. Publish it. That's what God longs for from this generation. Never has there been an hour like this where so much good news can reach the world so fast and have such great impact. Truly, the butterfly effect[8] is in operation. One life and one person can make a powerful and significant difference in our world today, for good or evil. You matter. Your words matter. Your life matters. God placed your importance in your DNA from birth. You are called to a life of significance. Don't ever forget that as you begin preaching the message, the gospel, that God Himself has placed on the inside of you.

The gospel resides in the believer. Paul declares, *"Clearly, you are a letter from Christ showing the result of our ministry among you. This 'letter' is written not with pen and ink, but with the Spirit of*

---

[8] In 1963, Edward Lorenz discovered the Butterfly Effect. That discovery was noted in his seminal paper called *Deterministic Nonperiodic Flow.* Later, one meteorologist remarked that if the theory were correct, one flap of a sea gull's wings would be enough to alter the course of the weather forever. The controversy has not yet been settled, but the most recent evidence seems to favor the sea gulls. Lorenz began to use the butterfly, due to its poetic brilliance, which is how we have the term Butterfly Effect. An excellent book that illustrates this point was written by Andy Andrews, *Butterfly Effect: How Your Life Matters.* I recommend it

the living God. It is carved not on tablets of stone, but on human hearts." 2 Cor. 3:3, *NLT*. Awesome! You are a living letter from the living Christ to convey His message to a dead world. No other book in history is like the book you are. You are God's masterpiece of literature written by Holy Spirit's ink in a heart of flesh. By that message inside of you, Christ's gospel, you are called and uniquely designed to inspire others to pursue the living Christ like no one else can. God has placed His gospel in you for that purpose, and He longs for that purpose to emerge in your life. You are the gospel to those you meet. Publish that gospel!

Books in Heaven and Books on Earth

Publishing the gospel is important. Gospel books are important. God has books that He has written. Heaven has books on innumerable subject. God writes and has written books. God publishes books. Jesus talked about books in heaven: *"rejoice, because your names are written in heaven."* Lk. 10:20. John, the Apostle, in the book of Revelation, speaks of a significant book in the hand of God the Father. *"And I saw in the right hand of Him that sat on the throne a book written within and on the backside, sealed with seven seals."* Rev. 5:1, *WBT*. Further, what was contained in that book was marked top secret: no one, in heaven or earth, could open that book, that is, until Jesus came. Jesus was found worthy to open that book. Rev. 5:5. That book may or may not be the Lamb's Book of Life.

The Bible speaks of a Lamb's Book of Life. *"They will bring the glory and wealth of the nations into the holy city. Only those whose names are written in the Lamb's Book of Life will enter it."* Rev. 21:27, *GWT*. Moses said to God, *"Now if You would only forgive their sin. But if not, please erase me from the book You have written."* Ex. 32:32, *HCSB*. God's response to Moses, *"I will erase whoever has sinned against Me from My book."* Ex. 32:33, *HCSB*. That book was the Lamb's Book of Life. David prays against his adversaries: *"Erase their names from the Book of Life; don't let them be counted among the righteous."* Ps. 69:28, *NLT.* So, there's a Book of Life.

But, according to Scripture, that's not the only book in heaven. There are other books in heaven. What are the other books in heaven? In Revelation 20:20, NLT, it says, *"I saw the dead, both great and small, standing before God's throne. And the books were opened, including the Book of Life. And the dead were judged according to what they had done, as recorded in the books."* Everything we do in this life is recorded in heaven. Jesus said, *"I tell you that on the day of judgment people will have to account for every careless word they speak."* Matt. 12:36, HCSB.

Your Voice is Heard in Heaven and What You Say on Earth Matters

Everything we say is recorded in heaven. And, we'll be held accountable for every word we speak, and write. That is why Scripture says, be *"quick to listen, slow to speak, and slow to anger..."* James 1:19, BSB. Solomon also instructs us that *"[a] fool gives full vent to his anger, but a wise man holds it in check."* Prov. 29:11, HCSB. Angry word lead to sin. Gospel words lead to blessing. Being able to keep what you say in check is an extremely important part of the Christian life. What we say matters.

The Bible has much to say about what we say. James says, *"The tongue is a fire, a world of evil. Placed among the parts of our bodies, the tongue contaminates the whole body and sets on fire the course of life, and is itself set on fire by hell."* James 3:6, ISV. What we say is important. And, what we write is important. *"Let no corrupt communication proceed out of your mouth, but that which is good to the use of edifying, that it may minister grace unto the hearers."* Eph. 4:29. In the *ABPE*, it says, *"Let not any hateful words come out of your mouth, but whatever is good and useful for improvement that you may give grace to those who hear...."* The sins of the tongue are some of the most devastating to our lives. Sins of the tongue are numerous: lying, slander, gossip, whisperings, rumors, false testimony, backbiting, inconvenient joking, swearing/cursing, harsh words, evil speaking, pessimism, sarcasm and other such kinds of speech. That would include contentious words, accusatory words and strife-filled speech. All of them are corrupt and will dilute the gospel.

Jesus' brother, James, says, *"From the same mouth come blessing and cursing. My brothers, these things ought not to be so."* James 3:10, *ESV*. Jesus taught, *"A good man produces good out of the good storeroom of his heart. An evil man produces evil out of the evil storeroom, for his mouth speaks from the overflow of the heart."* Lk. 6:45, *HCSB*. That means, for us to effectively share the gospel, we must have that gospel or good news stored in our hearts.

Open Hearts, Closed Eyes and Renewed Minds

How do we store the gospel in our hearts? By meditating on it. That's the secret to living the Christian life: we must allow the gospel to enter our hearts by making sure it's continually on our minds and in our mouths. If not, we risk meditating on the wrong thing. Like weeds, wrong thoughts can grow in our hearts, if allowed. We're called to tend that garden. *"The LORD God placed the man in the Garden of Eden to tend and watch over it."* Gen. 2:15, *NLT*. Eden's paradise is designed to flow from your heart, *"for it is the source of life."* Prov. 4:23, *HCSB*.

In the movie, *The Blindside*, there's a scene where Leigh Ann Touhy, played by Sandra Bullock, seeks to understand how Michael Oher, played by Quinton Aaron, was able to escape the evil that took place all around him. Oher was in the midst of evil, but he was a gentle giant in the midst of that evil. Oher didn't get caught up in the sin that was around him. In response to a question asked by Touhy, Oher says, "When I was little and something awful was happening my mama would tell me to close my eyes... And when she was finished or the bad things were over she'd say, 'Now when I count to three, you open your eyes. The past is gone, the world is a good place, and it's all gonna be okay.'" Oher escaped hell by closing his

[""]

eyes. That act enabled him to forget and forgive the evil taking place around him. And, that act opened doors to the hearts of men and women who wanted to help him escape that hell. Praise God!

I'm reminded of the children's song:

O be careful, little eyes, what you see
O be careful, little eyes, what you see
There's a Father up above
And He's looking down in love
So, be careful, little eyes, what you see

O be careful, little ears, what you hear
O be careful, little ears, what you hear
There's a Father up above
And He's looking down in love
So, be careful, little ears, what you hear

O be careful, little hands, what you do
O be careful, little hands, what you do
There's a Father up above

And He's looking down in love
So, be careful, little hands, what you do

O be careful, little feet, where you go
O be careful, little feet, where you go
There's a Father up above
And He's looking down in love
So, be careful, little feet, where you go

O be careful, little mouth, what you say
O be careful, little mouth, what you say
There's a Father up above
And He's looking down in love
So, be careful, little mouth, what you say. [9]

Guarding Your Heart, Keeping Your Soul and Obeying God's Voice

As children, we learn these lessons to keep us safe in this life. But, as we grow older, we often lose sight of those important lessons taught. We forget how important what we see, what we hear and what we say are to our lives. And, that we must constantly guard our hearts to ensure that we aren't allowing wrong things to fill our hearts. What we allow in our hearts – good or evil – will grow. If we allow the wrong things in our hearts, then our hearts will be polluted by them. Adam and Eve were placed in the garden of Eden to *"care for it and to maintain it."* Gen. 2:15, *NET*. Today, we're called to care for and maintain the garden of our hearts: *"Above all else, guard your heart, for everything you do flows from it."* Prov. 4:23, *NIV*.

---

[9] Copyright 1956 by Zondervan Music Publishers. All rights reserved. Used by permission.
[9] Copyright 1956 by Zondervan Music Publishers. All rights reserved. Used by permission.

Listen. Learn. Grow. You were designed by God to do that, and more. And, make sure you are listening to the right thing – truth. Make sure you are learning the right thing. Make sure you are growing in the right thing. *"How can a young person stay pure? By obeying Your Word."* Ps. 119:9, *NLT*. Moses spoke to Joshua when he was 80 years old these words: *"Study this Book of Instruction continually. Meditate on it day and night so you will be sure to obey everything written in it. Only then will you prosper and succeed in all you do."* Josh. 1:8, *NLT*. The Bible is a book of instruction to Mankind. Yet, most of us don't know it. Often, we don't study it. Neither do we follow its instructions for living life.

No wonder God says, *"If My people would only listen to Me, if Israel would only follow My ways, how quickly I would subdue their enemies and turn My hand against their foes! Those who hate the Lord would cringe before Him, and their punishment would last forever. But you would be fed with the finest of wheat; with honey from the rock I would satisfy you."* Ps. 83:13-16, *NIV*. Can you hear the aching in the heart of God? God's heart longs for Man to follow the instructions given. Yet, we often overlook the instructions and proceed on our own – to our own heartache. That's why we often fail to accomplish the desires and dreams implanted in our hearts by God: we fail to listen to the voice of His Word.

God's Words, God's Instructions and God's Ways

"All Scripture is inspired by God and is useful to teach us what is true and to make us realize what is wrong in our lives. It corrects us when we're wrong and teaches us to do what is right. God uses it to prepare and equip His people to do every good work." 2 Tim. 3:16,17, *NLT*. What should we fill our hearts with? Scripture. Prophecy. Christ. Nature. *"Man shall not live by bread alone, but by every word that proceedeth out of the mouth of God."* Matt. 4:4. Peter teaches: *"First of all, you must understand this: No prophecy in Scripture is a matter of one's own interpretation...."* 2 Pet. 1:20, *ISV*. Scripture is God inspired. God inspired men to speak the Scriptures. That makes Scripture inerrant.

Yet, Scripture's principles are subject to correct interpretation. Paul instructed us: *"Study to shew thyself approved unto God, a workman that needeth not to be ashamed, rightly dividing the word of truth."* 2 Tim. 2:15. Not every interpretation of Scripture is the right interpretation. No, there are many wrong interpretations. How do we know the difference? By their fruit. When we look at the fruit of a doctrine or message, we must determine if the fruit is good fruit. How do we know if the fruit is good? By observing the outcome of the message or doctrine. If the fruit is good, the root is good. If the fruit is bad, then the root is bad. Jesus made things simple.

Heaven's Instructions are Hidden in Plain Sight

God's instructions to Mankind are simple. And, God has made His instructions known to Mankind; they are readily available to us. Where? God gave Mankind a window into His mind through His creation. When we look at creation, we can see God's fingerprints. But, we have to look for His fingerprints. Many individuals have spent their lives studying God's mind through what is revealed in nature. In fact, some of our greatest achievements are connected to God's principles revealed in nature. Isaac Newton's laws of motion enabled Mankind to plot its course to the moon and back. The Constitution was framed by the Founders' understanding contained in the Declaration of Independence, which began with the statement: "We hold these truths to be self-evident...."

God's truth, His principles, are revealed by creation. When we know and follow His revealed truths, we succeed. When we ignore them, we fail. It was commonly understood by our Forefathers that no legislature, king or court had the ability to unwind the self-evident truths revealed to Mankind by God. And, that to ignore those truths meant certain disaster. For example, if a person jumps off the roof of a ten-story building flapping their arms claiming they can fly, we would call them crazy. Of course, that would be after we scraped them off the pavement in front of the building. The law of gravity is revealed and must be followed. And, we pay a dear price when we break it. But, that doesn't mean the law of gravity cannot be superseded. No, the law of gravity may be superseded by the law of aerodynamics, which enables us to fly across the world. But, just because the law of aerodynamics can supersede the law of gravity doesn't mean we ignore the law of gravity.

God's natural laws are hidden in nature. Mankind has had a hard time understanding and discerning those foundational laws. Today, we still have a very basic understanding of God's laws hidden in nature. And that's after several thousands of years of studying them. Since Adam, Mankind has been searching for the wisdom hidden in the creation. And, much of the good we have today comes from that hidden wisdom.

> **What Christ taught is nothing less than revolutionary; He revealed foundational principles hidden from Mankind since the beginning of the world.**

Cell phones are possible by use of that wisdom. So are refrigerators, microwaves, computers and other advances. Man has advanced as he has understood God's wisdom hidden in creation. In the same way, God has hidden His wisdom in a book of instruction to Mankind that was given by numerous prophets – the Bible. No other book is like it. Even other "holy" books written for other religions cannot compare to the matchless wisdom contained in the Bible nor do they have the tangible fruit offered by the Bible's wisdom. The Bible is superior in every way.

The Bible is God's Revealed Wisdom to All Mankind

The Bible contains God's hidden wisdom. Christ is the hidden wisdom of God. *"But to those Jews and Greeks who are called, He is Christ, God's power and God's wisdom."* 1 Cor. 1:24, *GWT.* Christ is the full manifestation of God's wisdom in human form. *"And the Word came in the flesh, and lived for a time in our midst...."* Jn. 1:14, *WNT.* Jesus Christ is God's wisdom revealed. What Christ taught is nothing less than revolutionary; He revealed foundational principles hidden from Mankind since the beginning of the world. And that revolutionary wisdom, if applied, has the ability to change the course and direction of our lives and nations. *"Every Word of God is flawless."* Prov.30:5, *WEB*. Flawless. Pure. That's what God's Word is when rightly understood.

The Bible is our instruction book for living life. But, we must search for its instructions to live our lives in line with those natural laws that existed prior to creation and that were set in motion at the beginning of creation. When rightly understood and applied to our lives, those laws benefit us. David wrote:

> *"The law of the Lord is perfect, refreshing the soul. The statutes of the Lord are trustworthy, making wise the simple. The precepts of the Lord are right, giving joy to the heart. The commands of the Lord are radiant, giving light to the eyes. The fear of the Lord is pure, enduring forever. The decrees of the Lord are firm, and all of them are righteous. They are more precious than gold, than much pure gold; they are sweeter than honey, than honey from the honeycomb. By them your servant is warned; in keeping them there is great reward."* Ps. 19:7-11, *NIV*.

The Bible's Increasing Importance to Mankind in the Last Days

Today, few understand the relevance of the Bible. Often its instructions are not sought prior to decisions being made. Many people don't see the Bible as relevant. Even professing believers have sought to change the Bible to make it relevant to culture. But in that process, hidden truths contained in the Bible often become more hidden. What we must understand in reading Scripture is: The Bible is relevant to our lives and we become relevant by understanding and applying its principles in our lives: We aren't to change the Bible's principles to fit our culture, but rather should seek to change our culture by knowing and applying the Bible's principles to our lives. There's coming a day on earth where this truth will be understood by Mankind. Isaiah prophesied:

> *"In the last days, the mountain of the LORD's house will be the highest of all – the most important place on earth. It will be raised above the other hills, and people from all over the world will stream there to worship. People from many nations will come and say, 'Come, let us go up to the mountain of the LORD, to the house of Jacob's God. There He will teach us His ways, and we will walk in His paths.' For the LORD's teaching will go out from Zion; His word will go out from Jerusalem."* Is. 2:2-3, *NLT*.

Micah mirrors Isaiah's prophetic utterance with his own prophecy:

> *"In the last days, the mountain of the LORD's house will be the highest of all – the most important place on earth. It will be raised above the other hills, and people from all over the world will stream there to worship. People from many nations will come and say, 'Come, let us go up to the mountain of the LORD, to the house of Jacob's God. There He will teach us His ways, and we will walk in His paths.' For the LORD's teaching will go out from Zion; His word will go out from Jerusalem."* Mic. 4:1-2, *NLT*.

Isaiah and Micah were contemporary prophets. Both lived in the Southern kingdom of Judah. And, both received identical prophetic words regarding the last days. Today, we're living in the last days, according to Scripture. How do I know? Under the unction of the Holy Spirit, Peter, the apostle said: *"'In the last days,' God says, 'I will pour out My Spirit upon all people. Your sons and daughters will prophesy. Your young men will see visions, and your old men will dream dreams.'"* Acts 2:17, *NLT*; see also, Joel 2:28. Peter quoted Joel, the prophet, in reference to what happened on Pentecost, as the Holy Spirit was poured out on the apostles and disciples in Jerusalem. Since 33 AD, it has been the last days. That means we're in the last days, today. Isaiah and Micah's prophetic Scriptures are applicable to us.

A Gospel Revolution is Coming

We're in the days of the fulfillment of Biblical prophecy. Knowledge of God's Word will increase. Daniel was told: *"And thou, Daniel, close the words, and seal the book, till the time of the end. Many shall run to and fro, and knowledge shall be increased."* Dan. 12:4, *DBT.* We're living in days where there has been an increase in knowledge. But, while knowledge has increased among the masses, knowledge of God's Word and wisdom hasn't. In many ways, we have spurned God's wisdom. Many have thought they are wiser than God. But, a revival is coming, first in our understanding of the hidden wisdom contained in God's law, as revealed in Scripture. Specifically, that law will be released from the mountain of the Lord's house. That center, located in Zion and Jerusalem, will teach God's law to the nations. The conflict over Israel is rooted in Israel's importance in releasing its understanding of God's law to the nations.

That reformation will bring about a transformation among the nations. Some have suggested that this transformation will take place post-rapture of the Church. But, I believe that transformation is just beginning and that it will continue to grow in the coming days. That the reformation among the nations of God's laws will bring about a radical emergence of Israel and that the nations will flow to it. That the emergence of Israel as a nation will transform the middle east from a place of conflict to a place of blessing among the nations of the world. I intend on writing a book detailing a scriptural understanding of prophetic revelation concerning that reformation and transformation among the nations. Get ready! We're in for some exciting days.

The Future of Gospel Publishing is Bright

There has been and will continue to be an increase in knowledge. As such, books, and the growing number of books will increase. As of the latest statistics, the number of books annually published is 2.2 million or more. [I was only able to find incomplete statistics that ranged from 1996 through 2013.] Of those books published, 440,000 books were published in China, 304,000 in America, 184,000 in the United Kingdom and 102,000 in Russia. That's 1.03

million books among these four nations. That means, the remaining nations of the world published the remaining 1.37 million books. Of those books published, no statistics were readily available as to how many were Christian or gospel-related books. But, I imagine it was a significant number. And, that number will grow. God is looking for men and women, young and old, to publish the gospel.

I've been in the publishing industry for 20+ years. I've learned that the average number of books sold by an author is an estimated 500 books. A bestselling Christian book is 40,000+ copies. A bestselling secular book is 100,000+ copies. With the advent of e-books and e-readers, the total number of books on the market is increasing, as is the availability of books. Today, it's very easy to publish your own book. With that increase in books, the increase in availability of books, and the increase in the ability to publish books, a real danger of the loss of vital knowledge exists. The flood of information can lead to lost knowledge in the midst of a sea of books. Yet, I believe publishing, especially gospel publishing, is one of the most important gospel works taking place on earth. We must remember that the gospel must be published. We must support the gospel, especially when published. People need the gospel in publication.

One of my favorite ministers, T.L Osborn, calls books "the printed preacher." I believe this statement holds true for magazines, blogs and other publishing formats. The printed preacher, he exclaimed, was always available to minister to the reader at their own convenience. The reader could choose a time and place to hear the preaching of the gospel. And, if they heard something that ministered to them, they could go back, again and again, and read what the printed preacher said.

The gospel preacher must take advantage of gospel publishing. When in doubt, publish the gospel. Write. Edit. Publish. Preach the gospel. Publish the gospel. The preached gospel is necessary for the gospel hearer. The published gospel is necessary to the gospel reader. Don't ever discount what you are called to write. Don't ever see it as offering no value. No, gospel publishing is of great value to God's kingdom. The publishing of the gospel establishes God's kingdom on earth.

Christ's Kingdom Advances by Gospel Publishing

Jesus has chosen the methods of preaching, publishing and proclamation to advance His kingdom. Christ's reign began 2,000 years ago. He said, *"I am the living one. I died, but look – I am alive forever and ever! And I hold the keys of death and the grave."* Rev. 1:18, *NLT*. Christ is reigning today. *"For Christ must reign until He humbles all His enemies beneath His feet."* 1 Cor. 15:25, *NLT*. That reign will continue until the last enemy, which is death, is destroyed. *"And the last enemy to be destroyed is death."* 1 Cor. 15:26, *NLT*. By His gospel, Christ longs to set men free from the fear of death, which is what holds Mankind in bondage to the devil. *"Since all of these sons and daughters have flesh and blood, Jesus took on flesh and blood to be like them. He did this so that by dying He would destroy the one who had power over death (that is, the devil). In this way, He would free those who were slaves all their lives because they were afraid of dying."* Heb. 2:14-15, *GWT*. Fear makes men slaves. Truth sets them free.

Christ's gospel sets Mankind free from Satan's bondages. Satan's two primary weapons against Mankind are deception and fear. Satan deceives men into believing lies, and then holds them in bondage to fear created by those lies believed. Satan uses that fear to hold Mankind in bondage. The gospel breaks the chains of fear, including the fear of death, which is the primary chain that holds humanity in bondage. Fear is Satan's #1 chain on the neck of Mankind. Fear is how Satan holds Mankind subject to chains of slavery to sin, iniquity, poverty, sickness, disease, addiction, shame, guilt, condemnation, racism and a host of other bondages that afflict Mankind. All of them are rooted in fear. The root of all fear is the fear of death. Mankind has been afflicted by the fear of death since the fall. But, Christ rose from the dead, broke the chains of the fear of death and set those who are captive to the fear of death free, if they will be free. Be free!

Knowledge releases power. Gospel knowledge releases God's power. Gospel knowledge published with gospel truth sets men and women free from bondage to fear. How? By faith, hope and love. *"Three things will last forever – faith, hope and love – and the greatest of these is love."* 1 Cor. 13:13, *NLT. "There is no fear in love; but perfect love casteth out fear: because fear hath torment. He that feareth is not made perfect in love."* 1 Jn. 4:18. Fear exists where there's a lack of experiential knowledge of love – especially, God's love. When we lack that knowledge, we're subjected to tormenting spirits of fear, from which Christ has already delivered us by His work on the cross. That's the gospel. The gospel message breaks the power of fear, especially its root, which is the fear of death. No fear!

Gospel Publishing, Kingdom Victories and Christ's Rule

No greater blessing exists for Mankind than to be free from fear's torment. Once delivered from fear, we're loosed from demonic bondages. What a blessing! God longs to set men and women free from fear. The devil holds men and women in continuous bondage to fear. One day, on seeing who Satan really is, we'll say, *"Is this the one who destroyed the world and made it into a wasteland? Is this the king who demolished the world's greatest cities and had no mercy on his prisoners?"* Is. 14:17, *NLT.* Satan destroys nations; he rules harshly over his prisoners. Why? He hates Mankind. Why? Because we're made in God's image. We remind Satan of God, of Satan's lower status than God and Man and of Satan's final doom, to be cast into the lake of fire. *"Now is the judgment of this world; now The Ruler of this world is hurled outside."* Jn. 12:31, *ABPE.* Where is his final place of judgment? The lake of fire. *"Then the King will turn to those on the left and say, 'Away with you, you cursed ones, into the eternal fire prepared for the devil and his demons...'"* Matt. 25:41, *NLT.*

Why does God allow evil to exist in the earth? Why does God allow the devil to run rampant in the earth? Why hasn't Christ returned? Why doesn't He return? For one reason, He is longsuffering and not willing that any should perish. Peter, the apostle said, *"The Lord isn't really being slow about His promise, as some people think. No, He is being patient for your sake. He does not want anyone to be destroyed, but wants everyone to repent."* 2 Pet. 3:9, NLT. No, it's God's mercy that has restrained Christ's return. *"Heaven must receive Jesus until the time when everything will be restored as God promised through His holy prophets long ago."* Acts 3:21, GWT. So, God is having mercy on Mankind by allowing His Church more time to preach and publish and proclaim the gospel to more people so that more people can believe the gospel. The souls of men and women hang in the balance, while the Church waits for Christ to come. This must change. God waiting for His Church, You and I, to get busy doing His gospel business.

The Harvest Fields are Ripe

The gospel sets Mankind free. But for that to happen, the gospel must be preached and published; it must be proclaimed. The proclamation of the gospel by preaching and publishing sets men and women free. Christ has committed the gospel message to His Church. Christ has called His Church to proclaim the gospel message to every tribe, tongue, people and nation. Whole nations and people groups are held in bondage because they have not heard the gospel. The devil is the one holding them in bondage. The devil keeps them in bondage through ignorance. Billions of men and women are ignorant of the gospel message. That's why the work of preaching and publishing the gospel is so important: to enable all Mankind to hear the gospel. Spiritual warfare is always about the preaching and publishing of the gospel. Why? Because the gospel message, when believed, breaks the devil's chains, always.

All spiritual warfare is designed to stop or hinder the spread of the gospel. If the enemy can stop the spread of the gospel, he's won:

billions of people, men and women, will join him in the lake of fire. The greatest act of love we, the Church, can show to the world: to preach, proclaim and publish the gospel. If we cannot, or will not, go and preach the gospel, then send someone in your place by supporting the work of gospel. Support gospel preachers. Support gospel writers. Support gospel television. Support the great gospel work taking place in the earth.

When we preach, proclaim and publish the gospel message, it changes lives forever. The greatest act that breaks the devil's power is to believe the gospel. Faith in the gospel message brings us under the gospel's power: that message weaves its way into every area of the fabric of our lives and binds every power that would hinder its effect in our lives. Whole nations hang in the balance. That's why the gospel must be preached, proclaimed and published. That's why the gospel must be believed. The question is: will we do it? Will we believe the gospel message enough to preach it, proclaim it and publish it to the end of the earth?

"The harvest is great and the workers are few; pray therefore the Lord of the harvest to send workers to His harvest." Lk. 10:2, *ABPE.*

Chapter Eleven

The Gospel Must be Believed

"Go into all the world and preach the Good News to everyone. Anyone who believes and is baptized will be saved. But anyone who refuses to believe will be condemned." Mk. 16:15-16, *NLT*.

The gospel is the greatest message in history. Yet today, many people don't know the gospel. Further, much of the Church fails to grasp the gospel message. Many don't believe the gospel. Many don't believe the gospel enough for it to actually transform their lives. That's why so few people in churches have been set free. We have a problem: a disconnect between what we practice and what we preach. We must be brutally honest with ourselves. We must examine ourselves to see if we in the faith. Paul commanded us to do this. *"Examine yourselves to see if your faith is genuine. Test yourselves. Surely you know that Jesus Christ is among you; if not, you have failed the test of genuine faith."* 2 Cor. 13:5, *NLT*. Are we passing or failing the test of real faith? That's the question.

Many people question their faith. Perhaps, you may examine your own faith, even daily. You question why things happened the way they did in your life. You wonder if God really truly does hear your prayers or care about you. You question whether God loves you. Sometimes, you even look at your life and question whether you are or ever were a believer. You see so much failure. Hear me! Faith doesn't always mean things happen the way we think they should. No. Nor does it mean that things always go our way. Often, things turn out differently than we thought they would. We get caught up in the struggles of life and lose sight of what really matters. When that happens, it's easy to question your faith. That's not the examination of which I'm speaking.

The Faith Tests that Everyone Will Experience

The examination of which I'm speaking is the fruit of real faith. Yes, real faith does have fruit. What is the fruit of real faith in God? I remember in my life when I was failing in life. I was driving my car home after an extremely hard day and I ran out of gas. I had a little money. I had to walk miles to get gas. And I wondered, God why? We have all had days like those, haven't we? In the middle of my struggles, I was reminded by the Holy Spirit of Peter standing next to Jesus after numerous disciples had chosen to walk away from Him due to Jesus' strange new doctrine: *"Except ye eat the flesh of the Son of Man, and drink His blood, ye have no life in you."* Jn. 6:53. Many left. Jesus asked the apostles: *"Will ye also go away?"* Jn. 6:67. Peter responded: *"Lord, to whom shall we go? Thou hast the words of eternal life. And we believe and are sure that Thou art that Christ, the Son of the living God."* Jn. 6:68-69. That's faith.

Faith chooses to stay when everything in you says leave. Faith doesn't base itself on understanding. No, faith is rooted in Christ. Many think real faith is what you confess, and that's part of it. But, real faith originates in the hearts of those who bases everything they believe on the person and work of Christ. Real faith locks onto Jesus. False faith tries to imitate real faith by understanding the principles of faith. We can understand faith and still fail to walk in it. Yet, when we walk in real faith, we truly begin to know who Christ is and what He did for us. That's the separation between real faith and false faith. What I've come to understand over the years is this: the distance we have departed from Christ is the distance we have departed from the faith. To examine ourselves and whether we're in the faith, we must first look at our individual relationship with Christ. That's the first and primary measuring stick of real faith.

Passing the First Test: Hungering for God's Word

Are we hungry for God? Do we read our Bible? Do we pray? Do we have kingdom thinking? Or, are we living for our own "thingdom"? If we're living for our own thingdom and not for Christ's kingdom, then we aren't living a real faith. No, we have a false faith. Further, beyond looking at our relationship with Christ, we must look at the fruit of that relationship. Fruit? Yes, fruit: *"love, joy, peace, longsuffering, gentleness, goodness, faith, meekness, temperance...."* Gal. 5:22. Yes, the fruit of wisdom, which is *"first pure, then peaceable, gentle and easy to be entreated, full of mercy and good fruits, without partiality and without hypocrisy."* James 3:17. We're to be filled with the fruit of righteousness. Phil. 1:11. By the fruit of our lips, we're to give thanks to His Name. Heb. 13:15. And, we're to have the fruit of signs, wonders and miracles. *"People of Israel, listen! God publicly endorsed Jesus the Nazarene by doing powerful miracles, wonders, and signs through Him, as you well know."* Acts 2:22, NLT.

Jesus was examined by God. And, He passed the test. Remember, Christ was led by the Spirit to be tempted by the devil. Lk. 4:1. Christ passed the test. When He passed the test, the devil left Him for a season: *"And Jesus returned in the power of the Spirit into Galilee: and there went out a fame of Him through all the region round about."* Lk. 4:14. Prior to the power is the test. Prior to the promotion is the test. Pass the test. Move to miracles. Fail the test. Repeat the test. That's where most believers live: Live, Fail, Repeat.

Break the cycle! Pass the test. How? By knowing when you're being tested. By knowing how to pass the test. Saints, there's always only one way to pass every test: *"Man shall not live by bread alone, but by every word that proceedeth out of the mouth of God."* Matt. 4:4. You will only overcome if you rely on God's Word to overcome. If you rely on other means, you'll have to take the test again and again and again, until you pass.

God Doesn't Test Your Faith, Satan Does

Your faith will be tested. Does God test our faith? *"No one undergoing a trial should say, 'I am being tempted by God.' For God is not tempted by evil, and He Himself doesn't tempt anyone."* James 1:13, HCSB. No, the devil tests our faith. Satan stands against faith in God. Job faced this test. Job 1:13-19; 2:7-9. Peter faced this test. Lk. 22:31. Paul faced this test. 2 Cor. 12:7; 1 Th. 2:18. We have a real adversary. Peter said, *"Be sober-minded and alert. Your adversary the devil prowls around like a roaring lion, seeking someone to devour."* 1 Pet. 5:8, BSB. That real adversary is seeking to devour you; he is seeking to steal, kill and destroy. Jn. 10:10. The Bible describes Satan as *"roaming throughout the earth, going back and forth on it."* Job 1:7; 2:2. What is he seeking? The devil is looking for anything that's a threat to his kingdom; he wants to stop or hinder every threat to his kingdom. The greatest threat is the seed of the gospel: *"Satan cometh immediately, and taketh away the word that was sown in their hearts."* Mk. 4:15.

Remember, we're in a war. That war has real weapons, real soldiers and real consequences. Where does this war usually take place? In our souls. The enemy seeks to torment our minds. How? By imaginations, knowledge and thoughts. 2 Cor. 10:5. That's the arena where we fight. The weapons we have to fight the devil are: truth, peace, righteousness, faith, hope, love, salvation, prophetic words and every kind of prayer. Eph. 6:18; 1 Th. 5:18. We often fail to use those weapons in spiritual conflicts that are taking place in our lives. When that happens, we lose. But, that isn't God's will. Rather, Scripture teaches, *"[T]hanks be to God, who always leads us in triumph in Christ, and manifests through us the sweet aroma of the knowledge of Him in every place."* 2 Cor. 2:14, NASB.

God wants us to win the very real war we're facing in our lives. That's His will.

Winning the War of the Mind

How do we win? By girding the loins of your mind. *"Wherefore gird up the loins of your mind, be sober, and hope to the end for the grace that is to be brought to you at the revelation of Jesus Christ...."* 1 Pet. 1:13, *WBT*. By being renewed in the spirit of your mind. *"Instead, let the Spirit renew your thoughts and attitudes."* Eph. 4:23, *NLT*. By renewing our minds. Paul taught the Roman believers: *"Don't copy the*

> ### What we think about is what dominates our lives.

behavior and customs of this world, but let God transform you into a new person by changing the way you think. Then you will learn to know God's will for you, which is good and pleasing and perfect." Rom. 12:2, *NLT*. When we think the right thoughts, we get the right results. When we think the wrong thought, we get the wrong results. Bad fruit originates from bad roots. In this imagery, the roots are thoughts. *"For out of the heart come evil thoughts – murder, adultery, sexual immorality, theft, false testimony, slander."* Matt. 15:19, *NLT*.

What we think about is what dominates our lives. We're controlled by what we think, *"[f]or as he thinketh in his soul, so is he."* Prov. 23:7, *DBT*. When we think evil, our lives become dominated by evil. Even seeking to do good, we can be motivated by the devil to do evil. Peter was motivated by good when he said to Jesus: *"Far be it from you, Lord! This shall never happen to you."* Matt. 16:22, *ESV*. But, Jesus knew its source: Satan. And Jesus said, *"Get behind Me, Satan! You are a hindrance to Me. For you are not setting your mind on the things of God, but on the things of Man."* Matt. 16:23, *ESV*. When our minds are consumed by the thoughts of this world, when we start to ask questions like, *"What will we eat? What will we drink? What will we wear?"*, Matt. 6:31, *NLT*, we have left the road of faith for the familiar.

The Road of Faith Versus the Familiar Path

Many men and women throughout history have left the road of faith for the familiar; it's easy to do. Worse yet, we can think we're still on the road of faith. When this happens, we have a choice: 1) Do I return to the road of faith? Or, 2) do I remain on the road of the familiar? When in that place, the only thing that can shake us free from the familiar is confrontation. When Jesus saw the Pharisees ingrained in the familiar, He said to them, *"How horrible it will be for you, scribes and Pharisees! You hypocrites! You are like whitewashed graves that look beautiful on the outside but inside are full of dead people's bones and every kind of impurity."* Matt. 23:27, GWT. But, they couldn't handle it and they killed Him.

How often, rooted in our need to remain in the familiar, the comfortable, we kill those sent to us. Why? Because we refuse to hear the message we need and choose the message we want. Gospel preachers must learn to bring words of comfort and grace as well as words of rebuke and correction. We must stop painting the world with rose-colored glasses. Everything is not okay. People are dying and they have a one-way ticket to hell. But, they don't know it. They have never heard the gospel, or they have left the gospel faith they once had and knew. Recently, Muhammed Ali passed away. But, he chose Islam over Christ. Bad choice! Ali denied the faith he once knew and turned his back on it. Ali needed confrontation. But, he received "love" and admiration. Yet, real love brings correction.

What We Believe Matters

God Himself preached the gospel to Abraham. Abraham and Sarah believed. By them, an entire nation was formed, Israel. That nation received the life-changing message of the gospel embedded in the words of the prophets. But, many missed it. Listen to what Scripture teaches: *"We have heard the same Good News that your ancestors heard. But the message didn't help those who heard it in the past because they didn't believe."* Heb. 4:2, GWT. They knew the Torah but didn't believe its message: *"You study the Scriptures in detail because you think you have the source of eternal life in them. These Scriptures testify on My behalf."* Jn. 5:39, *GWT.* Publishing the Bible isn't enough, neither is reading it. No, it must be believed.

What we believe matters. Today, many have forgotten this all-important message. Right believing matters. Wrong believing must be fixed. Not everyone's interpretation of Scripture is accurate. Correct interpretation of Scripture is vital to the health of the church and to believers. How do we know the difference? Fruit. Real faith has fruit. False faith doesn't. Jude 1:12. No, it has dead works. Heb. 6:1. We are to repent of dead works. That means we must change our mind regarding works that are dead. Dead works always have at their root a false faith. And, good works always have at their root real faith.

Right Faith, Right Words and a Right Heart

Real faith has good works. Jesus said, *"Let your light shine before men in such a way that they may see your good works, and glorify your Father who is in heaven."* Matt. 5:16, *NASB.* We're called to shine: not by what we say or by how good we say it, but by what we do. *"The tasks that the Father gave Me to carry out, these tasks which I perform, testify on My behalf. They prove that the Father has sent Me."* Jn. 5:36, *GWT.* Like Jesus, we have been assigned a specific task. But, often, we don't know what that task is. So, we just do anything rather than searching for the right thing. But, we aren't called to do everything or anything but the right thing. How do we find the right thing? By right believing.

Right believing produces right living. Right living produces right actions. Right actions produce good works. Simple. But, where do we start? By right thinking. We must begin to think the right way about things. To do that, we must have the right words stored in our hearts. I've met so many believers who have the wrong words stored in their hearts. Often, they will talk about the devil. Literally, they glorify and magnify the devil. But, they don't know it. Much of our teaching on spiritual warfare glorifies and magnifies the devil. We have become demon conscious, and we look for demons behind every bush, even burning ones. How foolish!

Once, I was talking to a man, a minister, and he kept on telling me what the devil was doing in his life. Then, when I had had enough, I said to him: "What is God doing?" That caught him off guard, and he stopped for a moment. Then, he went back to telling me what the devil was doing in his life, again. Then, a second time, I said to him: "What is God doing?" Needless to say, I wish I could tell you this story had a happy ending, but it didn't. That man couldn't stop himself: he had to tell everyone what the devil was doing in his life. How sad! A minister of the gospel who was intent on glorifying and magnifying the devil's works. And, what's worse, he didn't even know it. No, he thought he was being spiritual by identifying the devil in his life. I'd rather get rid of the devil. Isn't that what the Bible says? Cast out demons.

False Spirituality, Carnal Thinking and Vain Warfare

The gift of discernment of spirits isn't the gift of suspicion. No, it's an ability to peer into the unseen world and see behind the motives people have for what is really controlling and motivating them – good or evil. That's discernment of spirits. There's a right presence, God, and wrong presence, demons, and we should know both. Knowing where something proceeds is important to our spiritual walk; it will help us stay on the road of faith. Often, we can overcome the enemy by operating in the opposite spirit. When Satan approaches us with greed, we give. When Satan approaches us with anger, we forgive. When Satan comes at us with lust, we crave God's Word. That's how real spiritual warfare is won.

Much of the spiritual warfare being taught in churches today focuses on demons. Genuine teaching on spiritual warfare focuses on God.[12]

---

[12] I would highly recommend the following books on spiritual warfare: *Breaking Demonic Strongholds: Defeating the Lies of Satan,* Don Nori; *Breaking Controlling Powers,* Roberts Liardon; *Territorial Spirits: Practical Strategies for How to Crush the Enemy Through*

I believe the real spiritual battle is inside not outside. In 1989, Francis Frangipane published a wonderful set of books on spiritual warfare, which have become classics: *The Three Battlegrounds* and *Holiness, Truth and the Presence of God.* Both are relevant to spiritual warfare. Both focus on the battleground of the human heart. That's where the very real spiritual battles we fight take place. But, we often miss the fight not knowing that the fight we're fighting is the fight of faith and faith reside in our hearts. Paul encouraged us, *"And fight in the good contest of faith and seize eternal life, to which things you are called, and you have professed a good profession before many witnesses."* 1 Tim. 6:12, *ABPE*.

Learning the Lessons of Faith in Trials by Fire

The real faith is what is often missing among churches and believers today. Like Simon the Sorcerer, many try to conjure up their own faith for profit. Acts 8:9-10. But real faith cannot be bought on the auctions blocks of human achievement. No, it must be purchased in trials by fire. And for that, we must gain experience in those trials. That means we must learn the lessons of faith in the real world of human hardships. What do we do when we're betrayed? Persecuted for our faith? How do we handle slanderous accusations? Where do we turn when the going gets tough? Do we turn to God? Or, do we turn to ourselves? Others? Many fail tests of faith. Job did. Peter did. Moses did. David did. Elijah did. Will you be different?

We're called to be an example to those in the world. Paul taught Titus: *"And you yourself must be an example to them by doing good works of every kind. Let everything you do reflect the integrity and seriousness of your teaching."* Tit. 2:7, *NLT*. Paul taught Timothy: *"Be an example to all believers in what you say, in the way you live, in your love, your faith, and your purity."* 1 Tim. 4:12, *NLT*. How should we example our faith? By our good works. Listen to what James the brother of Jesus said, *"You fool!*

Spiritual Warfare, C. Peter Wagner; T*ruly Free: Breaking the Snares That so Easily Entangle,* Robert Morris; and *The Bondage Breaker,* Neil T. Anderson.

Do you have to be shown that faith which does nothing is useless?" James 2:20, *GWT.* Real faith from right believing produces real results that are easily discernable.

Just Say "NO!" to False and Fruitless Faiths

God doesn't believe in the COEXIST message being taught by many in the Church. CHRISLAM, MORMONISM, BUDDISM, TAOISM, CONFUSCISM and numerous other FALSE religions have no place in the Church. We are not supposed to let everything slide. No, we must have real discernment. Paul said, *"Have nothing to do with the fruitless deeds of darkness, but rather expose them."* Eph. 5:11, *NIV.* But, many today, are unwilling to expose the fruitless works of darkness. Instead, fruitless works are often celebrated in the Church. No, Paul states, *"How can righteousness be a partner with wickedness? How can light live with darkness? What harmony can there be between Christ and the devil? How can a believer be a partner with an unbeliever? And what union can there be between God's temple and idols?"* 2 Cor. 6:14-16, *NLT.* We must leave behind our foolish ways, and works, and thoughts. And, we must step into real faith.

The gospel must be believed. The gospel must be preached. The gospel must be published. Brothers and sisters, there are not many gospels. No, there's one gospel, and that gospel is a life changing message. The gospel is good news: *"All nations will be blessed through you [Abraham]."* Gal. 3:8, *NLT.* That good news is simple: God wants to bless Mankind. God has made provision to bless Mankind. But, that provision can only be found in God's Son. As John says, *"And this is that testimony: God has given us eternal life, and this life is in His Son."* 1 Jn. 5:11, *BSB.* Life is found only in the Son. Anyone, whether prophet, preacher or angel, who claims life can be found in any other place is spreading a false message, a false gospel. Gal. 1:9.

Chapter Twelve

There is a False Gospel

"Let God's curse fall on anyone, including us or even an angel from heaven, who preaches a different kind of Good News than the one we preached to you." Gal. 1:8, *NLT.*

Paul faced many enemies. He wrestled with wild beasts in Ephesus. 1 Cor. 15:32. Paul was shipwrecked. He was beaten. He was murdered. Paul suffered immensely to bring the gospel to the Gentiles. But, Paul's greatest threat didn't come from outside the Church, but rather came from within the Church. Paul faced a false gospel message being preached by false apostles. That false message almost ensnared two of the Church's main leaders, Peter and Barnabus and a host of other believers. Paul stopped it. How? He confronted it. Paul even implies James is the one who allowed this false gospel to permeate the Church. What false gospel? That we still needed to live by the law. In Galatians, Paul clarifies the gospel message as firmly rooted in grace.

The First Century's False Gospel

The gospel we preach is a gospel of grace. But, the false gospel is rooted in keeping the law. That root, fulfilling the demands of the Torah, is a bitter root containing corrupt fruit, for *"[i]f someone obeys all of God's laws except one, that person is guilty of breaking all of them."* James 2:10, *GWT.* By the teachings of the

Torah shall no flesh by justified. Gal. 2:16. *"Not one person can have God's approval by following Moses' Teachings. Moses' Teachings show what sin is."* Rom. 3:20, GWT. So, the false gospel is predicated on keeping the Torah. Put simply, the false gospel says Man can save himself by his own efforts. But, as we know, that's impossible. We all need salvation, which is only available by grace through faith. Eph. 2:8.

Is the law, Moses' Teachings, good or evil? Paul teaches us the law is good when used lawfully: *"We know that Moses' Teachings are good if they are used as they were intended to be used."* 1 Tim. 1:8, GWT. So, the law is good, if used in the right way. What does it mean to use the law legitimately? Paul states clearly, *"by the law is the knowledge of sin."* Rom. 3:20. So, the law is not meant for righteous men and women, but rather, it's meant for sinful men and women: *"For the law was not intended for people who do what is right. It is for people who are lawless and rebellious, who are ungodly and sinful, who consider nothing sacred and defile what is holy, who kill their father or mother or commit other murders. The law is for people who are sexually immoral or who practice homosexuality, or are slave traders, liars, promise breakers, or who do anything else that contradicts the wholesome teaching that comes from the glorious Good News entrusted to me by our blessed God."* 1 Tim. 1:9-11, NLT.

False Jews: Of Abraham But Not in Abraham

Some may ask, Are we not all sinful? Yes, all have sinned and come short of the glory of God. Rom. 3:23. So, how do we separate between men and women who sin/have sinned and sinful men and women? The difference is where the law is located. For sinful men and women, the law is located on the outside. For men and women who sin/have sinned, the law is located on the inside. *"No, a true Jew is one whose heart is right with God. And true circumcision is not merely obeying the letter of the law; rather, it is a change of heart produced by God's Spirit. And a person with a changed heart seeks praise from God, not from people."* Rom. 2:29. There are true Jews and there are false Jews. Rev. 2:9; 3:9. *"For not all who are descended from Israel belong to Israel...."* Rom. 9:6.

Who are those Jews that are false Jews? Those who, *"being ignorant of God's righteousness, and seeking to establish their own [righteousness], have not submitted to the righteousness of God."* Rom. 10:3, *DBT.* In the *DRB,* this verse says they do this *"not knowing the justice of God, and seeking to establish their own, have not submitted themselves to the justice of God."* False Jews refuse to submit to God's righteousness and justice. That righteousness and justice can only be found in God's Son, Jesus Christ. That's the dividing issue. And, it's an issue of faith. What we believe matters? We must believe the right thing – the gospel – whether a natural branch or grafted branch. Rom. 11:20-21.

Does that mean a false Jew can be of the Jewish people? Yes. Does that mean that a person who is a false Jew must remain a false Jew? No. The dividing issue is faith in the Messiah. We believe in the Messiah and as a result of that faith, we are saved. False Jews don't believe in the Messiah and as a result of that unbelief, they are damned, unless they repent of their unbelief. The dividing issue of faith in the Messiah must always be crossed before a person can claim to be a true Jew, whether of Israel or not. And, unless a person believes in the Messiah, they are not a true Jew, even if they are of Israel.

Discerning False Brothers & Sisters: The Gospel is Not Jewish

Today, in the Church, there has been a resurgence of Jewish customs, rituals and language. I understand the desire to understand the customs of Israel, and even to participate in those customs. I love Jewish music and dance, the blowing of the Shofar and the Hora. But, the danger is to believe that in doing Jewish customs, knowing the Jewish language or keeping the Jewish rituals makes us more righteous before God. When this happens, we're in danger of falling from grace. And, that's serious. We shouldn't trifle with Jewish customs, rituals and language as a betterment of our standing before God. No, our sole basis for righteousness before God is Christ.

Paul wrestled with false Jews. False Jews came in secretly to the Early Church to bring believers under the bondage of the law. Paul called those false Jews, false brothers. *"Now this matter arose because of the false brothers with false pretenses who slipped in unnoticed to spy on our freedom that we have in Christ Jesus, to make us slaves."* Gal. 2:4, NET. Paul often faced issues with and experienced danger from false brothers: *"In my frequent journeys, I have been in danger from rivers and from bandits, in danger from my countrymen and from the Gentiles, in danger in the city and the country, in danger on the sea and among false brothers...."* 2 Cor. 11:26, BSB. Paul faced very real dangers from and struggles with false brothers; they were, in fact, Paul's thorn in the flesh.[13]

Power is the differentiator between true apostles and false ones. No power, no apostleship.

What kinds of struggles did Paul face with false brothers? Paul describes this struggle in his letter to the Corinthians: *"For they say 'His letters are authoritative and forcible, but his personal presence is unimpressive, and as for eloquence, he has none.'"* 2 Cor. 10:10, WNT. To paraphrase, false brothers literally said, *"that brother surely can write, but when he speaks, it's boring and unimpressive."* Paul was concerned by what they said: *"I am afraid, however, that just as Eve was deceived by the serpent's cunning, your minds may be led astray from your simple and pure devotion to Christ."* 2 Cor. 11:3, BSB. Paul's concern was justified: *"People who brag like this are false apostles. They are dishonest workers,*

---

[13] Rick Renner has a wonderful teaching series on hidden meanings in Paul's thorn in the flesh. Renner describes Paul's thorn in the flesh as "different groups of people who covertly planned the problems and hassles he frequently faced in the ministry. A special messenger from Satan, perhaps even a demonic angel, had been sent to incite these people against Paul." *Sparkling Gems,* November 9, 2015.

since they disguise themselves as Christ's apostles." 2 Cor. 11:13, *GWT.*

Discerning False Apostles of Christ: Powerless Pretenders

Today, there has been a resurgence in apostolic ministry. Many men and women are calling themselves apostles: *"Many will follow their evil teaching and shameful immorality. And because of these teachers, the way of truth will be slandered."* 2 Pet. 2:2, *NLT.* But, these men and women who claim to be apostles lack the signs of an apostle: *"The true marks of an apostle – signs, wonders, and miracles – were performed among you with great perseverance."* 2 Cor. 12:12, *BSB.* To quote the grandmotherly woman hired by Wendy's, "Where's the beef!" Scripturally, no beef, i.e., no signs wonders and miracles – no apostleship. And, I'm not talking about once and a while. No, Paul continually moved in power. *"If it's the Lord's will, I'll visit you soon. Then, I'll know what these arrogant people are saying and what power they have. God's kingdom is not just talk, it is power."* 1 Cor. 4:19,20, *GWT.*

Power is the differentiator between true apostles and false ones. No power, no apostleship. That power is manifested in signs, wonders and miracles – not just talk. That's how God approves of His messengers. To have God's approval, we must carry His message with the right motives. Having the right message is not enough, we must also have the right heart. Paul said, *"Our message is not about ourselves. It is about Jesus Christ as the Lord. We are your servants for His sake."* 2 Cor. 4:5, *GWT.* That's the Biblical standard for a person named as an apostle. Anything less misses that mark. And, anyone who misses that mark and calls themselves an apostle, is not an apostle of Christ.

Isn't that a high standard? Yes, and rightfully so. Not everyone is called to be an apostle. Nor should anyone who is not an apostle claim to be one: it's dangerous to those who claim to be apostles and those who believe their claim. Paul set this true standard for apostles in Ephesus. Later, Jesus commended the Ephesians who held to the standard set by Paul: *"I know your works, your toil and your patient endurance, and how you cannot bear with those who are evil, but have tested those who call themselves apostles and are not, and found them to be false."* Rev. 2:2, ESV. Notice, Jesus and Paul didn't mince words when it came to identifying those who were false. Why? Because they were enemies to the gospel. How so?

When someone claims to be an apostle, but they are not, they impugn the dignity of that office. Further, their inability to demonstrate the signs of an apostle demean the apostolic ministry. Moreover, they cause the apostolic ministry to be treated as common when it's designed to be uncommon. An apostle is a special ministry in the church, and not everyone is called to function in the apostolic office. In fact, fewer are called into the apostolic office than any other office. Why? Because apostles are designated ambassadors for Christ in the earth; they are given unique authority in the church by virtue of the signs exhibited to establish doctrinal beliefs for large groups of believers. That's how important apostles are to the church. So, when we call everyone apostle, we demean the office and bring it into disrepute.

Paul wrestled with false apostles. Paul didn't mince words about these men and women: *"Such people are false apostles, dishonest workers who are masquerading as apostles of the Messiah. And no wonder, since Satan himself masquerades as an angel of light."* 2 Cor. 11:13-14, ISV. That was his thorn in the flesh. 2 Cor. 12:7. The gospel they preached was false: you must fulfill the law. Paul was incensed by their deception, for it made the genuine gospel of no effect. Gal. 2:21. Christ's death would be in vain if this false gospel was allowed to permeate the Church. Paul exclaimed: *"This false teaching is like a little yeast that spreads through the whole batch of dough!"* Gal. 5:9, NLT. No, God's blessing is reserved for those who accept Christ's completed work by faith – which is a work of grace, and grace alone, *"[f]or by grace are ye saved through faith; and that not of yourselves: it is the gift of God...."* Eph. 2:8.

Recognizing the False Gospels in the Church and World Today

Today, we have many different gospels. Some preach the gospel because they are in it for the money. Others preach the gospel out of selfish ambition, envy and strife. This is nothing new. Paul described to the Philippians: *"Those others do not have pure motives as they preach about Christ. They thus preach with selfish ambition, not sincerely, intending to make my chains more painful to me."* Phil. 1:17, *NLT.* Peter also describes this to the elders in the churches in Pontus, Galatia, Cappadocia, Asia and Bithynia: *"Be shepherds of God's flock that is among you, watching over them not out of compulsion, but because it's God's will; not out of greed, but out of eagerness; not lording it over those entrusted to you, but being examples to the flock."* 1 Pet. 5:2-3, *BSB.* Wrong motives can lead men and women into becoming deceitful workers, false brothers and sisters, even false apostles.

We need to recognize that false gospels are in our midst. Further, we must confront these false gospels by bringing the truth of the true gospel. Unless we know what the true gospel is, preach that gospel and disciple others to do the same, we'll enter a new dark ages. Paul describes this dark ages to the Corinthians: *"But if our gospel be hid, it is hid to them that are lost: In whom the god of this world hath blinded the minds of them which believe not, lest the light of the glorious gospel of Christ, who is the image of God, should shine unto them."* 2 Cor. 4:4. Without the gospel, Mankind is lost and perishing. With the gospel, we thrive. Today, our world needs the gospel more than it ever has. As such, we need the true gospel: Paul's gospel, Peter's gospel, and ultimately, Christ's gospel. That gospel brings salvation to all Mankind.

The real gospel is worth fighting for, and it's worth believing because it brings the salvation that Mankind needs. We cannot survive without it. America will not survive without the gospel. Any person or nation who fails to receive the gospel is missing out on the blessing that the gospel is intended to bring to them. Further, if we lack the truth of the gospel, we will perish. False gospels cause people to perish, hence their devastating and debilitating effect on churches and believers. Where false gospels exist, people will die spiritually. False gospels always produce death. That's their end. Moreover, that's why we must fight against them and protect the Church from them: false gospels bring death. That death always becomes apparent in any ministry where the gospel, true or false, is preached, for a tree is known by its fruit.

What are some false gospels being preached today? As believers, we should know what some of the major errors are in what is being preached. I want to discuss some of them. I'm not going to cover all of them, for that would take too much time and space, is not the focus of this book. As such, I'm focusing here on major false gospels affecting and afflicting believers and the Church today. I hope to present a complete enough list of false gospels to help you understand and identify the signs someone is preaching a false gospel. Where false gospels are preached, money and greed are often the primary motivators, though not always. Other reasons false gospels are preached are control, fearfulness, selfish ambition, foolishness, instability and ignorance.

Universalism. Some preachers teach the universal salvation of Mankind: that all men will be saved. Some even teach that Satan will eventually be saved. This is a false gospel. Major ministers and ministries have preached and continue to preach, this false gospel. To say that all men will be saved is a false gospel. The Bible clearly teaches us that all men will not be saved. In fact, Jesus said that the days prior to His return would be like Noah's day prior to the flood that destroyed Mankind. Factoid: Mankind. Only Noah and his family were saved. This, in and of itself, exposes the deception of Universal Salvation. Mankind was not spared from God's wrath and judgment: *"He did not spare the ancient world when He brought the flood on its ungodly people, but preserved Noah, a preacher of righteousness, among the eight...."* 2 Pet. 2:5, BSB. No, judgment took place, and nearly all of Mankind perished.

Listen to what Jesus said about the time before His return: *"When the Son of Man returns, it will be like it was in Noah's day."* Matt. 24:37, *NLT*. What was it like in Noah's day? Peter tells us what it was like in Noah's day: *"These who from the first were not convinced in the days of Noah when the long-suffering of God commanded that there would be an ark, upon the hope of their repentance, and only eight souls entered it and were kept alive by water."* 1 Pet. 3:20, *ABPE*. The people in Noah's day were given plenty of chance to repent, but they chose otherwise. Thus, they perished in the flood. Jesus describes what it was like in Noah's day: *"People went on eating, drinking, marrying and giving in marriage until the day Noah boarded the ark, and the flood came and destroyed them all."* Lk. 17:27, *HCSB*. When Christ comes, many people will perish in judgment.

I hope you hear me. Jesus said: *"On judgment day many will say to Me, 'Lord! Lord! We prophesied in your Name and cast out demons in your Name and performed many miracles in your Name.' But I will reply, 'I never knew you. Get away from Me, you who break God's laws.'"* Matt. 7:22-23, *NLT*. Jesus is not Santa Claus; He is a real King with a real kingdom, and He expects righteous living by people now, before judgment comes. When judgment comes, it will be too late. Your repentance now opens the door of salvation to you and your house. Only repentance from sin and turning from iniquity to Christ brings salvation. There's no other way. There's no other Name. There's no other Messiah. Jesus is it. Know Jesus, know salvation. No Jesus, no salvation.

Chrislam. One of the more dangerous deceptions that's entered the Church is the mixture of Islam with Christianity. Rick Warren was reported to have "embarked on an effort to heal divisions between evangelical Christians and Muslims by partnering with Southern California mosques and proposing a set of theological principles that includes acknowledging that Christians and Muslims worship the same God."[14]

What is Chrislam? Why is it dangerous? How is Chrislam false? Chrislam was reportedly formed in Nigeria in the 1980's. Its adherents believe in and accept the Bible and Qur'an as Scripture and accept Moses', Jesus' and Muhammed's teachings. Popular speakers have reportedly joined the ranks of those who have accepted, in one form or another, Chrislam. Rick Warren, Glenn Beck, Brian Houston, Richard Schuller, Richard Mouw and Pope Francis have all been accused of embracing Chrislam. Houston and Warren have specifically denied involvement with Chrislam or teachings that promote Chrislam. But, rumors continue to haunt them. And, some of their words, even if misspoken, are concerning to theological leaders. And, they should be. We must not allow confusion to exist in this area.

Chrislam is a false religion espoused by some seeking to build bridges between Jews, Christians and Muslims in the name of peace. It's a composite religion containing elements of Judaism, Christianity and Islam. Adherents celebrate Moses, Jesus and Mohammed, as prophets. And, adherents accept the teachings of all three, celebrate the holidays of all three and seek to build peace between all three. That's the essence of Chrislam, and it's dangerous to Christianity. We cannot have a mixture of Judaism, Christianity and Islam. To the early apostles, even a mixture of Judaism and Christianity was unacceptable. Paul didn't tolerate it. Gal. 2:11. And, neither should we: we must know what we believe, why we believe it and how important it is for the salvation of Mankind.

Islam, the second largest religion on earth, is not compatible with Christianity. Islam was founded by Mohammed in 600 AD. Mohammed purportedly received revelations that he claimed were from the angel, Gabriel. Mohammed wrote those revelations in a

---

[14] "Rick Warren Builds Bridge to Muslims," *The Orange County Register*, Feb. 26, 2012, http://www.ocregister.com/articles/muslims-341669-warren-saddleback.html.

book called the Quran. Islam teaches that Jesus Christ was a prophet. But, Islam also teaches that Allah has so son. That's one the major tenets of their faith. But, Christianity's major tenet is that Jesus Christ is God's Son. What does that mean? The God of Christians is not the god of Muslims. So, there can be no common ground between Christianity and Islam. A common faith is not possible between them. Christians must love men and women involved in the deception of Islam. Christians must seek to bring them out of the deception of Islam. But, Christians must never bow to the spirit of Islam.

We must never sacrifice our faith on the altar of expedience. No, we must be bold. Christ is not just one among many. No, Jesus said, *"I am the way, the truth, and the life. No one comes to the Father, except through Me."* Jn. 14:6, *WEB.* Peace between Judaism, Christianity and Islam is not possible. Islam opposes the gospel. We're

> **We must never sacrifice our faith on the altar of expedience.**

called to preach the gospel. We can serve Muslims. We can befriend them and love them for the purpose of showing Christ's love. But, we must not – no, we cannot water down the gospel for the sake of peace. The gospel is what sets men and women who are bound free, including those who are bound in the religions of Judaism and Islam. We may be the only hope they have to find freedom.

Globalism. Humanism has gone global. Humanists vary in what they believe, but the general thought patterns are in the primacy of Mankind without the need for the divine. Humanists contain a diverse group of individuals, from hedonism to atheism to Unitarianism. In the theater of humanism, atrocities reign. Nazism is the product of humanism taken to the extreme. Genocides occur when men place themselves above age-honored wisdom from our predecessors. Today, the gospel of globalism has permeated whole societies, including American society. And, it has created an environment rife with strife, a powder keg of human emotion. Whole nations are suffering under the globalist philosophy, including America.

In the Hollywood movie, *Deep Impact*, we see the impending doom of an asteroid, and Mankind builds a spaceship named, The Messiah, that's intended to, and does, save humanity. Humanists rely on the reason of Man for the salvation of Man: Mankind can think its way out of every problem. How? Greater choice. Greater freedoms. Less religion. Population control. Climate control. More Education. More government. More laws. Removal of national boundaries. Removal of moral restraint. Redistribution of wealth. Such reasoned moves are portrayed as intended to save the planet from destruction and prevent or restrain Mankind's eventual extinction.

The gospel of globalism portrays religion as weak, moralism as relative and evolution and climate change as fact. In the whole community of Mankind, human primacy can be found: it takes a village to raise a child, not parents. But, that primacy requires selection of the best and brightest: not everyone is welcome in the global community. Some are unwanted. Some are nuisances to the human community, which requires their neutralization or extermination. Sacrifices must be made in the name of the global community. Globalists seek control over external factors that could bring about the elimination of Man on the spaceship, Earth. For that reason, Globalists seek to bring Mankind under one government: one law to rule them all.

Globalism has noble goals but ignores original sin. Mankind cannot save itself from sin. God is real. Satan exists. Evil originates from the human heart, and often with the best of intentions. The road to hell is paved with good intentions. Lord Acton stated Man's parameters: "Power tends to corrupt and absolute power corrupts absolutely." Laws are being deliberately changed under the guise of progressivism and conservatism for the purpose of furthering globalist ideologies. Corporate and community cultures introduced to further globalist agendas. Rules of decency predicated on religious conviction challenged and eradicated. Christianity and Biblical values marginalized. The truths contained in the Bible is globalism's greatest threat, and globalist leaders know it and have sought to eliminate those truths from our conversation. And, it will increase.

Judaism. Judaism is not compatible with Christianity. Judaism opposes the gospel. We're called to preach the gospel. What is the gospel? *"In you, Abraham, shall all the nations of the earth be blessed."* Gal. 3:8. Aren't the Jewish people Abraham's children? No! Abraham's children are those who have accepted Jesus Christ as the Messiah. Aren't the Jewish people descended from Abraham? Yes, but their lineage is not the basis for being Abraham's children. To become Abraham's child, Jewish people must believe Jesus is their Messiah. Abraham's children can only found in the Messiah, whether Jew or Gentile. And, Judaism denies that Jesus Christ was/is the Messiah. Further, Judaism denies Jesus Christ's resurrection. Judaism trusts in the Torah for salvation. But, salvation cannot be found in the Torah. Mankind cannot keep the law. The law wasn't given to save Mankind; it was given to restrain Mankind's sin. By the law, we obtain knowledge of sin. *"The law simply shows us how sinful we are."* Rom. 3:20, *NLT*.

Mormonism. Mormonism is a false religion. It was founded by Joseph Smith. Smith purportedly received an angelic visitation from the angel, Moroni, where he was shown a golden book of revelation. That book was later captured by him in his writings, *The Book of Mormon.* Today, Mormonism has grown to include nearly 20 million adherents worldwide. What we must know about Mormons is this: Mormons are not Christians. Mormons do not believe what Christians believe. Nor do Mormons believe in the same Jesus Christ in which Christians believe. Mormons believe many things that Christians do not and should not believe about Jesus Christ:

1) Jesus and Lucifer were brothers,
2) Prior to creation, God was a man who became God, and
3) Mormons believe they can become gods.

Each belief precludes Mormonism from being a just another Christian sect. Mormons are not a Christian sect, but a false religion predicated on beliefs that are diametrically opposed to Christ's teachings.

Other False Gospels. There are numerous other false gospels.

1) The gospel of "once saved, always saved": believers who are once saved can habitually sin and still enter into eternal life.
2) The gospel of license, which is presented under the guise of grace: holiness is optional and unnecessary for salvation.
3) The gospel of greed: "money answers all things" and "give more to get more."
4) The seeker sensitive gospel: we must change the way we "do church" to reach our culture.
5) The gospel of inclusion: everyone is already saved, which is nothing more than Universalism repackaged.

There are numerous others. In essence, false gospels always have several things in common: they deny, in whole or in part:

1) Jesus Christ's deity,
2) Jesus Christ's humanity,
3) Jesus Christ's necessity,
4) Jesus Christ's supremacy,
5) Jesus Christ's legitimacy,
6) Jesus Christ's relevance, and
7) Jesus Christ's Body.

Scripture teaches us that we can be deceived: *"But evil people and impostors will flourish. They will deceive others and will themselves be deceived."* 2 Tim. 3:13, *NLT*. We can even deceive ourselves by our knowledge of Scripture into believing that we know the Scripture: *"Do not merely listen to the word, and so deceive yourselves. Do what it says."* James 1:22, *NIV.* Eve was deceived in the beginning: *"And it was not Adam who was deceived by Satan. The woman was deceived, and sin was the result."* 1 Tim. 2:14, *NLT.* Since the fall of Adam and Eve in the Garden of Eden, Mankind has fallen into even greater delusions. And, Christ warned us of this possibility: *"Be careful not to let anyone deceive you."* Matt. 24:4, *GWT.* Paul also warned us of this possibility: *"Don't be fooled by those who try to excuse these sins, for the anger of God will fall on all who disobey Him."* Eph. 5:6, *NLT.* And John, the Revelator, also warned us: *"My little children, let no man lead you astray: he that doeth righteousness is righteous, even as he is righteous...."* 1 Jn. 3:7, *ESV.*

Often, believers and church leaders have good reasons for their actions. Building bridges is good, but not at the gospel's expense. No minister should allow confusion to exist as to what they believe. That is unacceptable for gospel preachers. While political leaders may build political bridges between different faiths for the purpose of establishing common ground, gospel preachers must never compromise the gospel for the sake of peace. We can build friendships with men and women who are Jewish, Muslim, Hindu, Buddhist, Taoist or other religious philosophy, but we must never allow the gospel to be cheapened by those relationships. And, I'm concerned that many gospel preachers have sold out, or will sell out, for the sake of peace. We must continually guard against deception, especially in our own hearts. There is a false gospel.

Chapter Thirteen

The Gospel has Enemies

The gospel has very real enemies. We must know those enemies: who they are, what they believe and why they are enemies. We cannot be ignorant. Some people don't want the gospel message to be heard. The Bible describes men and women, including former ministers, who became enemies of the cross and enemies to the gospel. To dilute and/or pollute the gospel, those enemies introduce false gospels.

In Chapter Twelve, I described some but not all of the false gospels being presented in our day. Those false gospels are counterfeit messages intended to divert people from the true gospel message to prevent it from being heard. Satan introduces false gospels in an attempt to dilute, disparage, and ultimately, destroy the gospel's impact on and in our world. Peter warns all believers: *"Be clear-minded and alert. Your opponent, the devil, is prowling around like a roaring lion, looking for someone to devour."* 1 Pet. 5:8, ISV.

Who is Satan? What Does the Bible Say About Him?

We're first introduced to Satan in the book of Job. Job 1:6-12; 2:1-7. Job is likely the oldest book in the Bible and has a likely date of taking place between 2100 BC to 1700 BC. In Job, we see the devourer prowling in the earth seeking to devour his prey. We also see Job become Satan's prey. We see the thief at work. We gain a behind-the-scenes look at the invisible world around us, and we see how that invisible world interacts with our world. Job is attacked by Satan. That attack is ascribed to God. But, God wasn't behind Job's suffering. No, Job's suffering was clearly caused by Satan. Peter was likely referring to Job when he wrote the above passage. Peter was warning us that we have an adversary. Please let that sink in. You have an adversary. I have an adversary. We have an adversary.

In sharing his thoughts with the Corinthians, Paul said, *"I don't want Satan to outwit us. After all, we are not ignorant about Satan's scheming."* 2 Cor. 2:11, *GWT.* Satan is our adversary and he has real schemes, plots and plans, that he is implementing in our day. We must be aware of his plans. The Bible teaches us: *"The god of this age has blinded the minds of unbelievers, so that they cannot see the light of the gospel that displays the glory of Christ, who is the image of God."* 2 Cor. 4:3, *NIV.* Blinded minds and hardened hearts are the devil's work. When we see ignorance, we must recognize its source. Or, we'll be tempted to look at the person. And in doing that, we'll miss the real enemy: the tempter, devil, accuser, serpent and dragon. Interestingly, dragon is in the original Greek and comes from the Greek word, **drakón,** which has as its root word, **derkomai,** which means, "to look." We must know who our adversary is.

What does the Bible reveal about Satan? The Bible reveals that Satan was heavily involved in the decisions behind Jesus' crucifixion: *"None of the rulers of this age understood it [God's mysterious and hidden wisdom], for if they had, they would not have crucified the Lord of glory."* 1 Cor. 2:8, *NIV.* The Bible shows us how Satan motivated Herod, Judas, Pilate, Caiaphas and a host of others. Satan entered Judas for the express purpose of killing Jesus: *"When Judas had eaten the bread, Satan entered into him. Then Jesus told him, 'Hurry and do what you're going to do.'"* Jesus told Peter that Satan had targeted him: *"Simon, Simon, look out! Satan has asked to sift you like wheat."* Lk. 22:31, *HCSB.*

Hymenaeus and Philetus were *"taken captive by him [Satan] at his will."* 2 Tim. 2:26. Paul warned Timothy about placing the wrong men and women in positions of leadership: *"Neither should he be a young disciple, lest he be lifted up and would fall into the judgment of Satan; He ought to have an excellent testimony from outsiders, lest he fall into shame and into the trap of Satan."* 1 Tim. 3:7, *ABPE*. We are to have high standards for church leadership.

Cleansing Today's Church of Fakes, Flakes, Frauds, Fables and Fictions

Much of the Church has forgotten Paul's admonitions to Timothy. Today, church leaders are often chosen by charisma rather than character, or by cult and celebrity rather than long-term impact based on fruit. Further, no place is given for correction. Today, many church leaders are unteachable. They are unwilling to learn from others. Many believers don't honor men and women of God, and in some cases, for good reason. Today, many church leaders have fallen into disrepute before the world's eyes. Accusations abound. Real leadership is sparse. Believers follow inept leaders who fail simple tests, as outlined in Scripture. Prophetic accuracy is rarely tested. Apostolic authority rarely questioned. Apostolic signs rarely shown. Pastors and preachers behave more like hirelings. Greed. Lust. Pride. Selfish ambition. All are common in churches today. And, determination of actual authority rarely allowed or shown. The Church today has severe problems that must be rectified by a return to sound doctrine.

But, many believers don't want doctrine or teaching. Instead, it's all about the worship. The better the singing, the better the service. We have music. So does the world. We have motivation. So does the world. We have preaching and teaching. So does the world. And, the world has more: better music, better movies, better books and better leaders. But, the world doesn't have the gospel. The Church has, or is supposed to have, the gospel. That's what sets us apart from the world – our message. But, we have not known our message, the gospel. That's why I wrote this book. We've lost our message due to false gospels being presented by enemies of the gospel in the name of the true gospel. We have much fanfare and little actual fire. That must change. To do that, the pure gospel message must be rediscovered. And, the gospel's enemies exposed: *"Take no part in the worthless deeds of evil and darkness; instead, expose them."* Eph. 5:11, NLT.

Today, many are doing evil inside and outside the Church. We have false prophets, false apostles and false teachers that believers line up to see. Prophetic words abound. But, prophetic accuracy and authority are dismal. Not everyone who calls themselves a prophet is one. Not everyone who claims to be an apostle is one. Not everyone who has the title of pastor is one. Not everyone who claims to be of Christ is a Christian. John said, *"Beloved, do not believe every spirit, but test the spirits to see whether they are from God, because many false prophets have gone out into the world."* 1

Many are crying out for mercy, but few are allowing their hearts to be prepared to receive that mercy by repentance.

Jn. 4:1, NASB. In that passage of Scripture, the Greek word for false prophets is *"pseudoprophétes,"* which means, false prophets. John taught his disciples to watch out for false prophets. Peter did the same. 2 Pet. 2:1-3. Peter said false teachers would *"cleverly teach destructive heresies and even deny the Master who bought them."* 2 Pet. 2:1, NLT. Other translations say heresies will be secretly introduced. Why? *"In their greed, these teachers will exploit you with fabricated stories."* 2 Pet. 2:3, NIV.

I'm very concerned about all the stories I hear being shared in the Church. I'm skeptical by nature. And, I think that's a good thing. I check for fruit. The Bible teaches us to look for fruit: *"You will know them by what they produce. 'People don't pick grapes from thornbushes or figs from thistles, do they?'"* Matt. 7:16, GWT. The obvious answer, No. Good fruit is a requirement for true prophets. We cannot claim to be true when our fruit shows us to be false. We need a reality check. We need a Bible tune-up. We need to look under the hood to see what's there: good fruit or bad fruit. Why? *"A good tree can't produce bad fruit, and a bad tree can't produce good fruit."* Lk. 6:43, *NLT.*

Mass Repentance is Needed by Today's Church

I have been a believer for nearly 30 years. I began functioning in the prophet's office of prophet in 1991, 25 years ago. I have witnessed the rise and fall of numerous ministers and movements. I was saved immediately prior to the PTL scandal in the late 1980's. I watched Jerry Falwell step in to try to save PTL. I have also heard of numerous believers who were deeply wounded by the discipleship movement that took place in the 1970's. I have witnessed prophetic authority diminished by a deluge of inaccurate and, in many cases, false prophecies. I have witnessed major leaders involved in major scandals: Jim Baker, Jimmy Swaggart, Oral Roberts, Ted Haggard, Carlton Pearson, Clarence McClendon, Todd Bentley and others. I have been around the block. I have seen things taking place in the church that ought not to take place. Discernment is lacking and doctrine ignored. Biblically-based teaching is hard to find. Prophetic leadership is rare. Apostolic leaders rarer. Ministers regularly make merchandise of believers. Money is exalted and selfish ambition flouted. We need mass repentance.

Tragically, many ministers, some through ignorance and others by scheme, have become enemies of the very gospel they preach. Often, those same ministers don't even know the depth of their sin. Further, those ministers think God will continue to wink at their sins. But, judgment always comes. Peter warned: *"The time has come for the judgment to begin, and it will begin with God's family. If it starts with us, what will be the end for those who refuse to obey the good news of God?"* 1 Pet. 4:17, *GWT.* Many are crying out for mercy, but few are allowing their hearts to be prepared to receive that mercy by repentance. Instead, rebellion reigns. The spirit of lawlessness is in the world and the church. And, *"the mystery of lawlessness is already at work...."* 1 Th. 2:7, HCSB. Many believers' hearts are becoming cold due to that lawlessness. Jesus said, *"And because lawlessness is to be multiplied, the love of the many will grow cold."* Matt. 24:12, BLB. In the midst of this hell, these words stand tall: *"I will build My congregation, and the powers of hell will not conquer it."* Matt. 16:18, ISV.

Removing Idols and Breaking Religious Bondages

In that building process, much is required, including the tearing down of all that opposes and exalts itself against God. Idols are not allowed in Christ's Church. We have too many Dagons in the house of God. And, many will start to cry, *"We can't keep the Ark of the God of Israel here any longer! He is against us! We will all be destroyed along with Dagon, our god."* 1 Sam. 5:7, NLT.

Jesus said, *"Every plant not planted by My Heavenly Father will be uprooted...."* Matt. 15:13, NLT. And, believe me, to do that, Jesus will *"uproot and tear down, to destroy and demolish..."* all that opposes and exalts itself against Him. Jer. 1:10, HCSB. The Church has many false gospels and much false teaching, which we must no longer tolerate. It's time to get our houses and churches in order. Due to false gospels and false teachings, many people, including believers and ministers, are held in bondage. Christ came to set the captives free. First, from foolishness. Bondage to religious traditions should be abhorred, and expunged. How? Truth. That's the only thing that can bring freedom. Freedom begins when and where truth starts.

That's what we need in this hour – truth. But, as Pilate asked Jesus, *"What is truth?"* Jn. 18:38. Pilate, looking straight into the eyes of truth, did not recognize truth; he ignored it. And, that's what many are trying to do in our day. But, truth always comes to the surface. *"There is nothing hidden, which shall not be openly seen; nor anything secret, which shall not be known and come into the light of day."* Lk. 8:17, *WNT*. When Jesus made this statement, He wasn't speaking allegorically, metaphorically or hyperbolically, He was speaking truth. That truth is this: everything is going to come into the light. Why? *"[W]hoever does what is true comes to the light, so that it may become evident that his actions have God's approval."* Jn. 3:21, *HCSB*. And, we need a healthy dose of truth to counteract the lies permeating our churches.

Purging the Church of Hell's Leaven

"I am the way, and the truth, and the life. No one comes to the Father unless by Me." Jn. 14:6, *DBT*. Jesus' declaration stands against every other religion that seeks to claim the souls of men. No other religion is true and any religion, no matter where it originates, is not of Him. No, false religions are enemies to the gospel. And, false teachings and false teachers, false pastors, false apostles and false prophets are enemies to the gospel. These are very real enemies to the gospel and must be understood to be such. We cannot and should not enter into agreements with that which is false. *"What agreement has the temple of God with idols?"* 2 Cor. 6:16, *ESV*. *"Do two walk together unless they have agreed to do so?"* Amos 3:3, *NIV*. Any agreement with idols is anathema: neither church leaders nor believers should enter into agreements on matters of faith with those who oppose the gospel. Why? Because it dilutes and pollutes our message. Paul's example in this matter is instructive:

> *"One day as we were going to the place of prayer, we were met by a slave girl with a spirit of clairvoyance, a who earned a large income for her masters by fortune-telling. This girl followed Paul and the rest of us, shouting, 'These men are servants of the Most High God, who are proclaiming to you the way of salvation.' She continued this for many days. Eventually Paul grew so aggravated that he turned and said to the spirit, 'In the Name of Jesus Christ I command you to come out of her!' And the spirit left her at that very moment."* Acts 16:16-18, *BSB*.

Paul didn't allow an evil spirit to hijack God's work and neither should we. When we introduce falsity into the church, that leaven begins to leaven the whole. *"This false teaching is like a little yeast that spreads through the whole batch of dough!"* Gal. 5:9, NLT. Paul sharply rebuked the Corinthians for allowing sin to permeate the church: *"Your boasting about this [the sexual sin of a man sleeping with his father's wife] is terrible. Don't you realize that this sin is like a little yeast that spreads through the whole batch of dough?"* 1 Cor. 5:6, NLT. Paul's response to this sin: *"Get rid of the old 'yeast' by removing this wicked person from among you. Then you will be like a fresh batch of dough made without yeast, which is what you really are."* 1 Cor. 5:7, NLT. Sin is serious as hell, and it should be; false gospels bring demonic bondages. False ministers spread false gospels; they are enemies of the gospel.

Remaining Faithful to Christ's Doctrine

To overcome false gospels, we need pure unadulterated truth. Jesus prayed: *"Use the truth to make them holy. Your words are truth."* Jn. 17:17, GWT. And, *"If you hold to My teaching, you are really My disciples. Then you will know the truth, and the truth will set you free."* Jn. 8:32, NIV. In the King James version, it says, *"If ye continue in My word...."* We can only become disciples as we hold to Christ's teachings. To hold to Christ's teachings, we must continue in His Word. That's how true disciples are made. Disciples are disciples because they learn. Disciples follow; they don't lead. But, many today want to lead rather than follow. Jesus is looking for disciples, and disciples are followers. That's where the apostles started – as disciples. Then, they were promoted. Faithful disciples are promoted. Unfaithful disciples are demoted. Simple.

Many believers are looking at what it takes to be a minister of the gospel. All ministers start as disciples, whether called into the fivefold ministry or not. Disciples learn. They follow. They grow. They remain faithful. They stay planted. They aren't easily moved. When things get tough, they don't leave. No, they stay. That's what the requirement is for the ministry – faithfulness. Paul instructed Timothy in regards to choosing elders: *"The things which you have heard from me in the presence of many witnesses, entrust these to faithful men who will be able to teach others also."* 2 Tim. 2:2, NASB. Moses was chosen because of his faithfulness. Heb. 3:2. Abraham was chosen because of his faithfulness: *"For I know him, that he will command his children and his household after him, and they will keep the way of the LORD, to do justice and judgment; that the LORD may bring upon Abraham that which He hath spoken of him."* Gen. 18:19, WBT. Christ Himself was chosen because he was faithful; he was, in fact, more faithful than any other man or woman, ever. Heb. 3:2.

> **To overcome false gospels, we need pure unadulterated truth.**

Self-promotion is the Seed of False Doctrine

Paul considered faithfulness a necessary quality for leadership. Ministers, including their wives, were required to be faithful. Faithful to sound doctrine and what they had learned. To be a good minister, leaders and their wives are required to be *"inwardly feeding on the lessons of the faith and of the sound teaching of which you have been, and are, so close a follower."* 1 Tim. 4:6, WNT. In other translations, that Scripture says, *"nourished in the words of faith and of sound doctrine."* We need sound doctrine. To have sound doctrine, we must rightly divide the word of truth. That right division always looks to whom the teaching glorifies. Paul said of himself: *"Our message is not about ourselves. It is about Jesus Christ as the Lord. We are your servants for His sake."* 2 Cor. 4:5, GWT. That's where all ministry begins. True teaching starts with Him. False teaching is about self-promotion. Jesus said, *"How can ye believe, who receive honor one from another, and seek not the honor that cometh from God only?"* Jn. 5:44, WBT.

A servant doesn't seek his own. How do we know if a man or woman is serving God? We know them by their fruit: their words and their actions. Jesus said true servants were instructed to say this: *"In the same way, when you obey Me you should say, 'We are unworthy servants who have simply done our duty.'"* Lk. 17:10, *NLT.* Today, we have many who are not saying what they were taught to say. Is it any wonder why false doctrine abounds? We aren't doing what Jesus said. Instead, we're doing our own thing. Then, in possibly the greatest insult we could hurl at God, we claim it was Him who told us to do what we did. We say what Frank Sinatra sang, "I did it my way." Falsity begins by doing things our way. Like Burger King, false leaders tend to say, "You can have it your way." While this may work for Burger King, it doesn't work for the King. And, I'm not speaking about Elvis. No, Jesus is the master and we're called to be His disciples. We are to do the kingdom His way. And, bluntly, we cannot serve Him if we will not follow Him.

Discipleship: Christ's Calling to Today's Church

That's what happened to the twelve called as apostles. Jesus invited them to follow Him: *"Follow Me, and I will make you fishers of men."* Matt. 4:19, *ESV.* Many did, but not all. Then, those who followed Him learned the gospel of the kingdom from Him. How? By listening and learning from Jesus: *"He opened His mouth and began to teach them...."* Matt. 5:2, *NASB.* Jesus taught the gospel to His disciples, the twelve. We see Christ explaining the gospel of the kingdom to His disciples in the Sermon on the Mount. Matt. 5:2-7:27; Lk. 6:20-49. Then, He set apart certain disciples, twelve apostles, and He ordained them to preach the gospel and empowered them to demonstrate the gospel: *"He gave them power against unclean spirits, to cast them out, and to heal all manner of sickness and all manner of disease."* Matt. 10:1. Why is this important? Because power and authority are given by Christ to those who are disciples. Disciples, first. Then, apostles or prophets or pastors or evangelists or teachers or any number of other ministry assignments given by Christ. But, discipleship is first and foremost.

What does it take to be Christ's disciple? Jesus plainly said, *"You cannot become My disciple without giving up everything you own."* Lk. 14:33, *NLT*. But, some will say, "that's too hard!" Others will say, "Jesus didn't really mean that we need to give up everything; it was allegorical." What?! Yes, Jesus meant what He said, said what He meant, and expects what He said from us, His disciples. What does He expect? Total commitment and complete sacrifice. Wow! Some will say, "I'm not sure I can do that." I understand. Good. That means you have just understood your first lesson in Christ's school of discipleship: We cannot fulfill Christ's commands in our own strength.

The second lesson is like the first: we cannot fulfill Christ's commands in our own strength, but we can fulfill His commands by His Spirit. The Bible plainly teaches: *"Not by might, nor by power, but by My Spirit, says the LORD of hosts."* Zech. 4:6, *ESV*. "By My Spirit" is not just a catch phrase. No, it's a living reality for us. Jesus said to us: *"For apart from Me, you can do nothing."* Jn. 15:5, *NLT*. Jesus said of Himself, *"I can do nothing on My own."* Jn. 5:30, *NLT*. Jesus didn't do what He did in His own strength, and we cannot do what we're called to do in our own strength. We rely on Christ, as Jesus relied on the Father. The Bible teaches us: *"A disciple is not greater than his teacher, but everyone when fully trained will be like his teacher."* Lk. 6:40, *NET*.

The third lesson is corollary to the first and second: A real disciple doesn't try, he does. To quote Yoda from the popular movie, *Star Wars: The Empire Strikes Back*: "Do. Or do not. There is no try." Long before Yoda, Jesus' mother Mary said, *"Whatever He tells you, do it."* Jn. 2:5, *NET*. Now, we know where Nike got its slogan, "Just do it!" Discipleship is about doing; it's not about trying. We cannot try to be disciples. No, we're either disciples or we're not disciples. That's the crux of being a disciple: we learn, we grow, we do. What do we learn? What the teacher teaches. How do we grow? By following the instructions given by the teacher. How do we do? We just do. Or, we don't. Sink or swim. That's it.

John G. Lake: An Apostolic Example for Today's Church

One of my favorite ministers is John G. Lake. Lake learned much from Alexander Dowie. Dowie learned what he learned by revelation and perspiration. Dowie learned that Christ was a healer by revelation. One day, he read the passage in Acts 10:38: *"How God anointed Jesus of Nazareth with the Holy Ghost and with power: who went about doing good and healing all that were oppressed of the devil; for God was with Him."* Dowie believed all sickness was of the devil. Dowie would literally rip tumors off people in the Name of Jesus, and they came out roots and all. Lake had family members who were sick, and he brought them to Dowie's healing homes in Chicago, Illinois. Lake's family members were healed. Lake joined Dowie for a season, and he learned. One day, Lake was critical of Dowie. Dowie responded: "When you have done what I have done, you can criticize me, but for now, follow me." Lake did, and he learned. Years later, over a five-year period, Lake founded 500 churches in South Africa. After that, Lake moved to Seattle, Washington. While there, Lake had 100,000+ persons who were healed – verified healings.

Lake used Jesus' method to train his Bible school students: Sink or Swim. Lake would send his Bible school students to the homes of those who were sick and infirm. For what purpose? To heal them. In Lake's mind, healing wasn't optional. No, the sick were healed, always. As Lake sent out his students, he would say to them: "Don't come back until they're healed!" Lake knew healing was God's gift to Mankind. Lake taught this, and he expected it. Lake wanted his students to expect it. Lake taught them the healing ministry by hands-on training, and his students learned fast if they wanted to continue in Bible school. While some of us may look at Lake's training methods as harsh, few of us have ever had his results. We have much to learn. We must become disciples, first. Then, we can become teachers.

Letting Go and Holding On

Christ was the Father's disciple. Jesus learned everything He knew from the Father. He said, *"I can guarantee this truth: The Son cannot do anything on His own. He can do only what He sees the Father doing. Indeed, the Son does exactly what the Father does."* Jn. 5:19,20, GWT. We're called to be Christ's disciples. How? By letting go of all we own. That's the first step. But, we cannot take that step in our own strength. No, we must rely on the power of the Holy Spirit. That's the second step. To accomplish this, we just have to do it. There's no try in disciple, just do. How do we do? Jesus said, *"If any man will come after Me, let him deny himself, and take up his cross, and follow Me."* Matt. 16:24, WBT.

Further, on letting go, we must learn to hang on. What?! Yes, Jesus moves quickly and we must hold on to Him. Jesus moved too quickly for His disciples. Often, Jesus would literally throw them in the water and say, *"Come."* Matt. 14:29. Peter did. But, then he doubted. That's how discipleship works. We learn by doing. Jesus said to Peter: *"Follow Me, and I'll make you fishers of people!"* Mk. 1:17, ISV. Jesus does the making. We do the following. We cannot make ourselves His disciples. Neither can we make ourselves apostles. Jesus makes us. First, into disciples. Then, into what He wants us to be. How does Christ make us? He teaches us. He trains us. He guides us. He instructs us. He directs us. And, He expects us to follow Him in this process.

To follow Christ means there are times when we'll go into places we would rather not go. Christ will send His disciples into dangerous and difficult places: *"For this reason, I am sending you prophets and wise men and experts in the law, some of whom you will kill and crucify, and some you will flog in your synagogues and pursue from town to town...."* Matt. 23:34, NET. Sometimes, being a disciple means doing things that we don't want to do or going places we don't want to go. Sometimes, it means eating or drinking or sitting down with people that we don't like. That can be stretching to the human will and ego. But, to be His disciples, we must be willing to be stretched. And please understand, that stretching process can take place over months, years or decades and lifetimes.

God's Process: Times of Temptation, then Promotion or Demotion

Why do we need to be stretched? Because each of us will be tempted. Christ was tempted. What was He tempted to do? By whom was He tempted? In Matthew 4:1-10, we see Christ's temptations by the devil. The Greek word for devil is *diabolos. Diabolos* comes from the Greek word *diaballó,* which means to slander, complain of, accuse, and implies malice, even if true. To secular Greeks, the word *diabolos* meant to backbite and lay charges against someone with the intent of bringing them down or destroying them. Christ was tempted by Satan in three primary areas:

1) to disbelieve in His calling,
2) to misuse and/or abuse His calling, and
3) to turn from His Father's calling to Satan's calling.

Satan tempted Christ by saying to Him, *"If you be the Son of God...."* Matt. 4:3,6, *AKJV*. Satan tempted Christ by saying to Him, *"It is written...."* Matt. 4:6. Satan tempted Christ by saying, *"All these things will I give thee, if Thou wilt fall down and worship me."* Matt. 4:9. Like Christ, and in exactly the same areas, we'll be tempted. There's no escaping it.

How we handle our times of temptation determines our place and position of promotion in God's kingdom. The reward of being a disciple is promotion. We cannot and will not be promoted unless we become disciples. And, our place and position of promotion is determined by the quality of our discipleship: *"The [authority] to reward someone does not [come] from the east, from the west, or [even] from the wilderness. God alone is the judge. He punishes one person and rewards another."* Ps. 75:6,7, *GWT*. That's why it's important to become a disciple: we want to be promoted into better places and positions in God's kingdom.

Yes, God promotes. He also demotes. How does God judge? He reviews our discipleship record, especially how we act and react in times of testing. God asks the question: "Were you faithful?" In His discipleship lessons to the apostles, Jesus said, *"Whoever can be trusted with very little can also be trusted with a lot. Whoever is dishonest with very little is dishonest with a lot."* Lk 16:10, *GWT*. Jesus taught His disciples: *"The master was full of praise. 'Well done, My good and faithful servant. You have been faithful in handling this small amount, so now I will give you many more responsibilities. Let's celebrate together!'"* Matt. 25:21, *NLT*. Temptations create opportunities for us to fall or rise.

Christ was promoted after temptation. After His greatest temptation – the cross – Christ was promoted to the highest place: *"God elevated Him to the place of highest honor and gave Him the Name above all other names...."* Phil. 2:9, *NLT*. By doing what He saw the Father do, Christ turned the negative of the cross into a positive: *"For the joy set before Him, He endured the cross, scorning its shame, and sat down at the right hand of the throne of God."* Heb. 12:2, *NIV*. Christ did not enjoy the cross. No, He despised it. Yet, He endured it. Why? To save Mankind. To Christ, you and I were worth the shame He endured on the cross. Today, Jesus Christ still thinks that we're worth it. Talk about turning the tables on the devil, Christ conquered the tempter by overcoming His greatest temptations. Christ beat temptation and said, *"It is finished!"* Jn. 19:30, *NLT*.

We Need Faithful Friends in the Faith

How do men and women, even well-known and well-respected ministers, become enemies of the gospel? By giving in to temptation. How are they/we tempted? The Bible teaches: *"Temptation comes from our own desires, which entice us and drag us away."* James 1:14, *NLT*. We're tempted by desires that drag us into sin: *"You lust, and don't have. You kill, covet, and can't obtain. You fight and make war."* James 4:2, *WEB.* Many have succumbed and will succumb to temptation. That's why Scripture teaches: *"From now on, whoever thinks that he stands, let him beware lest he fall."* 1 Cor. 10:12, *ABPE.* Temptation is common to everyone: *"The temptations in your life are no different from what others experience."* 1 Cor. 10:13, *NLT.* We need one another to overcome the temptations we all face.

Jesus needed His disciples during His final temptations: *"And ye – ye are those who have remained with me in my temptations...."* Lk. 22:28, *YLT.* Christ needed their prayers. But, the disciples were tempted too. To do what? Sleep. Jesus asked His disciples: *"Why are you sleeping? Get up and pray that you may not enter into temptation."* Lk. 22:46, *NASB.* Not once, nor twice, but three times. In Christ's hour of greatest need, His disciples failed Him, they gave in to the temptation to sleep. But, *"[a]n angel from heaven appeared to Him and strengthened Him."* Lk. 22:43, *NIV.* No one should try to walk through temptation alone. No, we need others. We need prayer. *"Then Jesus told them a parable about their need to pray at all times and not lose heart...."* Lk. 18:1, *BSB.* We need to pray: for ourselves and for one another. Don't walk alone. Or, you will be tempted and fall.

> **We all need friends to whom we can turn for prayer.**

Jesus said to Peter: *"But I begged for you, that your faith may not fail. And you, when you have turned back, strengthen your brothers."* Lk. 22:32, *BLB.* I have a question for you: Who is begging for you? I have another question: Who is at your side praying for you that your faith doesn't fail? Believe me, temptations come. But, those who endure have friends who are faithful in prayer. We all need friends who stand with us when things get rough and the going gets tough. It will. You will be tested. You will be tempted. Jesus was. Peter was. And, Paul was. As a spiritual father, Paul didn't consider it impossible to fall. No, Paul said, *"I discipline my body like an athlete, training it to do what it should. Otherwise, I fear that after preaching to others I myself might be disqualified."* 1 Cor. 9:27, NLT.

Paul considered his life's journey the fight of his life. Near the end of his life, Paul said, *"I have fought an excellent fight; I have finished my race and I have kept my faith."* 2 Tim. 4:7, ABPE. Paul finished well. But, Paul was tempted: *"The first time I was brought before the judge, no one came with me. Everyone abandoned me. May it not be counted against them."* 2 Tim. 4:16, NLT. And, *"You know that everyone in the province of Asia has deserted me, including Phygelus and Hermogenes."* 2 Tim. 1:15, NIV. Paul could have succumbed to discouragement and doubt. But, he didn't. Paul said, *"the Lord stood by me and gave me strength so that I could finish spreading the good news for all the nations to hear. I was snatched out of a lion's mouth."* 2 Tim. 4:17, GWT.

Paul remembered those who walked with him, worked with him and endured hardship with him. Although many were tempted to leave and did leave, some remained true. Paul had prayer partners: they prayed for and with him, and they continued with him in his time of temptation. But, many believers were shipwrecked in their faith. Not everyone finished well. Paul's warning to the Ephesians was prophetic: *"I know that false teachers, like vicious wolves, will come in among you after I leave, not sparing the flock. Even some men from your own group will rise up and distort the truth in order to draw a following. Watch out!"* Acts 20:29-31, NLT. We all need friends to whom we can turn for prayer. We need people who will stand with us when, like Jesus, we're tempted to: 1) disbelieve in our calling, 2) to abuse our calling, or 3) to turn from our calling.

Fighting, Running and Pressing On

As some have said, it's not how you start the race but how you finish it. *"So run to win!"* 1 Cor. 9:24, NLT. That should be our outlook on life each and every day: we're running the race of faith to win it. That's why we must always remember, the clock is always ticking.

None of us are guaranteed tomorrow. As such, we must *"[m]ake the most of every opportunity in these evil days."* Eph. 5:16, *NLT*. We have an opportunity to make a difference in our world and in the lives of others while we're still alive. Paul said, *"I press toward the mark for the prize of the high calling of God in Christ Jesus."* Phil. 3:14. We, too, must press forward toward that mark.

Most men fail for want of trying. Try! Or die. One of my favorite Bible heroes of the faith is Noah. Noah preached for 500+ years to wicked men and women in wicked generations. And, we think we have people living for the devil. In Noah's day, women were having sex with demons. Ugh! And, Noah was a great preacher. You think T.D. Jakes is good?! Noah was great! Yet, in all his years of preaching, Noah only had eight converts – his family. I'd be discouraged. How big is your church, Noah? We have eight. Week after week, month after month, year after year, decade after decade and century after century. Discouraging! Then, God gave him a huge building project, code named ARK. For 100+ years, Noah worked on that project. I can only imagine what happened daily as Noah worked on his ARK project for over 100 years: he was heckled, mocked, slandered, accused, vilified and persecuted. But, he continued building. Why? For the prospect of rain. Remember, it had never rained before. But, Noah held true. That's faith.

I'd rather have someone, when trying to walk on the water, step out of the boat and fail, than to have everyone stay in the boat and fail to try. Trying to walk on water is not being false. Even failing to walk on water is not being false. Saying you walked on water when you didn't, that's false. Making up stories and telling others you walked on water, that's fraudulent. Try, but don't lie. We need real miracles. We need real prophecies. We need real power. But, we need to put an end to worthless stories of miracles that never happened. We must stop lying about what actually took place for profit. And, we much check what is claimed against recorded fact. Jude warned about such false ministers: *"These are hidden reefs at your love feasts, as they feast with you without fear, shepherds feeding themselves; waterless clouds, swept along by winds; fruitless trees in late autumn, twice dead, uprooted...."* Jude 1:12, *ESV*.

Defending the Gospel by Fearing God

Fact checking is not faithless. And, failure is not fruitless. No, failure's fruit is success. Fear of failure is fruitless and worthless. False stories are fruitless and worthless. And, that's where the church has dwelt for far too long. We have been afraid to fail. And, often, we have accused those who tried and failed of being false. No, it's not a sin to try and fail. Rather, it's a great sin to fail to try. To give up before we start, may be the greatest of all sins: *"'Sir, look! Here's your coin. I've kept it in a cloth for safekeeping because I was afraid of you. You're a tough person to get along with. You take what isn't yours and harvest grain you haven't planted.'"* Listen to God's response: *'I'll judge you by what you've said, you evil servant!'"* Lk. 19:20-22, *GWT*. The man who failed to try was tried for that failure and it wasn't good.

I don't want that to happen to me. I don't want to be before the Father on the day of judgment and hear Him say, *"Depart from Me, you accursed, into the eternal fire that has been prepared for the devil and his angels!"* Lk. 25:41, *NET*. Nothing that we face in this life is worth hearing those awful and dreadful words. We should fear God. *"Fear Him who, after your body has been killed, has authority to throw you into hell. Yes, I tell you, fear Him."* Lk. 12:5, *NIV*. Jesus taught His followers to fear God. Eternity hangs in the balance. In sin, many foolishly hang by a very thin thread over hell. Many think, "I don't need God in my life!" Some think, "I'm not sure if God exists!" And, a few even say, *"There is no God."* Ps. 53:1. And, the day of reckoning is coming: *"All of us must appear in front of Christ's judgment seat. Then all people will receive what they deserve for the good or evil they have done while living in their bodies."* 2 Cor. 5:10, *GWT*.

Hell is real. Heaven is real. Believing the gospel is the only way to heaven. Jesus said, *"I am the way, and the truth, and the life. No* one comes to the Father unless by Me." Jn. 14:6, *DBT*. And, *"I am the resurrection and the life. He who believes in Me will live, even though he dies."* Jn. 11:25, *BSB*. That's why the gospel message is so important. And for that reason, we must defend the gospel message from the gospel's enemies: those men and women who preach false gospels.

Whole nations have been deceived into believing false gospels. Whole generations have been deceived into believing false gospels. Churches and church leaders have been deceived into believing false gospels. Dowie thought he was Elijah. John and Charles Wesley believed a lie, one many others also believed, that people were predestined for heaven or hell. No choice. Just chosen. Today, we have men and women who are preaching false gospels, like the gospel of inclusion, i.e., all will be saved. False gospels abound because the Church has failed to defend the gospel. And as a result, the gospel has been diluted and polluted. And, we tolerate it for the sake of peace. But, the gospel is the only way into heaven. For that reason, we must defend the gospel. Or, we risk losing it.

Chapter Fourteen

The Gospel Must be Defended

"The latter do so from love because they know that I am placed here for the defense of the gospel." Phil. 1:16, *NET.*

The gospel is irreplaceable. No other message on earth is like it. And, the Church, doesn't realize this simple truth. Instead, we try to appease the world and impress the world by the greatness of our religion. But, the Church, in many ways, has become like the world. And, many leaders think that's OK, and even necessary, to reach the world. But, that assumption is wrong. No, the Church cannot and should not look, or act, like the world. We are to be different: *"But you are a chosen people, a royal priesthood, a holy nation, a people for God's own possession, to proclaim the virtues of Him who called you out of darkness into His marvelous light."* 1 Pet. 2:9, *BSB.*

Being Lights in the World by Sharing Good News

We are to be lights. Like Paul, the defense of the gospel requires us to be lights in this world: *"That ye may be blameless and harmless, the sons of God, without rebuke, in the midst of a crooked and perverse nation, among whom ye shine as lights in the world; Holding forth the word of life; that I may rejoice in the day of Christ, that I have not run in vain, neither laboured in vain."* Phil. 2:15-16. But, it's easy to let our light be covered and concealed. We can hide from sharing the gospel. When we do, we silently surrender to the world. And, in doing so, ignorance of the gospel grows, and the Church retreats.

Much of the Church is on the retreat. We're not advancing or conquering. Instead, we're holding on until Christ comes again. But, the promise of His coming wasn't designed to keep us from participating in the world. No, it was designed to motivate us to reach the world. *"Go into all the world and preach the Good News to everyone."* Mk. 16:15, *NLT.* That's our mission. That's our mandate. To reach the world with the gospel is what Christ intend. We are to be advancing His kingdom on earth. How? By sharing the good news. But, to do that we must know what the good news is. We must know our content so that we can communicate it.

Fleecing the Flock: Ignorance is Dangerous and Deadly

Ignorance is one of the deadliest weapons on earth, and drives men to the edge of madness and insanity. If men remain ignorant, it's easy to mold them to do that which is ridiculous and hypocritical. Men don't need a reason to do evil if their reason is taken from them. No, when reason is taken from Mankind, we're left with barbarism. Many church leaders have become fools ignorantly playing the world's game of folly. Entire denominations and associations are playing the fool, but they don't know it. They are ignorant. But, they wear their ignorance well. And, with it, an entire generation is being lost to the world. Sad!

Recently, I was watching a rerun of the *I Love Lucy* show. In it, Lucy learns to play golf from her husband, Ricky Riccardo, and his friend, Fred Mertz. Riccardo teaches Lucy a strange version of golf. His goal? To cause her to lose interest in golf. One day, Lucy and her friend, Ethel Mertz, are playing on the golf course that version of golf they were taught by their husbands, and they meet a well-known professional golfer, Jimmy Demaret, and, try to teach him "golf". The scene is hilarious. Later, when Lucy and Ethel learn from

Demaret their husbands have used their ignorance to dupe them into acting foolishly on the golf course, Lucy and Ethel recruit Demaret, to play a ruse on their husbands: Demaret plays the game Riccardo and Fred taught their wives, to their embarrassment. Funny!

Watching Lucy and Ethel teach Demaret how to play golf is hilarious. Demaret is completely caught off guard by Lucy's and Ethel's complete ignorance of the game of golf. Laughter fills the audience. Demaret tells them that they are not playing golf. Then, Demaret learns the reason for their ignorance, they were deceived. Like Lucy and Ethel, much of the Church has been deceived. We're ignorant of Satan's devices: to our own hurt. False gospels permeate the Church. False ministers pervade the Church. Why? For personal gain and profit. They know how easy it's to fleece the flock of God. And, fleeced is being generous in describing how false ministers' con believers for personal profit and gain.

From Genesis to Revelation: Satan's Plan for World Domination

There's a movie, *Leap of Faith*, where Steve Martin plays a wild and crazy evangelist. Martin presents himself as a miracle worker in a rural community. Throughout his meetings, the fix is in. The music is fantastic. The program electrifying. Martin is even wearing a suit fitted with lights that light up. People claim to be healed. Words of knowledge are given. But, we learn it's all a ruse. Then, something amazing happens, a true miracle takes place. Martin, so convicted by his fleecing of the flock, leaves behind his electrifying act. Would to God that such a thing would happen in the Church. We need the real. But, we mustn't be so hungry for the real that we fall for anything. Otherwise, we're an accident waiting to happen.

Deceived men and women are easy to control. And, it's easy to deceive men and women. People want to believe the truth. That's why church leaders must be on guard: the flock will often eat things that are not good for them. And, when they do, there's always a bitter harvest. Many church leaders know that deception is prevalent, but out of fear are afraid to confront it. Instead, they allow it to continue. But, fallacies and falsehood must be confronted. People, once deceived, cling to deception and delusion; it can be very hard to set them free. The lie is often easier to swallow than the truth. Truth can be a bitter pill. But, truth sets us free. Lies keep us in a state of bondage. Ignorance can be bliss, but it eventually leads to hell. How easily are ignorant men and women kept bound by chains in their minds.

The enemy seeks to fashion hidden chains of ignorance to hold Mankind in bondage to slavery to sin and sickness. Satan keeps the whole world locked in that prison of ignorance. Paul said, *"Satan, who is the god of this world, has blinded the minds of those who don't believe. They are unable to see the glorious light of the Good News. They don't understand this message about the glory of Christ, who is the exact likeness of God."* 2 Cor. 4:4, *NLT*. Isaiah prophesied of a coming day: *"Everyone there will stare at you and ask, 'Can this be the one who shook the earth and made the kingdoms of the world tremble? Is this the one who destroyed the world and made it into a wasteland? Is this the king who demolished the world's greatest cities and had no mercy on his prisoners?'"* Is. 14:16,17, *NLT*. All Mankind will be shocked by what they see. Why? Because, at that time, Satan will be fully exposed and brought into the light, and we'll see him for who he really is.

Briefly, I want to explain to you that our adversary, the devil, has grown throughout Mankind's history. In Genesis, we see Satan as a serpent: *"Now the serpent was the most cunning of all the wild animals that the LORD God had made. He said to the woman, 'Did God really say, 'You can't eat from any tree in the garden?'"* Gen. 3:1, *HCSB*. In Revelation, we see Satan as a Dragon: *"Then another sign appeared in heaven: an enormous red dragon with seven heads and ten horns and seven crowns on its heads."* Rev. 12:3, *NIV*. Big difference. Satan has gone from being a crafty and cunning serpent to a huge dragon with seven heads and ten crowns. How? By increasing his kingdom and dominion in the earth. How did Satan increase his kingdom and dominion in the earth? By schemes, cunning and wile.

The Gospel Revolution: Satan's Nightmare

We're facing a very real enemy. That enemy, Satan, is fearful of the gospel. Jesus explained what happens when Mankind is ignorant of the gospel: *"Someone hears the word about the kingdom but doesn't understand it. The evil one comes at once and snatches away what was planted in him. This is what the seed planted*

Satan keeps the whole world locked in that prison of ignorance.

along the road illustrates." Matt. 13:19, *GWT.* Satan will use our ignorance against us. How? By preventing us from knowing the truth of the gospel. Gospel truth is different from all other truth. Gospel truth has power to set Mankind free from slavery to sin. Gospel truth, when believed, translates us from Satan's kingdom to God's kingdom. Heaven is populated and hell is plundered. That's what happens when the gospel is preached. And, it's why the gospel must be defended.

Paul defended the gospel from enemies. He foretold what would happen to the Church after his death: *"I know that false teachers, like vicious wolves, will come in among you after I leave, not sparing the flock."* Acts 20:29, *NLT.* Jude warned the churches: *"I say this because some ungodly people have wormed their way into your churches, saying that God's marvelous grace allows us to live immoral lives. The condemnation of such people was recorded long ago, for they have denied our only Master and Lord, Jesus Christ."* Jude 1:4, *NLT.* Today, like then, we have men and women, immoral people, who have chosen to live in constant sexual immorality and perversion, leading churches and preaching at conferences. Despicable.

God's Charge: Defend the Gospel

We must defend the gospel. We must defend churches from hucksters and charlatans who fleece God's flock. Jeremiah saw God's flock being fleeced and prophesied to Israel's leaders: *"'How terrible for the shepherds who are destroying and scattering the sheep of My pasture!' declares the LORD. Therefore, this is what the LORD God of Israel says about the shepherds who are shepherding My people, 'You have scattered My flock and driven them away. You haven't taken care of them, and now I'm about to take care of you because of your evil deeds,' declares the LORD."* Jer. 23:1-2, *ISV*. James pleaded with believers: *"Dear brothers and sisters, not many of you should become teachers in the church, for we who teach will be judged more strictly."* James 3:1, *NLT*. I hope you understand what a gift, and responsibility, there is in preaching the gospel. We shouldn't take it lightly.

We, church leaders, should be embarrassed by the rampant deception in our midst, and by our powerlessness to confront it. We tolerate the intolerable, and we refuse to confront the abominable. We need a revival of truth and righteousness. We need a revival of sound doctrine and good teaching. Truth is at a premium. Confronting false gospels is a necessary and primary task of genuine apostles. Paul's epistles were written to correct, instruct, reprove and rebuke. Correction leads to life. But, in a consumer driven culture, leaderless flocks are addicted to smooth words laced with deceptive teachings. Rare is the leader that can actually confront the flock. Even rarer is the flock that will allow pastors to confront. Instead, they leave.

Hearing the Instruction that Leads to Life

David taught Solomon that *"the commandment is a lamp, and the teaching a light, and reproofs of instruction are the way of life...."* Prov. 6:23, *DBT*. In the *NET*, it says, *"For the commandments are like a lamp, instruction is like a light, and rebukes of discipline are like the road leading to life...."* A believer's, or church's, failure to receive instruction, correction, reproof and rebuke is evidence that they are not walking on the path of life. Solomon says, "He is in the way of life who heeds correction, but he who forsakes reproof leads others astray." Prov. 10:17, WEB. Lack of discipline has driven the Church into the wilderness of sin, and want of correction keeps it in the valley of the shadow of death. We need discipline. We need correction. We need instruction. That's how the gospel is defended.

The gospel is defended when godly men and women, preach the uncompromising truth, and stand up against ungodliness by confronting it. Paul, as a father in the faith, spoke to his son in the faith: "Preach the Word of God. Be prepared, whether the time is favorable or not. Patiently correct, rebuke, and encourage your people with good teaching." 2 Tim. 4:2, NLT. Peter, as a father in the faith, spoke to his children in the faith: "And if someone asks about your Christian hope, always be ready to explain it." 1 Pet. 3:15, NLT. Without this ability, gospel preachers are like toothless tigers; they have not the resolve or conviction to hold believers accountable. But, that's exactly what believers and churches need, to be called to account for their lives.

Seeing Beyond: The Lens of Eternity

By godly fear, I say this with all gravity, each of us will be called to account for our lives. You will be called to account for your beliefs, your time, your talent, your money and your words. So will I. God will open the books to make a determination of how we lived our lives, and what we did with our lives, and what we accomplished with our lives. Rev. 20:12. Many will say on that day, "I was afraid of you, because you are a hard man. You take out what you did not put in and reap what you did not sow." Lk. 19:21, NLT. Here is God's response to them: "'You wicked servant!' the king roared. 'Your own words condemn you. If you knew that I'm a hard man who takes what isn't mine and harvests crops I didn't plant, why didn't you deposit my money in the bank? At least I could have *gotten some interest on it.'"* Lk. 19:22,23, *NLT.* Are you making eternal deposits? Or, is your life all about that which is temporary?

The gospel brings an eternal perspective of life to our minds. We see our world through the light of eternity. And, we need that kind of soberness. We need to be reminded that what we do in this life is important. We should live on purpose. Our time on earth is limited. Focus is important. Make the most of your time by following God's plan. God's vision is greater than your vision. God's plan is greater than your plan. God, before you were born, had something in mind just for you. Your value is in identifying your place and position of importance. And, the only way you can do that is by instruction, correction, reproof and rebuke. We need those elements of discipline to keep us on the path of life. Without them, we stray.

"End Times" and "Last Days" Deceptions

Keep this in mind, in the New Testament, many strayed. Even men and women trained by apostles, like Paul and John, strayed. Peter strayed. Judas betrayed. Your mentor doesn't determine your ability to stay the course and/or stray from that course. Many, when the way became too narrow, failed to stay the course. Many, in the midst of difficulty, have lost faith. Others, in the midst of

We must know what we believe, why we believe what we believe and how we are to live what we believe in this world – today.

prosperity, lost their way. Jesus made this clear to His disciples: *"Watch out that you don't get led astray, for many will come in My Name, saying, 'I am he,' and, 'The time is at hand.' Therefore, don't follow them."* Lk. 21:8, *WEB.* Deception caters to men and women focused on end times theology.

Many have claimed to know the exact coming of Christ. Harold Camping predicted Jesus' exact date of return, May 25, 2011. But, he wasn't the first. Nor was 2011 his first attempt at predicting when Christ would return. Camping's first prediction of Christ's return was 1994. He was wrong, twice. Edgar Whisenant wrote about 88 reasons why the rapture will be in 1988. But, 88 reasons weren't enough, so Colin Hoyle Deal wrote 101 reasons why Christ would return by 1988. Both were wrong. Today's resurgence of end times theology means the Body of Christ is especially ripe for deception. We have bestselling books like *The Harbinger, the Shemitah* and *Four Blood Moons*. And, who can forget, *Left Behind*? And, there are many more. But, Jesus said, *"go yet not therefore after them."* Lk. 21:8.

Being Grounded in the Here and Now

Instead, our focus must be on the here and now. We have much to do. Christ is coming, and we're not ready. No, our hearts are hard with stubbornness and heads thick with unbelief. We don't know what the Bible actually says. And, we wrestle over fine points that have little bearing on the quality of eternity. Paul soundly rejected this kind of foolishness:

> *"So teach and exhort. If any one is a teacher of any other kind of doctrine, and refuses assent to wholesome instructions – those of our Lord Jesus Christ – and the teaching that harmonizes with true godliness, he is puffed up with pride and has no true knowledge, but is crazy over discussions and controversies about words which give rise to envy, quarrelling, revilings, ill-natured suspicions, and persistent wranglings on the part of people whose intellects are disordered and they themselves blinded to all knowledge of the truth; who imagine that godliness means gain."* 1 Tim. 6:3-5, WNT.

We, too, must reject such foolishness. Instead, our focus must be grounded on solid doctrines that produce long-lasting fruit. We must know what we believe, why we believe what we believe and how we are to live what we believe in this world – today. Instead of living in what might come, we must live in the here and now. And, we must build our defense for the gospel. Why? Because there's coming a time when we'll need to defend the gospel we believe. And, unless we know what we believe, we'll not be able to defend the gospel we preach. The gospel is enough; it's sufficient for this day. And, if we know our message, that message will produce the radical results we seek. But, to ignore that message, creates a vacuum for false gospels and false ministers to flourish. And, that's what we have today.

Paul's Defense of the Gospel

Paul was prepared to defend the gospel. Paul defended the gospel. In Philippians 1:16-17, Paul said, *"I am put here for the defense of the gospel."* In another translation, it says, *"I am appointed for the defense of the gospel."* Still another says, *"I am set for the defence of the gospel."* Paul understood his purpose: to defend the gospel. To do that, he wrote. Paul's epistles became and have become the backbone of the Church. Paul's writings have become the touchstone for determining if the gospel preached is true. God meant for that to happen. But, in the same way Paul was prepared to defend the gospel, we must also be prepared to defend the gospel. We're here to defend the gospel.

Paul's defended the gospel against false ministers. Paul called them *"false apostles, deceitful workers, masquerading as apostles of Christ."* 2 Cor. 11:13, BSB. What they said of Paul was this: *"His letters are weighty and powerful, but his physical presence is weak, and his public speaking is despicable."* 2 Cor. 10:10, HCSB. Paul plainly tells the Corinthians: *"I will give you all the proof you want that Christ speaks through me. Christ is not weak when He deals with you; He is powerful among you. Although He was crucified in weakness, He now lives by the power of God. We, too, are weak, just as Christ was, but when we deal with you we will be alive with Him and will have God's power."* 2 Cor. 13:3-4, NLT. Paul had the goods – signs wonders and miracles – and he was ready to bring it.

Paul had his "A game" going: he was ready to defend the gospel, and the Church. From what? The Corinthians were deceived. By who? Men who claimed to be apostles. What did these false apostles look like? Paul describes their *modus operandi: "When someone makes you slaves, consumes your wealth, seizes your property, orders you around, or slaps your faces, you put up with it."* 2 Cor. 11:20, *GWT.* The Corinthians were literally being robbed by false apostles, and they didn't know it. How? *"You happily put up with whatever anyone tells you, even if they preach a different Jesus than the one we preach, or a different kind of Spirit than the one you received, or a different kind of gospel than the one you believed."* 2 Cor. 11:4, *NLT.*

Paul defended the gospel before the Jews. Paul *"spent all his time preaching the word. He testified to the Jews that Jesus was the Messiah."* Acts 18:5, *NLT.* From that, *"Many of the Corinthians, when they heard, believed and were baptized."* Acts 18:8, *HCSB.* In Acts 21:28-40, Paul is placed on trial before the Jews. In Acts 22:1-21, Paul defends himself. The Jews refuse to hear Him, and desire to kill Him. In Acts 22:25, Paul is to be scourged, but he says, *"I am a Roman."* Paul testifies to the Jewish "chief priests and all their counsel." Acts 22:30. Division arises: Sadducees versus the Pharisees. And, the Pharisee sect says, *"We find no evil in this man...."* Act 23:9. Jesus tells Paul: *"Be encouraged, Paul. Just as you have been a witness to Me here in Jerusalem, you must preach the Good News in Rome as well."* Acts 23:11, *NLT.*

Paul answered his critics, false apostles, in the church, before the Jews, false brothers, in Jerusalem, and, finally, he before Caesar in Rome. Paul appealed to Caesar Augustus. Acts 25:25. Paul is taken to Rome to appear before Caesar. In Acts 27:23, *WEB,* God's angel appears to Paul, and says, *"Don't be afraid, Paul. You must stand before Caesar."* Paul was taken to Rome, and later, he was martyred in Rome. Many scholars believe that it was Nero who had Paul beheaded. That Nero after beheading Paul committed suicide. Paul describes his death to Timothy before it happens: *"My life is coming to an end, and it is now time for me to be poured out as a sacrifice to God."* 2 Tim. 4:6, *GWT.* But, Paul isn't discouraged. No, Paul tells Timothy: *"I have competed well; I have finished the race;*

I have kept the faith!" 2 Tim. 4:7, *NET*. Paul completed his course: to preach and defend the gospel

Paul did not remain silent. Paul was placed on trial: 1) before the Corinthians by false apostles, 2) before the Jews in Jerusalem, and 3) before Caesar in Rome. In each case, Paul exercised wisdom to defend the gospel. In the church, he exercised true apostolic authority. Before the Jews, he submitted to Scriptural and Roman authority. And, in Rome, he submitted to divine authority. Paul understood the battle he was facing, and the calling on his life, to defend the gospel from all enemies, foreign and domestic. In Acts 28:31, *GWT*, Paul, in Rome, can be found doing what he knew to do: *"He spread the message about God's kingdom and taught very boldly about the Lord Jesus Christ. No one stopped him."*

Paul at the end of Acts is preaching and teaching the gospel. But, he is also still defending the gospel. Paul stands as pillar of truth, and is unhindered from sharing that truth. Paul rises each morning celebrating the day ahead, knowing, what he is called to do: preach, teach and defend the gospel. Paul's fight, although delayed, is not over. Paul fought, and finished. Paul gained something of immense value: *"And now a crown of righteousness is kept for me, which my Lord shall award to me in that day when He shall judge the just, but not only to me, but also to those who will have loved his revelation."* 2 Tim. 4:8, *ABPE*. Talk about finishing strong. Paul finished strong, and his strength still stands as a testimony today. Paul's blood sprinkled the Church's future with hope, even in death. As Tertullian said, "The blood of the martyrs is the seed of the Church." Paul's life illustrates this point.

For Today, Tomorrow and Forever

Paul labored. Paul suffered. Paul gave. The Christian life isn't always easy. Sometimes, it can be hard. While not everyone is called to be an apostle, like Paul, or to defend the gospel as Paul did, we're all called to defend the gospel by knowing it, believing it and demonstrating its reality in our lives. Paul was placed on trial. Paul was brought before Herod, Felix, Agrippa and, lastly, Caesar. Paul stood. Paul finished. Paul won. And, so will we, if we cling to the gospel. Hold on to it. Don't let the afflictions of the gospel stop you. You can persevere. You can overcome. Paul did. He wasn't superhuman. No, he was a man, like you and me, but he was driven to fulfill his purpose: to defend the gospel.

You, like I, have been called, for such a time as this, to defend the gospel. We mustn't let the seed of the gospel be watered down by wicked and perverse men and women intent on fleecing the flock of God by elaborate fables and fairytales to profit from the ignorance that currently exists in the Church. No, we must cling to the hope of the gospel, and believe in the sufficiency of the gospel, for it's in that sufficiency that we're called to rest. Paul came to that realization: he couldn't do it himself. That in Paul's weakness, Christ's strength was shown. In your weakness, Christ's strength will shine. Then, you will experience the power of the gospel. And, you will know that the gospel is enough – for you, your family and this world.

Chapter Fifteen

The Gospel Has Afflictions

"May the Lord show special kindness to Onesiphorus and all his family because he often visited and encouraged me. He was never ashamed of me because I was in chains."
2 Tim. 1:16, *NLT*.

When describing the gospel he preached, Paul often mentioned the afflictions, persecutions and hardships associated with preaching the gospel message. In other words, preaching the gospel wasn't for the faint of heart. Paul was well acquainted with suffering for the sake of the gospel; he lists his sufferings as a badge of honor: *"Five times I received at the hands of the Jews the forty lashes less one. Three times I was beaten with rods. Once I was stoned. Three times I was shipwrecked; a night and a day I was adrift at sea...."* 2 Cor. 11:24-,25, *ESV.* Paul was undeterred in his mission to preach the gospel: he passionately pursued Christ and boldly declared Him to his generation and to generations yet to follow.

Paul trained his son in the faith, Timothy, to understand that afflictions were part and parcel of the gospel message. Timothy, the pastor of the Ephesian megachurch, was told by Paul: *"Do not be ashamed then to bear witness for our Lord and for me His prisoner; but rather share suffering with me in the service of the*

Good News, strengthened by the power of God." 2 Tim. 1:8, *WNT*.
Paul equated the gospel with suffering and power. To the Romans,
Paul said, *"I'm not ashamed of the Good News. It is God's power
to save everyone who believes, Jews first and Greeks as well."*
Rom. 1:16, *GWT*. Paul's formula for success in preaching the gospel
was simple: gospel + suffering = power. That formula worked. Paul
changed his world by following it. And, we can do the same.

The Gospel, and Its Afflictions

But, for that to happen, we must return to that formula. We cannot
expect to have Paul's results unless we use Paul's formula for
success. Why is suffering so important to the gospel message?
Because, it shows those who don't believe in the power of the gospel
to change the human heart, the human reality of the gospel. Men
and women who can endure the hardships associated with the
gospel are real. Non-believers can understand God's reality in the
face of hardship. Sometimes, that's the only thing that can awaken
their conscience to God's righteousness. But, it's the pattern of
evangelization that Christ used, Paul used, Peter used and John used.
All of them suffered for the gospel. And, none were afraid of suffering
for the sake of the gospel. All suffered.

Why is it important to know of the sufferings associated with the
gospel? Because unless we know that suffering is associated with
the gospel, we can misunderstand the opposition we face when the
gospel is preached. We can believe that we have done something
wrong, when, in reality, it's the gospel that's what offends. Paul
called the cross an offense. Gal. 5:11. Paul also called the preaching
of the cross a stumbling block and foolishness. 1 Cor. 1:23. John
Wimber plainly stated this truth: "God offends the mind to reveal
the heart." Why does God offend our minds? Because it was by the
pursuit of wisdom that Mankind fell into sin. Sin used Mankind's
desire to know more to deceive us into believing that the pursuit of
knowledge was the answer to Mankind's hunger and thirst for more.
But, it's not.

Penance Isn't the Right Path

No, besides the tree of the knowledge of good and evil in the middle of the garden of Eden, there's also a tree of life. That's what we're called to pursue, Life. That's where the answer is found. Speaking to Moses, God said, *"I call on heaven and earth as witnesses today that I have offered you life or death, blessings or curses. Choose life so that you and your descendants will live."* Deut. 30:19, GWT. We have been given a choice. The power to choose carries with it the consequences of the choice made. Free will demands that we account for the choices we make. We cannot escape our choices, good or bad, for they follow us.

Paul made a choice to suffer for the sake of the gospel to bring men and women out from Satan's prison. Please understand: the jailhouse doors have already been opened. How? By Christ's completed work. As such, we're free to voluntarily leave the prison house of sin, sickness, sorrow and fear. Why then do so many remain in that prison?

> *Paul's formula for success in preaching the gospel was simple: gospel + suffering = power.*

Because they don't know what Christ has done; they believe the lie. What lie? They are paying for their own sins. Most people, when confronted by their sins, think of ways to do penance for them. Their thought: If only I can do enough to wipe the slate clean.

In the Hollywood movie, *The Avengers,* Scarlett Johansson, playing the Black Widow, a.k.a. Natasha Romanoff, says to the villain, Loki, "It's really not that complicated. I've got red in my ledger, I'd like to wipe it out." To which, Loki says, "Can you wipe out that much red? Dreykov's daughter, Sao Paulo, the hospital fire? Your ledger is dripping, it's GUSHING red, and you think saving a man no more virtuous than yourself will change anything? This is the basest sentimentality. This is a child at prayer... PATHETIC! You lie and kill in the service of liars and killers. You pretend to be separate, to have your own code. Something that makes up for the horrors. But they are a part of you, and they will never go away!" Here, Loki is lying. Why? To hide his plan. How? Deceit. Disinformation. Misdirection.

Breaking People Out of Satan's Jails

Satan is a liar. Satan, through his lies, keeps men in prison. To get out of jail, Mankind is convinced it must make up for the wrongs it has done. But, in our attempt to wipe the slate clean, we hear the voice of the accuser saying, "Can you really wipe away that much red?" And we know, the answer is, No! But, instead of giving up, we keep trying to wipe the slate clean. Paul described this ignorance: *"For they [the Jews], being ignorant of God's righteousness, and seeking to establish their own righteousness, have not submitted themselves to the righteousness of God."* Rom. 10:3, *WBT*. That's why the gospel is vital to Mankind: it's Christ's declaration to Mankind that we're free to come out of Satan's jail. We don't have to remain in bondage. We're free. And, all we have to do is walk out of jail.

But for many, that first step outside the cell is the most difficult; it's easy to want to return to the comfort of that cell. And, as you can imagine, the gospel is an observable threat to the system of the prison's guards and warden. Paul's gospel was a threat to Satan's system of imprisoning people. That gospel is still a threat. Now that you know what the gospel is, you are a threat to that system. Why is the gospel such a threat to Satan's system? Because Christ's gospel destroys Satan's kingdom. Jesus Christ chose the preaching of the gospel as the primary means by which He would establish His reign on earth. Christ could have chosen armies to establish His reign, but He didn't. No, He chose the force of faith over the force of arms.

Paul chose to preach the gospel, despite the conflict it created. Paul did not intentionally seek to create conflict or offend people. No, the gospel itself was offense enough. Jesus said, *"Don't assume that I came to bring peace on the earth. I did not come to bring peace, but a sword."* Matt. 10:34, *HCSB.* But, many have presumed the end of the gospel is peace, and it is, but it's also an instrument of combat. Remember, *"[n]one of the rulers of this age knew this wisdom, for if they had known it, they would not have crucified the Lord of glory."* 1 Cor. 2:8, *HCSB.* Satan controlled and motivated those rulers. Christ allowed that motivation and used it for His glory to break demonic chains.

Freedom is Available to All... Today

The chains have been broken, but demons still try to keep Mankind bound, to extend their futile effort to escape the hell prepared for them. To do that, demons turn the hearts and minds of men and women against those who preach the gospel. As a result, the gospel offends the minds and hearts of Mankind, especially religious men and women. Religion and the gospel don't mix. The gospel frees men from religious ritual into a living reality of freedom in Christ. But, not all men or women want freedom. Some like the ritual and find comfort in religion's ritual. Religion uses ritual to create ruts and rot in the minds of men and women, to hold them in bondage. The gospel threatens religion's rituals.

We have many religions today that are threatened by the gospel:

- the religion of politics and law,
- the religion of greed and gluttony,
- the religion of license and promiscuity,
- the religion of pornography and perversion,
- the religion of homosexuality and transgender,
- the religion of gender and racism,
- the religion of ecology and science,
- the religion of psychology and psychiatry,
- the religion of capitalism and business,
- the religion of nationalization and immigration,

and many more.

The gospel threatens those religions; it's in conflict with them. No religion can stand against the gospel. The gospel has and will prevail. The gospel is enough.

Understanding the Conflict the Gospel Creates

But, the battle is intense. To the Hebrews, Paul wrote, *"Remember the earlier days when, after you had been enlightened, you endured a hard struggle with sufferings,"* Heb. 10:32, HCSB, *"At times you were made a public spectacle by means of insults and persecutions, while at other times you associated with people who were treated this way,* Heb. 10:33, ISV, *For ye had compassion of me in my bonds, and took joyfully the spoiling of your goods, knowing in yourselves that ye have in heaven a better and an enduring substance."* Heb. 10:34. There's great warfare over the gospel. That conflict was evident in Paul's life. Paul understood the reasons for the conflict. And we, too, must know why the gospel causes such conflict. Why? To endure it and overcome when the conflict comes. And, it will.

When the conflict comes, remember that you can endure. Further, remember, a special blessing is offered to those who endure. What could possibly be worth going through the afflictions described herein to preach the gospel? Paul identifies them:

1) We participate in Christ's sufferings;
2) We partake of Christ's power;
3) We partner in Christ's salvation; and
4) We're promoted in Christ's kingdom.

In the remainder of this chapter, I'd like to take a look at each of these areas. If we truly understood the blessings offered for enduring the gospel's afflictions, we would never again, in response to them, ask the question, "Why me, God?" We would know.

With Christ... in the Fires of Affliction

When we endure the gospel's afflictions, we participate in Christ's sufferings. Further, through our participation in Christ's sufferings, we truly begin to understand Christ's love. Christ's love is discovered in the furnace of affliction and fires of adversity. The Psalmist, in Psalm 119:71, *NLT*, said, *"My suffering was good for me, for it taught me to pay attention to your decrees."* To the Philippians, Paul said,

> *"More than that, I now regard all things as liabilities compared to the far greater value of knowing Christ Jesus my Lord, for whom I have suffered the loss of all things – indeed, I regard them as dung! – that I may gain Christ, and be found in Him, not because I have my own righteousness derived from the law, but because I have the righteousness that comes by way of Christ's faithfulness – a righteousness from God that is in fact based on Christ's faithfulness. My aim is to know Him, to experience the power of His resurrection, to share in His sufferings, and to be like Him in His death, and so, somehow, to attain to the resurrection from the dead."* Phil. 3:8-11, *NET.*

Paul found a deeper relationship with Christ in the sufferings he endured for the sake of the gospel. 2 Tim. 3:12-13. Paul learned things he otherwise couldn't have known. By choosing to suffer the gospel's afflictions, Paul invested his life in the gospel. By that investment, he became Christ's partner and a stakeholder in Christ's kingdom. Like any partnership or relationship, personal or business, both parties must understand the other. Paul's gospel afflictions enabled him to understand the value of what Christ offered and the price Christ paid. Paul's willingness to endure the gospel's afflictions to learn Christ's love made him into the apostle he became.

Christ considered Paul's willingness to suffer worthy of a general in the faith. Christ, in the middle of Paul's afflictions, said, *"My grace is all you need. My power works best in weakness."* 2 Cor. 12:9, *NLT.* Jesus stood by Paul in his afflictions: *"Be encouraged, Paul. Just as you have been a witness to Me here in Jerusalem, you must preach the Good News in Rome as well."* Acts 23:11, *NLT.* God sent angels to Paul in his afflictions: *"Do not be afraid, Paul.*

You must stand trial before Caesar...." Acts 27:23, *NIV*. Paul was brought by providence before Caesar to preach the gospel. And, what a witness that was – divine.

Partaking of Christ's Afflictions... and Christ's Power

When we endure the gospel's afflictions, we partake of Christ's power. Paul taught, *"Be not thou therefore ashamed of the testimony of our Lord, nor of me his prisoner: but be thou partaker of the afflictions of the gospel according to the power of God...."* 2 Tim. 1:8. When we suffer for the gospel, power is released to us. Paul said, *"For our light and temporary affliction is producing for us an eternal glory that far outweighs our troubles."* 2 Cor. 4:17, *BSB*. While some believe Paul speaks of the hereafter, it's my understanding that Paul spoke of the here-and-now and the hereafter. According to the measure of our sufferings and afflictions endured for the sake of the gospel, God deposits in us a glory that's equal to or greater than those sufferings and affliction.

In the Greek language, there are six different words for power: 1) *dunamis,* 2) *energia,* 3) *ischus,* 4) *kratos,* 5) *exousia* and 6) *biastes.*[17] The first four Greek words reveal demonstrative power, and the last two Greek words reveal authoritative power. Power and authority are different. When we accept Christ as Lord, we have power, *exousia,* to become God's sons. Jn. 1:12. But, that power is different than the power we receive after being baptized in the Holy Spirit. When we're baptized in the Holy Spirit, we receive power, *dunamis,* from on high. That same word, *dunamis,* is used in 2 Tim. 1:8. Or, when we suffer for the sake of the gospel, it releases *dunamis* power, i.e., miraculous power, into our lives. Miracles are made manifest in the lives of believers who suffer for the gospel's sake. Phil. 3:10.

---

[17] Teaching from Dennis & Diane Teague, Pastors of River of Grace Fellowship in Olympia, Washington. See www.riversofgrace.org/power.html.

Miracles and Afflictions Go Hand in Hand

Why is it important for us to know the miraculous power is associated with the afflictions and sufferings associated with the gospel? Because, if we don't know that miraculous power is available when we're suffering, we'll try to endure suffering in our own strength. Paul's secret sauce to effective evangelism was suffering and affliction. Paul's suffering enabled him to move in **dunamis** power. God deposited **dunamis** power in Paul's life, as he suffered for the sake of the gospel. Paul was bathed in miraculous power, glory was deposited into his life, as he suffered for the gospel's sake. And, I'm convinced that suffering afflictions and persecutions for the gospel's sake will release new levels of miraculous power into the Church.

When we endure the gospel's afflictions, we partner in Christ's salvation. Possibly, this may be the least understood piece of the gospel's afflictions. And, its implications are overwhelming for those who endure suffering for the gospel's sake. In Colossians 1:24, *NASB*, Paul states, *"Now I rejoice in my sufferings for your sake, and in my flesh I do my share on behalf of His Body, which is the Church, in filling up what is lacking in Christ's afflictions."* Lacking in Christ's afflictions? Yes, Christ's afflictions were not enough: Christ's Church is built on the backs, and by the blood of its martyrs. Paul said, *"For you have been given the privilege for the Messiah's sake not only to believe in Him but also to suffer for Him."* Phil. 1:29, *ISV*. Christ needs gospel preachers who are willing to suffer so His Body may be completed.

Apostolic Leadership: When the Gospel Takes Center Stage

Today, the Church is suffering because gospel preachers aren't willing to suffer. Instead, we focus on the prosperity offered in this life. Yes, and God does offer prosperity... with persecutions and afflictions. The Church Jesus builds requires gospel preachers willing to be afflicted for the sake of the gospel. I'm convinced that many of the churches we attend are not the churches that Christ is building. What do I mean? When Jesus does the building, the gospel is center stage. Today, we have many things that replace the gospel message as the primary motivation behind what is being done in churches. Jesus isn't building that church.

No, Jesus builds His Church in His own way. How does Jesus build His Church? By stripes. By afflictions. By necessities. By imprisonment. By work. By prayer. By long hours of groaning intercession. In God's kingdom, we earn our stripes. What? Yes, grace is for salvation, but stripes are required for church leadership. Christ promotes men and women who have suffered and are willing to suffer for the gospel. God's generals always have more stripes. Here's what Paul said about true apostles and genuine apostolic ministry:

> *"Giving no offence in any thing, that the ministry be not blamed: But in all things approving ourselves as the ministers of God, in much patience, in afflictions, in necessities, in distresses, In stripes, in imprisonments, in tumults, in labours, in watchings, in fastings; By pureness, by knowledge, by longsuffering, by kindness, by the Holy Ghost, by love unfeigned, By the word of truth, by the power of God, by the armour of righteousness on the right hand and on the left, By honour and dishonour, by evil report and good report: as deceivers, and yet true; As unknown, and yet well known; as dying, and, behold, we live; as chastened, and not killed; As sorrowful, yet alway rejoicing; as poor, yet making many rich; as having nothing, and yet possessing all things."* 2 Cor. 6:3-10.

The Genuine Apostolic Pattern and Paradigm

If Paul were on the earth today, he would likely not recognize men and women who claim to preach the gospel. Why is that? Paul expected gospel preachers to suffer the gospel's afflictions. Why? To fill up what was lacking in Christ's afflictions. Paul knew that afflictions were needed for men and women to find salvation. And, he considered that a small price to pay for guiding them to salvation. Paul knew that afflictions were needed for salvation and healing to be manifested. Why are so few healed? For want of suffering. We don't have enough stripes. Am I saying that our stripes bring healing? NO. That would be heresy. What am I saying then? I'm saying gospel preachers receive supernatural power as they endure afflictions for the gospel's sake. Living in need is necessary for gospel preachers. And, so are stripes. And, so are martyrs.

True apostles set this pattern for the New Testament Church. Of Christ's twelve apostles, one betrayed Christ, 10 were martyred, and one was confined to an island, Patmos. Not that men didn't try to kill him. They did. But they failed, many times. So, failing to kill him, they confined him to prison, Patmos. That's where John received "The Apocalypse" of Christ. Paul, arguably the greatest of all the apostles, except Christ, was martyred: he was beheaded. Paul said of himself: *"But even if I am offered upon the sacrifice and service of your faith, I rejoice and triumph with all of you...."* Phil. 2:17, ABPE, and *"My life is coming to an end, and it is now time for me to be poured out as a sacrifice to God."* 2 Tim. 4:6, GWT.

When we endure the gospel afflictions, we're promoted in Christ's kingdom. Today, many want the promotion, but few are willing to endure the suffering. Persecution and affliction equals promotion. If we suffer with Him, we're promoted by Him. Gospel preachers who never suffer lack weight; their message is untested and untried. And, they also lack gospel power. Where men and women suffer for the gospel's sake, power is always present. And, that power leads to promotion. Why? *"For the kingdom of God is demonstrated not in idle talk but with power."* 1 Cor. 4:20, NET.

Following Christ... Into the Furnace of Affliction

We demonstrate our lack of understanding of the gospel by our unwillingness to suffer for it. In Christ's kingdom, every preacher is required to attend Christ's school of suffering. We, church leaders, cannot lead until and unless we're willing to suffer and have suffered for the gospel's sake. Today, that's the missing ingredient in church leadership. We have many men and women who want to lead but are unwilling to follow Christ in His sufferings. In Christ's kingdom, only those willing to walk with Christ in His school of suffering are qualified to lead His Church. Otherwise, we're hirelings. And today, we have plenty of men and women in the church who are hirelings. They get paid to preach. And, we get what we pay for – hirelings not pastors or apostles or prophets or teachers or evangelists. No wonder we're lukewarm.

Listen to Paul teaching on church leadership:

> *"Now ye are full, now ye are rich, ye have reigned as kings without us: and I would to God ye did reign, that we also might reign with you. For I think that God hath set forth us the apostles last, as it were appointed to death: for we are made a spectacle unto the world, and to angels, and to men. We are fools for Christ's sake, but ye are wise in Christ; we are weak, but ye are strong; ye are honourable, but we are despised. Even unto this present hour we both hunger, and thirst, and are naked, and are buffeted, and have no certain dwellingplace; And labour, working with our own hands: being reviled, we bless; being persecuted, we suffer it: Being defamed, we intreat: we are made as the filth of the world, and are the offscouring of all things unto this day. I write not these things to shame you, but as my beloved sons I warn you. For though ye have ten thousand instructors in Christ, yet have ye not many fathers: for in Christ Jesus I have begotten you through the gospel. Wherefore I beseech you, be ye followers of me."* 1 Cor. 4:8-16.

Paul said, *"Follow my example, as I follow the example of Christ."* 1 Cor. 11:1, *NIV*. Paul didn't speak idle words. No, he meant what he said and said what he meant. Paul's yes was yes, and Paul's no was no. And, that's what we should example: *"Simply say yes or no. Anything more than that comes from the evil one."* Matt. 5:37, *GWT*. But, today, we have many men and women who are smooth gospel preachers who intermingle soft words in exchange for hard truths. Christ doesn't build His Church by smooth silky words, but tangible demonstrations of power. How does that happen? By gospel preachers who are pray-ers. Paul said, *"My little children, of whom I am in labour again, until Christ be formed in you."* Gal. 4:19, *DRB.* Paul labored in prayer. Then, he labored in the gospel. And, with that labor came many afflictions. That's Paul's example.

Paul's Apostolic Message and Apostolic Fires

In 1995, I received a heavenly dream. In that dream, Paul, the Apostle, quoted to me the Scriptures that I just quoted, 1 Cor. 4:8-15. By that dream, I understood the necessity of suffering and affliction to be qualified for church leadership. Like Paul, my qualifications don't come from my eloquence. No, I have endured significant hardships for the sake of the gospel. I know what it's like to carry the gospel's

Christ doesn't build His Church by smooth silky words, but tangible demonstrations of power.

afflictions. And, I know it's easy to walk away from those afflictions. That's the temptation all gospel preachers face. But, if we want to be promoted in Christ's kingdom, then afflictions and sufferings are required. There's no exception. As the Psalmist said, *"Exaltation does not come from the east, the west, or the desert, for God is the Judge: He brings down one and exalts another."* Ps. 75:6-7, *HCSB.*

Some will ask the question: Why would I want to endure the gospel's afflictions to preach the gospel? Others will say I'm wrong, afflictions are not required. They will say, God wants us to have divine prosperity. I know. Yes, and that's part of the gospel message. But, for gospel preachers, the gospel requires endurance of gospel afflictions. We cannot serve others unless we're willing to follow Christ. Christ endured sufferings for our sake. Gospel preachers endure sufferings for the sake of those who are lost: to bring them the gospel message. And, we'll face hardships and afflictions as we bring the gospel to the lost.

In our world, there are roughly 1.6 billion Muslims. Of that number, five million follow Wahhabism, which is the sect known for its brutality. But, that sect is well financed and rising fast. A day is coming where a dynamic collision of faiths will occur. And, we must be prepared for it. Gospel preachers will face what Paul faced: the edge of the sword. In Paul's day, it was Rome. In our day, it will be Islam. Islam is the one of the greatest threats to gospel preachers today. And, persecution and affliction is the gospel's greatest fan: to raise the gospel's flame among gospel preachers. Get ready! The fire, like the flame in Nebuchadnezzar's furnace, is about to get seven times hotter. The Church is going to once again experience the gospel's afflictions. Then, we'll have the fire. Amen.

My prayer for us:

Fire, fall on us, we pray.

Chapter Sixteen

The Gospel on Display: Signs, Wonders & Miracles

"Through mighty signs and wonders, by the power of the Spirit of God; so that from Jerusalem, and around to Illyricum, I have fully preached the gospel of Christ." Rom. 15:9, *WBT*.

Paul preached. That was his mission. That was his mandate. And, he did not stray from that task. Paul wasn't sidetracked from preaching the gospel. Nor did he fail to fully preach the gospel. Paul described his mission and mandate: *"I have fully preached the gospel of Christ."* Rom. 15:9. How? Paul clearly states: *"with power of signs and wonders, in virtue of the Spirit of God...."* Rom. 15:9, *JUB*. Why is it so important that we know Paul considered signs, wonders and miracles an integral part of fully preaching the gospel? Because, for many years, much of the Church has considered signs, wonders and miracles secondary to preaching the gospel and not a vital part of it. But signs, wonders and miracles are vital to the preaching of the gospel, and we risk not fully preaching the gospel if they are absent.

That describes the Church in America. For many years, we ignored signs, wonders and miracles. What happened? People turned to humanism, spiritism, demonism and self-actualization. We became our own gods. America has sown to the wind and is reaping the whirlwind. Hos. 8:7. That's why our nation is in danger: we, the Church, have failed to fully preach the gospel. That failure has resulted in a gaping hole, a breach between generations, that has robbed our nation of its greatness. That greatness cannot be restored unless and until the gospel is fully preached. And, the gospel can only be fully preached when it's accompanied by signs, wonders and miracles. As such, we need a restoration in our understanding of the importance of signs, wonders and miracles so that we're fully equipped to preach the gospel.

Working Miracles and Walking in Signs and Wonders

In this chapter, I want to arm you with an understanding of how the gospel is displayed by radical signs, wonders and miracles. Everyone in the Church is called to the ministry of signs, wonders and miracles. We're all part of the Body of Christ. As such, we all have the necessary power resident inside us to work miracles. I want you to begin to see yourself as you are: a vital member of Christ's Body. To do that, I want to challenge some of the misconceptions that have pervaded the Church concerning signs, wonders and miracle. I'm going to teach you how to walk in the realm of signs, wonders and miracles. This chapter is worth the price of this book, for it will enable you to move into a new dimension of your walk with Christ – the realm of the miraculous. All believers are called and should desire to move in this realm.

Since February 23, 1987, the date of my salvation, I have experienced many miracles. I have heard God's audible voice. Through an open vision, I have seen God's glory. I have experienced angelic visitations, dreams, visions and other supernatural manifestations. I have seen the sick healed, the demon possessed set free and supernatural protection in extremely dangerous situations. By the power of the Holy Spirit, I have survived and thrived. My walk has been a walk of faith. I have learned how the supernatural can become natural, as we depend on the person and power of the Holy Spirit. Remember, we have the Holy Spirit residing in us. Amazing!

The Holy Spirit is here right now living on the inside of us, you and me. Because He lives in us, we all have the power and ability necessary to work and walk in signs, wonders and miracles. But, to do that, we need to learn how to walk in this spiritual realm, and that doesn't necessarily come naturally. We grow and can grow in living in the realm of the miraculous. And, we can become more and more proficient in walking in the miraculous and working miracles, as we learn how miracles happen.

Miracles Happen in the Here and Now... Today

Miracles happen in this world; they are a suspension of this world's natural laws. No miracles are needed in heaven for natural laws do not exist there. We're called to live in the realm of miracles now. We're anointed to live in that realm. But due to ignorance and unbelief, much of the Church has failed to realize their potential to walk and work in this supernatural realm. That can and will change, if you let it, right now. You can see miracles happen in your life. That's God's will.

> *[T]he gospel can only be fully preached when it's accompanied by signs, wonders and miracles.*

How do I know? Jesus walked in miracles. He is our example. The Christian life is more than being good or doing good: it's about doing the impossible. Christ's resurrection was impossible. Christ's birth was impossible. Christ's sinless life was impossible. Christ's ascension was impossible. Everything Jesus did was impossible, and often, it had never been done before. And, so it is with you and I. We are called to do the impossible.

Why are some more proficient at walking in and working miracles? Why do some people experience more miracles than others? Why do some experience more results? Why do some experience no results? I have asked these questions, and others, which have led me to write this book and a series of study guides, to help believers begin to walk in the power of the gospel. I want you to experience the gospel's power, daily. Paul said, *"I am not ashamed of the gospel, because it is the power of God for salvation to everyone who believes, first to the Jew, then to the Greek."* Rom. 1:16, *BSB.* Paul spoke these words to a church located in the heart of Rome. Rome was a wicked city, a pagan palace. Rome was ruled by demons and dominated by demonic power. Brutal. Godless. Pagan. Perverted. All describe Rome. But in Rome, Paul spoke: *"the gospel is God's power."* Listen and believe. The gospel is raw power – God's power – to those who believe.

The Gospel is God's Power Revealed

Since the gospel is God's power, when did the gospel begin? That's a good question. The gospel did have a beginning: *"The beginning of the gospel of Jesus Christ, the Son of God."* Mk. 1:1, *ESV.* When did the gospel begin? Galatians 3:8 says, *"The Scripture foresaw that God would justify the Gentiles by faith and foretold the gospel to Abraham: 'All nations will be blessed through you.'"* By that Scripture, we know Abraham heard and believed the gospel. Further, we discover the gospel was preached to the Jewish people prior to Christ's birth: *"We have heard the same Good News that your ancestors heard. But the message didn't help those who heard it in the past because they didn't believe."* Heb. 4:2, *GWT.* Or, the true gospel + real faith = raw power. The Jewish people heard the gospel, but didn't believe it, and as a result, the gospel became ineffective to them. For that reason, the gospel was taken from them and given to those who would believe it – the Gentiles, i.e., the nations.

From the beginning of creation, the gospel was intended for all Mankind, all nations, not one nation, Israel: *"In you shall all the nations be blessed."* Gal 3:8, *ESV*. As such, Jesus commanded His disciples: *"Go the whole world over, and proclaim the Good News to all Mankind."* Mk. 16:15, *WNT*. The gospel was given to the Jewish people: *"He has chosen you to be His people, prized above all others on the face of the earth."* Deut. 7:6, *NET*. Why did God choose the Jewish people? *"The LORD did not set His heart on you and choose you because you were more numerous than other nations, for you were the smallest of all nations! Rather, it was simply that the LORD loves you, and He was keeping the oath He had sworn to your ancestors."* Deut. 7:7-8, *NLT*. God chose the Jewish people to preach the gospel to the nations: *"When the Most High divided to the nations their inheritance, when He separated the sons of Adam, He set the bounds of the people according to the number of the children of Israel."* Deut. 32:8, *WBT*. But they didn't preach the gospel. Instead, they isolated themselves as a nation.

Tradition & Religion: Hindrances to Walking in God's Power

When Jesus came, the Jewish people had little to no contact with the outside world. The nations were ripe for harvest: *"I tell you, open your eyes and look at the fields! They are ripe for harvest."* Jn. 4:35, *NIV*. The nations needed the gospel, but the nation assigned to preach the gospel, Israel, didn't believe the gospel. Instead, the Jewish people chose religious tradition: *"You revoke God's Word by your tradition that you have handed down."* Mk. 7:13, *HCSB*. Israel refused to preach the gospel, even though they knew it, due to their religious tradition handed down by the elders. Religious tradition stopped the Jewish people, Israel, from preaching the gospel to the nations.

What tradition? Many traditions. Jesus said, *"Woe to you Scribes and Pharisees, pretenders, who wash the outside of the cup and of the dish, but within are full of plunder and evil!"* Matt. 23:25, ABPE. What happened? Jesus said, *"Blind Pharisee! First, clean the inside of the cup and dish, and then the outside also will be clean."* Matt. 23:26, NIV. Where were the Jewish people blind? *"Watch out and beware of the leaven of the Pharisees and Sadducees."* Matt. 16:6, NIV. What leaven? Jesus said, *"Why can't you understand that I'm not talking about bread? So again I say, 'Beware of the yeast of the Pharisees and Sadducees.' Then at last they understood that He wasn't speaking about the yeast in bread, but about the deceptive teaching of the Pharisees and Sadducees."* Matt. 16:11-12, NLT. The Jewish people were deceived by the teachings of the leaders of Israel. That's what stopped them from moving forward and declaring the gospel to the nations.

Peter's Vision and the Breaking of Jewish Tradition

After Pentecost, Peter received a vision in a trance that enabled him to see what was still hidden: God wanted the gospel to be preached to the nations. In that vision, Peter heard these words: *"What God has made clean, you must not consider ritually unclean!"* Acts. 10:15, NET. Prior to this visitation, Peter had this mindset: *"You are well aware that it is against our law for a Jew to associate with or visit a Gentile."* Acts 10:28, NIV. That mindset gripped the entire nation of Israel. Deception had clouded Israel's vision of the truth: the gospel was meant to be preached in all nations. Since Abraham, that mandate has not changed. And, that mandate is still in effect today. We the Church are called to carry the gospel to the nations. What about Israel? Because the Jewish people chose isolation and refused to preach the gospel, they lost the gospel: *"That, I tell you, is the reason why the Kingdom of God will be taken away from you, and given to a nation that will exhibit the power of it."* Matt. 21:43, WNT.

For nearly 2,000 years, the Jewish people remained in darkness. Most Jewish people refused to receive the gospel's light. Instead, they chose the darkness of ignorance. God allowed them to make that choice, knowing that, through their choice, the nations would receive the gospel. Paul said: *"I do not want you to be ignorant of this mystery, brothers, so that you will not be conceited: A hardening in part has come to Israel, until the full number of the Gentiles has come in."* Rom. 11:25, BSB. *"Did God reject His people? By no means!"* Rom. 11:1, NIV. What happened? Paul tells us: *"I have reserved for myself seven thousand who have not bowed the knee to Baal."* Rom. 11:4, BSB. Even today, a remnant exists who are called to preach the gospel to the nations: *"Thus, then, in the present time also there has been a remnant according to election of grace."* Rom. 11:5, DBT. That remnant, chosen by grace, carries the gospel to the nations.

Why does God still choose men and women from among the Jewish people to preach the gospel? Through them, God secures the gospel. By grace, they are called to share the gospel of grace. We, too, have received grace to believe the gospel and to share that gospel. God, in His wisdom, has used the unbelief of the Jewish people, and the nations, to bestow His mercy on all Mankind. Rom. 11:30-33. How? By the gospel.

Using the Kingdom's Keys of Power

The gospel is revelation of what God has done through Christ for all Mankind. That revelation is the only key by which we can enter into the kingdom of God: *"For flesh and blood has not revealed this to you, but My Father who is in heaven."* Matt. 16:17, ESV. And, it's by that revelation, we advance the kingdom of God: *"And from the time John the Baptist began preaching until now, the Kingdom of Heaven has been forcefully advancing, and violent people are attacking it."* Matt. 11:12, NLT. How does the gospel advance? By preaching the gospel... with power.

The Church has failed to realize its importance in establishing Christ's reign on earth: *"For He must reign until He has put all His enemies under His feet."* 1 Cor. 15:25, NIV. When did Christ's reign begin? At His birth. Matt. 2:2. For nearly 2,000 years, the Church has been waiting on Jesus to bring His kingdom, but Christ is waiting on us, His Church, to establish His kingdom. How do we establish God's kingdom? By preaching the gospel with power and teaching things pertaining to the kingdom of God. The apostles understood this reality: *"It is not right that we should give up preaching the Word of God to serve tables."* Acts 6:2, *ESV*. Paul also understood this reality: *"Paul stayed there two full years in his own rented house, welcoming all who came to visit him. Boldly and freely he proclaimed the kingdom of God and taught about the Lord Jesus Christ."* Acts 28:30-31, *BSB*. That's how the Acts of the Apostles ends: with Paul preaching the gospel, and teaching on things pertaining to the kingdom of God.

Gospel preaching is vital. Gospel teaching, essential. We need more gospel. We need the pure gospel. But to preach the gospel, we must first know the gospel. And in that regard, we, the Church, have fallen woefully short. We do not know our message, for we fail to demonstrate its power. Paul said, *"For our gospel did not come to you in word only, but also in power, in the Holy Spirit, and with much assurance."* 1 Th. 1:5, *HCSB*. Demonstration of the gospel is an integral part of preaching the gospel: *"My message and my preaching were not with wise and persuasive words, but with a demonstration of the Spirit's power,"* 1 Cor.

The Church has failed to realize its importance in establishing Christ's reign on earth...

2:4, *NIV*. But, we can only demonstrate what we know. And, because we don't know the gospel, we have been unable to demonstrate its validity. That's where the Church has failed – where we have failed. Like Israel, we the Church have failed to fully preach the gospel. How? By disregarding the necessity of signs, wonder and miracles.

Heal the Sick... Raise the Dead

Recently, I was forced to examine my own calling. I was challenged by a word that I received: *"Heal the sick, cleanse the lepers, raise* the dead, cast out devils: freely ye have received, freely give." Matt. 10:8. When I heard that word, I immediately understood it wasn't a request. No, Christ had given me a direct command. For the first time, I realized that I was being commanded to do the miraculous. Then, I felt woefully underqualified. I thought of excuses for my failures to walk in more supernatural power. But, I realized there was no good excuse. I was being required to walk in signs, wonders and miracles at a level to which I had not walked up to that point in my life. But, I had been walking in the miraculous for 25 years to a degree at which many never walk. I witnessed the miraculous and walked in miracles. I did the impossible. But, what I experienced wasn't enough. I was underqualified for what I was called to do. And, so is the Church.

But, the command remains. Christ expects the impossible. Jesus doesn't blink when we say we can't. No, Christ's immediate response to us is: *"I tell you the truth, anyone who believes in Me will do the same works I have done, and even greater works, because I am going to be with the Father."* Jn. 14:12, *NLT*. So, like Peter, we're called to walk on water, heal with our shadow, see the lame walk and preach the gospel. Like Paul, we're called to raise the dead, experience unusual miracles and preach the gospel. Like John, we're called to heal the lame and preach the gospel. Like Jesus, we're called to open the eyes of the blind, restore limbs to the maimed, bring wholeness the hurting, feed the hungry and poverty stricken and bring deliverance to demonized. That's our calling. Like Jesus, we the Church must be about our Father's business. Lk. 2:49. And, our Father's business is miracles.

Doing God's Business God's Way

But, the Father's business is suffering. Why? Because, although humanity's need is immense, the workers are few. Jesus said, *"The harvest is vast, but the workers are few. So ask the Lord of the harvest to send workers out into his harvest."* Lk. 10:2, *ISV*. In the Greek, the word for workers is ***ergatés,*** which is derived from *ergazomai,* to work, and *ergon,* work. But, each word has deeper meaning. *Ergon* means to accomplish something and implies someone who makes something work or an employee who gets the job done. *Ergazomai* means someone who has a business or is employed in a professional trade and earns a living by it. So, laborer carries the meaning and understanding of someone who gets the job done no matter what, because they derive their living and earn their keep by what they do. When employed in the Father's business, doing is essential. The Father employs every son and daughter, you and me, in His business.

We're called to do a supernatural work. But oftentimes, we feel overwhelmed and underqualified for that work. The work will appear impossible. Miracles will be required to fulfill the work. And, we're rewarded on whether we complete the work or not. We have been assigned a task. We're expected to fulfill that task. What task? To preach the gospel to the nations with power. But, how will we fulfill that task? You may have been taught that the day of miracles is past. Others have Scriptures that appear to justify that position. But the fact remains, Christ expects us, His Church, to fully preach the gospel. And the gospel, according to Paul, cannot be fully preached unless there are accompanying signs, wonders and miracles. What shall we do? We can lean on our own understanding like the Jewish people did. Or, we can learn what we need to know to move into the realm of walking in and working miracles.

The HOW Behind the Working of Miracles

I'm here to teach you. I want to share with you what I know. I trust that what I share will help you. I believe that you will gain insight into "the how" behind the miraculous. Further, I believe you will partake of the anointing to walk in and work miracles. Grace will enter your life for that purpose. Expect it! So then, where do we start? We start by understanding how Jesus moved in the realm of the miraculous. Then, we can learn how He taught His disciples to move into that realm. Yes, Jesus taught His disciples and apostles how to walk in miracles. The miracles we see in Scripture are a short list of the miracles that Jesus did. John said, *"Jesus also did many other things. If they were all written down, I suppose the whole world could not contain the books that would be written."* Jn. 21:25, *NLT*. Miracles were a normal part of Jesus' life and ministry and they should be so in our lives and ministries. We're called to walk in miracles. But, how? That's what I want to share with you: the "how" behind the miracles.

Step 1: Seeing and then Doing

Let's begin. Briefly, we'll study what Jesus did. I have noticed several things that were a constant part of His life and ministry. And, it's from that place that I'd like to start. First, Jesus did nothing of Himself. *"I tell you the truth, the Son can do nothing by Himself. He does only what He sees the Father doing. Whatever the Father does, the Son also does."* Jn. 5:19, *NLT*. Christ started from the position of completely relying on the Father. That reliance shaped His entire life and ministry. And, that's a good place for us to start. We must learn to follow the Father. We must learn to listen to His instructions. In following and listening, we gain authority to work miracles with Him, through Him and for Him.

Step 2: Being Anointed

Jesus was anointed. *"The Spirit of the Lord is on Me, because He has anointed Me to preach good news to the poor. He has sent Me to proclaim deliverance to the captives and recovery of sight to the blind, to release the oppressed...."* Lk. 4:18, *BSB*. Jesus did what He did by the anointing. The Holy Spirit that was in Him and on Him enabled Him to do what He did. And, He realized this. That's why Jesus said, *"I tell you the truth: it is to your advantage that I go away, for if I do not go away, the Helper will not come to you. But if I go, I will send Him to you."* Jn. 16:7, *ESV*. When speaking of the Helper, Jesus was talking about the Holy Spirit. The Holy Spirit is vital to the working of miracles. Miracles are performed by the Holy Spirit. We cooperate with Him in the miracle ministry.

Step 3: Not My Will

Jesus did the Father's will not His own will. Jesus said, *"I have come down from heaven, not to do My own will, but the will of the one who sent Me."* Jn. 6:38, ISV. Jesus said, *"My food is to do the will of Him who sent Me and to finish His work."* Jn. 4:34, BSB. Jesus lived, breathed and drank God's will and work. Listen to what He said, *"My Father is always working, and so am I."* Jn. 5:17, NLT.

On the cross, Jesus' final words were, *"It is finished!"* Jn. 19:30, NLT. Jesus finished His work. Paul worked toward the same end. He said, *"I have worked harder than any of the other apostles; yet it was not I but God who was working through me by His grace."* 1 Cor. 15:10, NLT. At the end of His life, Paul said, *"I have fought the good fight, I have finished the race, I have kept the faith."* 2 Tim. 4:7, ESV.

Step 4: Fulfilling Prophecy

Jesus did what the Scriptures said. *"This was to fulfill what was spoken through the prophet Isaiah: "He took on our infirmities, and carried our diseases."* Matt. 8:17, BSB. The Scriptures were an integral part of Jesus' life. He read them. He studied them. He relied on them. By Scripture, He overcame the devil's temptations. Matt. 4:1-11. Jesus, in response to each temptation, said to the devil, *"It is written."* Matt. 4:4, 7 & 10. Christ believed in the integrity of Scripture, even the hard sayings. In response to the Jews objection to His claim to be the Son of God, Jesus said, *"And you know that the Scriptures cannot be altered. So if those people who received God's message were called 'gods'...."* Jn. 10:35, NLT. Further, Jesus said, *"I can guarantee this truth: Until the earth and the heavens disappear, neither a period nor a comma will disappear from Moses' Teachings before everything has come true."* Matt. 5:18, GWT.

Step 5: Prayer and More Prayer

Jesus prayed. *"He frequently withdrew to the wilderness to pray."* Lk. 5:16, *BSB*. Notice, He prayed frequently and often. Jesus took time to pray. Jesus didn't assume; He prayed. So impressed by Jesus' prayer life, one of His disciples asked Him, *"Master, teach us to pray, just as John taught his disciples."* Lk. 11:1, *WNT*. In response, Jesus said, *"When you pray, say,"* Lk. 11:2, *WEB*,

> *"Our Father which art in heaven, hallowed be Thy Name. Thy kingdom come. Thy will be done in earth, as it is in heaven. Give us this day our daily bread. And forgive us our debts, as we forgive our debtors. And lead us not into temptation, but deliver us from evil: for Thine is the kingdom, and the power, and the glory, for ever. Amen."* Matt. 6:9-13.

That's how Jesus prayed. Jesus prayed to the Father. Jesus honored the Father. Jesus prayed for the Father's will to be done. Jesus relied on the Father for His provision. Jesus relied on the Father to deal with debts. Jesus relied on the Father for deliverance from temptation and evil. Jesus recognized the reality of God's kingdom. Jesus was kingdom focused, minded and centered. And, we should be too. Everything is about manifesting and establishing God's kingdom. And, kingdom reality is always birthed in prayer. There's no other way. Everything in the kingdom is by prayer.

Step 6: Fasting is Required

Jesus fasted. *"For forty days and forty nights He fasted and became very hungry."* Matt. 4:2, *NLT*. Fasting was integral to Christ's calling. Fasting prepared the way for Christ to move forward in His calling. Without fasting, He could have been unprepared for the temptations thrown at Him. Fasting was necessary. Jesus said, *"When you fast...."* not if you fast. Matt. 6:16. And, it's necessary for those who desire to walk in the miraculous. *"And your Father, who sees in secret, will reward you."* Matt. 6:18, *NET*. Fasting prepares the way for miracles. *"Then your light will*

*break forth like the dawn, and your healing will spring up quickly;
and your vindication will go before you, and the glory of the LORD
will guard your back."* Is. 58:8, ISV.

But, fasting must be done for the right reasons and the right way.
*"[T]his is the kind of fasting I want: Free those who are wrongly
imprisoned; lighten the burden of those who work for you. Let the
oppressed go free, and remove the chains that bind people. Share
your food with the hungry, and give shelter to the homeless. Give
clothes to those who need them, and do not hide from relatives
who need your help."* Is. 58:6,7, NLT. Fasting, for it to be effective,
requires right motives and right actions.

Step 7: Honoring Authority

Jesus honored, and walked in divine authority. Jesus told John,
*"This is the way it has to be now. This is the proper way to do
everything that God requires of us."* Matt. 3:15, GWT. *"The people
were amazed at His teaching, for He taught with real authority –
quite unlike the teachers of religious law."* Mk. 1:22, NLT. When
someone has real authority, others will notice it. When we lack that
authority, others will see that. *"The men were amazed and asked,
'What kind of man is this? Even the winds and the waves obey
Him!'"* Matt. 8:27, NIV. Jesus continually walked in this kind of
authority. Usually, He instructed. Matt. 5:2. Often, He commanded.
Matt. 10:5. And on occasion, He rebuked Peter (Mk. 8:33), James
and John (Lk. 9:55).

Jesus had authority and He knew it. The Jewish leaders demanded
of Christ: *"Tell us by what authority do you do these things, and
who is he who has given you this authority?"* Lk. 20:2, ABPE.
Rather than acquiescing to their demands, Jesus asked them one
question: *"John's baptism – was it from heaven, or of human
origin?"* Lk. 20:4, NIV. Paul expressly said concerning his own
sphere of authority, *"Neither do we go beyond our limits by
boasting of work done by others. Our hope is that, as your faith
continues to grow, our sphere of activity among you will greatly*

expand...." 10:15, *NIV*. As such, stay in your lane, operate in your authority and allow that authority to expand in the right way: by what you do and the impact your works have had on the lives of others. Don't spend time talking about what others have done. Walk in your authority. Focus on what you have done and are doing. This is how genuine authority functions, always. True leaders know this and operate from this place of authority.

Step 8: Preach the Gospel

Lastly, Jesus practiced and preached the gospel. *"And Jesus went about all Galilee, teaching in their synagogues, and preaching the gospel of the kingdom, and healing all manner of sickness and all manner of disease among the people."* Matt. 4:23. Preaching the gospel was one of the most significant works done by Christ. Jesus said, *"The sower sows the word."* Mk. 4:14, *ESV*. Jesus was sent to the Jewish people. Matt. 15:24. Jesus sent His disciples to the Jewish people. Matt. 10:6. John preached, Jesus preached and Jesus' disciples preached. Matt. 3:1; 4:7; 10:7. After His ascension, Jesus worked with His disciples and confirmed the word preached with signs following. *"And the disciples went everywhere and preached, and the Lord worked through them, confirming what they said by many miraculous signs."* Mk. 16:20, *NLT*.

Jesus has not stopped working. No, He is working today. Where? When? How? In confirmation of what is preached by those whom He sends to preach the gospel. Signs, wonders and miracles follow the preaching of the gospel. That's why the gospel must be preached, and it's only fully preached where signs, wonders and miracles are manifested.

Beginning Your Miracle Ministry

Where do we start? We start by beginning. And, beginning starts by doing. We all learn by doing what we know and then we grow. Although some may be endowed with extraordinary gifts in specific areas, the vast majority of us learn to do what we do as we do what we do. We get better through practice. And, preaching the gospel is no different. We should practice preaching as much as we should practice what we preach. Many have been taught to practice what they preach, but few have been taught to practice their preaching. We must practice preaching the gospel. Before we practice preaching the gospel, let's ensure that our content is accurate.

In media, content is always king. In preaching, it's no different – we must have the right content. What is that? To preach, we must know. To know, we must study. To study, we must be willing to learn. To learn, we must go to the right source. Our source is the Scripture. Also, our source is godly men and women who have learned the Scriptures.

We must always listen to the message being preached to determine if its foundation is Scripture. No matter who is preaching, if the foundation of the message shared is not Scripture, it's flawed. The same is true of prophecy. We preach as we learn and our ability to preach grows as we learn. Then, our language of preaching develops and matures. That maturation process is one of the things I'm detailing in this book. I want you, the reader, to understand the process of growth in, of and for the kingdom of God.

I have spent years learning and listening to the gospel. I have seen what works, and I have seen what doesn't work. Men/women who have succeeded in preaching the gospel well aren't always the most spiritual. But, they have learned a secret. What secret? They have learned how to skillfully preach under the unction of the Holy Spirit and communicate their message in stories that people can relate to. Besides the previous understanding of operating in the miraculous, those two keys will help you practically see miracles manifest as you preach the gospel message. The KISS (Keep It Simple, Saints) principle works.

Keep it Simple, Saints (KISS)

One of my favorite ministers, T.L. Osborn, believed in the simplicity of the gospel message: he taught others to keep the gospel message simple and to focus on God's love. There, he discovered, people had faith to receive miracles and find their way to salvation. Remember, Jesus is real. And, He longs to intervene in people's lives. God is good and the devil is bad. That simplicity enables others to overcome their fears: fear of the unknown, fear of failure and even a false fear of God. Clarity is key to sharing the gospel, and seeing miracles follow the preaching of the gospel requires that kind of simplicity.

Osborn shares the story of how he began in the miracle ministry. Osborn and his wife, Daisy, had come back from a missionary journey in India; it was a complete failure, no converts. Then, while back in the United States, Osborn went to a famous evangelist's healing crusade. As he saw miracles being done, Osborn said within himself, "I can do that!"

> **_Faith is not impossible; it's just difficult._**

Then, he went out and did it. That's the key. What was the difference in his missionary journey and the ministry that followed his failure? Osborn believed. Osborn had a simple faith in God that he acquired by seeing miracles being done in Jesus' Name. You can do it! Only believe!

Faith is not impossible; it's just difficult. And, the first step is always the hardest one to take. Preaching is like that. Miracles are like that. The first step is always the scariest. Why? Because the question comes to mind: What if? What if God doesn't do miracles? What if I look like a fool? What if it doesn't work for me? What if? To move forward, you have to turn your "What if?" into an "I can!" That the strength of faith. Faith makes the impossible possible. Faith changes a "no way" into "yes, I did." I'd rather take a foolish step in faith and miss it than remain in the land of unbelief and doubt. Doubt is no place for a saint to live. Live in faith.

Finding Grace to Fulfill God's Call

As we practice preaching and practice what we preach, we must also practice entering into the realm of miracles. Our lives should be, as

Paul described, living epistles, known and read by all men. 2 Cor. 3:2-3. Miracles don't just happen; they begin forcefully, by faith. Faith doesn't sit back and wait; it moves forward when it should be afraid. You may be scared by this concept. Maybe you agree, but you have not yet experienced miracles in your own life. Or, maybe you don't believe in the concept of signs, wonders and miracles being central to the gospel message. I understand. I'm not going to try to dissuade you. I'm only sharing my belief and experience with you.

We're called to do a supernatural work. And, that work may be dangerous. But, whether or not it's dangerous to have faith, we must choose to believe. In moving forward in faith, our fears are overcome and grace is released. Grace is always gained as we step out in faith. Grace is where the gospel grows. The gospel requires grace and faith. Miracles also require grace and faith. The gospel and miracles go hand-in-hand and they point to the person of Jesus Christ. That's the purpose of the gospel and miracles, or the gospel of miracles. God is a God of miracles; He delights in working miracles. He did in Jesus' day and He has not changed.

But, often, we feel overwhelmed by the necessity of the work, and we can feel underqualified to do it. But, that's where we find the grace given is sufficient for the work assigned. You have an assignment. I have an assignment. Your assignment isn't my assignment. My assignment isn't your assignment. Each of us has been given grace according to our own particular assignment and calling to a particular work. And, if we're faithful to that assignment, we're rewarded for our faithfulness. God doesn't measure us like we measure ourselves or others. No, He measures us based upon our accomplishment of the task assigned. So, our focus should be squarely on determining what our assignment is and how we're called to fulfill that assignment.

Are Miracles for Today?

Before closing this chapter, I want to answer an objection some may have about all of us being called to work miracles. To do that, I'll respond to a Scripture in 1 Corinthians 12:28-31, *NASB*, which says, *"Not all are apostles, are they? Not all are prophets, are they? Not all are teachers, are they? Not all perform miracles, do they? All do not have gifts of healings, do they? All do not speak with tongues, do they? All do not interpret, do they? But earnestly desire the greater gifts. And I show you a still more excellent way."* Does this Scripture contradict my statement that all of us have been called to walk in the realm of working miracles?

At first glance, it would seem to, but as we take a deeper look we can see that it does not. How so? In the same way, all do not speak with tongues via the gift of tongues, all do not work miracles via the gift of working of miracles. The gift of working of miracles is a special endowment given to certain men and women for the express purpose of demonstrating the miraculous and teaching others to walk in the miraculous. So, some may have a greater propensity to work miracles than others, but all are called to walk in the realm of signs, wonders and miracles. How do I know? The Scriptures teach: *"I and the children whom the LORD has given me are for signs and for wonders in Israel from the LORD of hosts, who dwells in mount Zion."* Is. 8:18. All God's children are called to move in the realm of signs, wonders and miracles.

Think about it for a second. On Pentecost in Jerusalem, nearly 2,000 years ago, God's miraculous power was poured into and onto the entire Body of Christ. That means, Christ's entire Body is anointed. As such, the entire Body of Christ is anointed to live, work and walk in signs, wonders and miracles. That how God approved of Christ, isn't it? Acts 2:22. Even the fringe of Christ's clothing was anointed, how much more His body? Matt. 9:20. Jesus was anointed. You are anointed. After Jesus was anointed, He began to work miracles; they were a natural expression of the anointing on His life. And, so it will be with you. Miracles are a natural extension of your life as a believer.

Only Believe!

Please understand: you have a special gifting to work miracles. I'm not taking away from that. Apostles are known by their propensity to work miracles. I'm not taking away from that either. No, miracles are a ministry in the church that we desperately need, and so is genuine apostolic ministry. We should investigate whether those who claim to be apostles are really apostles by checking to see if signs, wonders and miracles are following them. Also, as believers, we should check to see if our faith is real by looking to see if signs, wonders and miracles are following us.

> *Only believe! Preach the gospel! Expect miracles! Repeat!*

In closing, prior to His ascension, Jesus gave His disciples – His apostles – this last and final command to them:

> "As you go into all the world, proclaim the gospel to everyone. Whoever believes and is baptized will be saved, but whoever doesn't believe will be condemned. These are the signs that will accompany those who believe: In My Name they will drive out demons, they will speak in new languages, and they will pick up snakes with their hands, even if they drink any deadly poison it will not hurt them; and they'll place their hands on the sick, and they'll recover." Mk. 16:15-18, *ISV*.

Now what? Only believe! Preach the gospel! Expect miracles! Repeat! Amen.

Chapter Seventeen

The Gospel Message is Foundational

To this point, I have focused on providing a framework for the gospel's theology. I have done this to create a point of reference to understand the gospel. I have focused the substance of this book on gaining an understanding of what the gospel is and how it works in practice. But in this chapter, I want to move into a more practical understanding of the gospel. I want to share my vision for advancing the gospel in the vocabulary of local churches. My goal is to enable local churches to equip and enable their members to share the gospel with family, friends and acquaintances. This, more than anything else, will enable churches to preach the gospel to their communities, impact those communities and reverse the modern trend toward local church's obsolescence within the community. We must reach our communities with the gospel.

For that to happen, I'm convinced of the local church's need to equip its members to learn how to proclaim the gospel. The success of churches is dependent on its members learning how to proclaim the gospel to family, friends and acquaintances. Local churches stand or fall on this singular attribute. When church members are equipped to proclaim the gospel, churches thrive. When church members fail to proclaim the gospel, churches die. And in today's society, church members are becoming increasingly devoid of understanding as to how and when to preach the gospel. That's why the majority of local churches in our nation are struggling. That must change. But, the question is: How?

The Church Triumphant: The Gospel's Goal

First, I want to share a statement of significant importance in relation to the gospel and the Church: Jesus said, *"You are Peter, and I can guarantee that on this rock I will build My Church. And the gates of hell will not overpower it."* Matt. 16:18, *GWT*. Christ said, *"I will build My Church."* The Church isn't Man's idea but Christ's conception. Jesus gave Himself to give birth to the Church. We're here today because of what Christ did. And, we'll continue in our significance by listening to what Christ says. We must never lose our positional understanding that Jesus Christ is in charge of His Church. My boss, and yours, is a former Jewish carpenter from Galilee.

In building the Church, we must further understand that revelation of Christ is the rock upon which the Church is built. And revelation, by its very nature, is a work of the Holy Spirit. The Holy Spirit reveals who Christ is. *"When the Spirit of truth comes, He will guide you into all truth. He will not speak on His own but will tell you what He has heard. He will tell you about the future. He will bring Me glory by telling you whatever He receives from Me."* Jn. 16:13,14, *NLT*. We obtain revelation by and from the Holy Spirit of the person of Christ. So, from the ground up, the local church must have a clear revelation of Christ, which it obtains by the Holy Spirit.

Empowering Churches, Transforming Lives

Pastors are responsible for and required to create an environment where the Holy Spirit can work to bring that revelation to the church members. When that environment exists, church members thrive, for the Holy Spirit works in the church members to change the hardest of human conditions – the heart. Only the Holy Spirit can change hearts. And pastors, if you want to see your church succeed, hearts must be transformed. From what? Congregants must be motivated by more than self. The average church member, like many in the world, when it considers the church, says, "What's in it for me?" But, that question reveals a wrong heart attitude. Instead, congregants must learn to ask, "How may I serve you, Lord?" or "Pastor, what I can I do to help?"

But pastors, that's not enough. We cannot just ask church members to serve. Participation isn't transformation. And, the gospel is transformative. If the gospel preached doesn't transform, then a problem exists. Paul revealed a simple cause and effect formula: gospel preaching + gospel believing = gospel transformation. When faith is present, the true gospel always transforms the recipient. That's the power of the gospel. The gospel always transforms the believer. And, that's what we should expect from church members: for a transformation to take place in the hearts and minds of members and those in attendance.

The gospel is transformative. And, that transformation begins in the heart. But, not everyone is transformed by the gospel. The gospel only transforms those who believe it. When there's an absence of faith, no transformation takes place. And, from observation, church members are not being transformed by the gospel. Rather, churches are changing the Church, and in some cases, the gospel, to acquiesce to church members. That type of transformation is not good. Rather, it's motivated by hardness of heart. And, our hearts are hard. We church members can no longer differentiate between what is gospel and what is not gospel.

Reclaiming the Gospel's Clear Sound in the Local Church

We must reclaim our understanding of the gospel and its importance. We must regain lost ground in spreading the gospel. We must relearn how to proclaim the gospel to a new generation without changing the gospel. We must rethink how to reach a new generation with the gospel. We must look to a new future that's filled with gospel vision for a bright future. We must retool churches and believers with new hope to proclaim the gospel. I'm convinced of this need: local churches need the gospel and pastors must equip their members to proclaim the gospel. And for that to happen, major changes must take place in our understanding of the gospel.

The local church is the bastion of the global Church. The local church is where the global Church meets the community. Many have tried to replace the need for local churches. And, some have sought to change or redefine it. Some have denied that the local church is needed. But, the gospel must have a context from which it flows to the world. And, that context is the local church. Being part of the global Church is not enough. We must also be submitted and committed to a local church. And for many, that's a problem. Believers have left local churches. Why? For various reasons. But in general, believers have felt that they aren't receiving what they need. And in many cases, they're right. But, who's fault is that? And, what is the right response?

I believe that local churches are failing because believers are unable or unwilling to commit. That lack of commitment is demonstrated in the following areas: 1) lack of attendance and/or regular tardiness, 2) lack of involvement or volunteerism and 3) lack of tithing and/or giving. Pastors regularly give much of themselves to their churches. Annually, pastors are leaving the ministry by the thousands. Why? Burnout. But, pastors shouldn't be burning out. And, church members should understand Christ's requirements in His kingdom. In His kingdom, discipleship is mandatory, not optional. But, pastors have made discipleship optional. That's why the local church is suffering. And, that lack of discipleship is a clear contradiction of the gospel.

The Transformative Message of the Cross

The gospel requires discipleship. The gospel requires commitment. The gospel requires sacrifice and service. The gospel requires giving. The gospel requires obedience. That's the cross we're all called to bear. Paul exhorted Timothy: *"Teach these things and insist that everyone learn them."* 1 Tim. 4:11, *NLT.* But in many churches, that's not being taught. Instead, pastors have focused their energies on giving church members what they want... Feed me! Give me! and Mine! are still problems pastors deal with every day. Pathetic. To quote the title of David Ravenhill's book, *For God's sake: Grow Up!* But, that's from his prophetic vantage point of frustration with many modern-day believers. And, mine.

> **We must retool churches and believers with new hope to proclaim the gospel.**

Yes, there's a cross to carry. Yes, sometimes the church services will be boring. Yes, sometimes, we won't feel like going to church. Yes, sometimes we'll feel excluded by leaders. Yes, pastors will often ask more than they should. Yes, believers will ask more than they should. Yes, transgressions will abound. That's life. And in life, we learn how to deal with issues. We confront. We love. We share. We cooperate. We make things work, if possible. And if we can't, or if others won't, we move on and find greener pastures. But first, discipleship means there's a commitment to learn. And to learn, we must be willing to hear what we may not want to hear. The truth hurts sometimes.

Jamie Buckingham, known for his satiric wit, wrote the book, *The Truth Will Set You Free, But First It Will Make You Miserable.* I think many can say, "Amen!" The gospel has a price. And that price is described by the Greek word, **Koinonia**, meaning participation, communion and fellowship. In the Greek, the idea is one of sharing. That means we learn to share. To give and take. To participate and interact. We aren't born again with these abilities. No, we learn them by living in a community of caring believers. That's what the local church is called to be: a loving and sharing community of believers who love one another, pray for one another and support one another. And, we all need that, don't we?

Moving Toward Genuine Discipleship... Everyday

How does that kind of community form in local churches? By discipleship. By preaching the gospel. By loving and listening to one another. By studying and learning. By prayer. My belief is that local churches are failing because of lack of commitment. Discipleship is a major issue in churches. Many believers have no concept of discipleship. Today, many believers that "worship," leave a "tip" in the offering for the music... and leave untransformed. Participation is optional. Prayer non-existent. And, most believers never share the gospel... with anyone. Why? Fear. Believers are scared to share. And, fears arise in hearts because of feelings of inadequacy. We don't think we can and we don't know how. Why? Because believers have not been equipped.

I want to change that. I want you to believe you can preach the gospel. Does that mean I'm expecting you to preach the gospel on the street corner of your local community? No. Does that mean I'm going to ask you to go house-to-house to total strangers and share the gospel? No. Am I going to encourage you to share the gospel with your friends and family member? Yes. How can you be involved in spreading the gospel message once you know what it is? That's what I want to explore. I want to provide a structure, framework and context whereby believers in everyday life can preach the gospel in a non-confrontational way... and see results.

How I Found Grace to Preach the Gospel

From the beginning of my salvation, I had an overwhelming desire to preach the gospel. I was hungry and excited. I had been lost. And, I knew what it was like to be found. I wanted others to know what I had gained. I loved listening to the gospel. And, I'd spend countless hours listening: by tape, by television and in person. I'd often look forward to special evangelists coming to preach the gospel on the University of Iowa campus at the Pentacrest. Several hundred students would gather to listen. The atmosphere was electric and the evangelists were dynamic. I once tried preaching this way and failed miserably. I wasn't called to preach like that. I was called to preach like I'm called to preach.

I didn't know much. And, the gospel I shared was simple. But, I would share it with everyone I met. I looked for opportunities to share the gospel. And, some were saved. The reward of seeing the lost saved was exhilarating. But in my personal relationships, I came across as preachy. My family was unable to receive from me. My friends were few and primarily Christian. I became isolated. And, that isolation persisted... for years. I have finally come to see what happened: I became lost in the gospel to the needs of the lost. By God's grace, I was willing to change. And, I have changed. I'm much more approachable, teachable and graceful in my approach to preaching the gospel. I have become a "smooth man of God" as one prophecy I received stated I would become.

To reach others, I changed. I became more than I was. How? By discipleship. I allowed other men and women of God to mentor me. I believe the Biblical model for discipleship is mentoring. We learn what we learn one-on-one with someone we trust. Pastors, I want to encourage you to learn how to disciple by mentoring those closest to you. Paul taught Timothy: *"What you have heard from me through many witnesses entrust to faithful people who will be able to teach others as well."* 2 Tim. 2:2, *ISV.* That's the discipleship model outlined in Scripture. Jethro taught Moses: *"But select from all the people some capable, honest men who fear God and hate bribes. Appoint them as leaders over groups of one thousand, one hundred, fifty and ten."* Ex. 18:21, *NLT.*

America: A Gospel Revolution is Brewing

A revolution is brewing. The winds of change are blowing. And, we can be carried on them or we can be carried away by them. I don't want to see believers and churches carried every which way by the winds of doctrines that are currently blowing in the church. False gospels, false ministers and false words have led to dismal results. Instead, I desire to see a gospel revolution. To that end, I'm creating a series of study guides to assist pastors and church leaders to help their members learn how to preach the gospel. In them, I'm going to share practical ways you can take what we have learned in this book and begin to use it to proclaim the gospel. I hope that you will use them to learn how to preach the gospel. [For more information, see the catalog at the end of this book or go to the Web site: www.thegospelisenough.com or www.gospel-revolution.com.]

The gospel is enough to transform any nation, including America.

In America, a different kind of revolution is brewing. Many Americans are upset with the leaders of our political system. Many are disillusioned. Justice has fallen in the streets. Is. 59:14. Terror and violent crimes are on the rise. Police shootings are a significant issue, as is government corruption. Americans are afraid. Why? Hopelessness. Helplessness. Many don't feel they can stop the deterioration of our nation. But, I want to encourage you, in the power of the gospel's transformative message. There is hope. The gospel is enough to transform this nation. To that end, I want to cultivate an American gospel revolution. I want the gospel to become the singular focus of the church. That we would truly believe The Gospel is Enough.

The Gospel Revolution Has Begun

The gospel is revolutionary. The gospel is the most powerful force on earth today; it's the greatest agent of change known to Mankind. The gospel is enough to transform any nation, including America. We can change our nation. How? By applying what I have written in this book. To do that, I want to create and publish study guides of various facets of the gospel to help believers understand and share the gospel message with others. So, this book is not an end in itself. Rather, it's a beginning.

Will you begin to share the gospel? Will you join the gospel army? Will you join the army of gospel laborers who have been equipped to share the gospel? Will you become a gospel laborer? I hope so. Jesus is recruiting. I believe that your decision to sign up to his all-volunteer army will set the course of your life toward victory. And to that end, I'm prophesying breakthrough over your life.

When facing Goliath, David said to his brothers, *"Is there not a cause?"* 1 Sam. 17:29. Today, like David, many are facing Goliaths. Goliath was intimidating and represents intimidation. You may feel intimidated by the concept of sharing the gospel. And like David, we must rise up and say, "Yes, there is a cause." Church, we have the greatest cause on Planet Earth today and its rewards are eternal. The gospel is powerful. The gospel is needed. The gospel is enough. You can trust in and rely on the gospel. Believe that. Now, step out in faith. Believe the gospel. Share the gospel. Preach the gospel. You can do it.

In the Bible, four lepers were sitting at the gate of the city of Samaria and waiting. For what? They were waiting to die. Why? Food was scarce and they were lepers. No one cared if they lived or died... except God. God sparked something inside them that made them ask this question: *"Why just sit here until we die?"* 2 Kgs. 7:3, HCSB. That question sparked in them the desire to move forward in life. They were no longer content to sit back and wait for something to come to them. No, they arose and went to get what they wanted – food and clothing. The four lepers wanted to live.

I want you to live. The gospel is life. The gospel is health. The gospel is blessing. The gospel is provision. We need the gospel. We must hear the gospel. We must preach the gospel. We must believe the gospel. Pastors, your church needs the gospel. Believers, you need the gospel. Fathers, your children need the gospel. Mothers, your children need the gospel. Families need the gospel. Communities need the gospel. Cities need the gospel. Nations need the gospel. The gospel is enough: for you, your church, your city, your state, your nation and the world. Be transformed by the power of the gospel. Believe it! Amen.

Other Books Available from Lighthouse Publications

These and other Christian books from Lighthouse Publications are available at participating local Christian bookstores, *Amazon.com* & *Bn.com.*

To order books directly from Lighthouse Publications:

Lighthouse Publications
www.lighthouse-publications.com
Ph: (224) 200-5175

Apostolic Team Ministry

Scott Wallis, Pastor/Prophet, provides practical answers to the questions that many believers have, such as: "How can I overcome lack in my life?" Learn why apostles are so important to the purpose and plans of God, and how apostolic teams release tremendous supernatural power and wealth into the Church.

Author: Scott Wallis
Retail Price: $11.99
ISBN: 0964221128

The Third Reformation is Coming

Prophetic leaders have been declaring for several years that a third reformational movement of the Holy Spirit was about to begin. Find out what this third reformation is and how it will radically change the Church and your life.

Author: Scott Wallis
Retail Price: $9.99
ISBN: 0964221144

How to Know if Your Prophecy is Really from God

One of the most important books on prophecy available for Believers. If you have ever received a prophetic word, then this book will help you discern if that word was from God, and if it was, what to do with it to see it fulfilled.

Author: Scott Wallis
Retail Price: $11.99
ISBN: 1931232415

Plugging into the Spirit of Prophecy

God has designed every believer to walk in the prophetic. You can learn how to flow in the Holy Spirit of prophecy. This exciting book will teach you how to do this and more. You will experience God's awesome power through the prophetic word.

Author: Scott Wallis
Retail Price: $13.99
ISBN: 1931232210

Entering the School of the Prophets

Scott Wallis' third book in his series on understanding prophetic ministry that answers questions regarding the prophetic office and its value to the Body of Christ today. A great resource for those desiring to understand more about the prophetic office and ministry.

Author: Scott Wallis
Retail Price: $13.99
ISBN: 1-933656-04-2

Decade of Destiny

A powerful prophetic word detailing what God is doing in our days. First written in 1991, this timeless book has proven to be an accurate window into the future. Discover what God is saying to His Church today!

Author: Scott Wallis
Retail Price: $11.99
ISBN: 0964221195

Secret Corruption

www.SecretCorruption.com

A provocative, insightful and honest look at America's legal system from the perspective of an outsider, a non-attorney, someone who is an experienced *pro se* litigator. The litigation industry has become our nation's most corrupt enterprise, a place where dishonesty, bribery and corruption reigns.

Author: Scott Wallis
Retail Price: $14.99
ISBN: 9781619965458

The Gospel is Enough

NEW STUDY MATERIALS!

www.TheGospelisEnough.com
www.Gospel-Revolution.com

TEACHER'S MANUAL: For a more serious discussion and classroom study of this compelling work, a companion soft-cover **Teacher's Manual** is available in module sets. Please visit the Web site below or contact Lighthouse Publications for more detailed information and to order.

Author: Scott Wallis
Retail Price: Available upon request

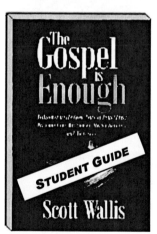

STUDENT GUIDE: For a more serious discussion and classroom study of this compelling work, additional soft-cover **Student Guides** are available in quantity. Please visit the Web site below or contact Lighthouse Publications for more detailed information and to order.

Author: Scott Wallis
Retail Price: Available upon request

Contact the Author, Scott Wallis

 Scott Wallis was called into ministry through an open vision where he saw the glory of God. Since then, he has sought to fulfill that heavenly mandate: to school coming generations in the things of God.

Wallis, a prophet, brings a wealth of wisdom obtained through 25+ years of ministry. He has travelled in ministry as a prophet, pastored a local church, owned and/or operated several businesses, including a multi-million dollar international business.

Wallis is available for speaking engagements and prophetic ministry to local churches and congregations. To schedule ministry engagements or business consultation, please contact him at the information given below.

For Correspondence, Donations or Prayer:

Scott Wallis
All Nations Worship Center
PO Box 6462
Elgin, IL 60121
(224) 200-5175

NOTES

NOTES

NOTES

NOTES

NOTES

NOTES

NOTES

NOTES

NOTES

NOTES

NOTES

NOTES

NOTES

NOTES

NOTES

NOTES

NOTES

NOTES

NOTES

NOTES

NOTES

NOTES

NOTES

NOTES

NOTES

NOTES

NOTES

NOTES

NOTES

NOTES

CPSIA information can be obtained
at www.ICGtesting.com
Printed in the USA
FFOW02n1606020417
34133FF